Crescent Moon Over Laos

by Mark Boyter

TO DEBBIE

Thanks for making
Township 7 such.
a fun experience for us

MARK

PROMONTORY
PRESS

CRESCENT MOON OVER LAOS

Copyright © 2014 by Mark Boyter

Promontory Press Inc.
Victoria, Canada
www.promontorypress.com

First Edition: May 2014

ISBN: 978-1-927559-38-3

Typeset at SpicaBookDesign in *Horley*

Printed in India

0 9 8 7 6 5 4 3 2

Acknowledgements

After all these many years that *Crescent Moon Over Laos* has sat ready, ever pregnant, waiting for me to finally breathe the last breath of air into it and set it free, there are many, many, many people to thank. After these many years, too, of trying so hard to be solitary, of demanding of myself that I succeed on my own or risk compromising my success, I have finally come to understand, to see—to know—that success alone is not simply lonely, but impossible. I stand on the collectively supportive shoulders of hundreds of people; some that I see every day, some that I see when the fates allow, some that have fallen away from my life, some that I met only once, for brief minutes. I would not be who I am today without having had each of you in my life. I thank them—you—all.

To Ed Trevisi, Jane Allan (nee Steindl), Rod Anderson: my oldest and dearest friends; who have always supported me, always loved me, and never once said, "Who gave you that pencil?" A single sentence (or even two) feels lacking, and yet how to put a lifetime's appreciation into words without those words turning into a book itself. If we are judged by the company we keep, then I am held very highly, for I walk with people who embody integrity, dedication, honesty, and love; and for being near those qualities, I embrace and become them too. I love you all. Thank you.

To S. Ballantyne, who had the good sense to come with the friend of the friend of the friend of the person that was invited to that fateful Minesing barn dance, and the brave sense to take a chance and accept that offer scratched in the dry end-of-summer dirt. I am eternally thankful for the time we had together, for the experiences we were able to share, for the growth as a human that I found through it all. *Crescent Moon Over Laos* would not exist if not for you (there I go, quoting George Harrison songs again). But perhaps most importantly, I have to thank you for Chris Rea. Since then, he has been a mainstay in my musical and emotional life. Thank you, and God bless.

To George Payerle, my editor, my friend, my first professional acceptance; who thinks that I'm from NYC because I watch TV through the bottom of the set instead of the front screen, and who upon reading *Crescent Moon Over Laos* in its oh-so-self-polished-roughness told me that both I and the book were amazing, and who insighted that I probably couldn't be told that enough. Of the second, at least, he was right, and for that—for believing in me—and for all the hours we spent working on the manuscript, for all the hours he spent teaching me how to think like a writer, I am forever thankful. Thank you.

To the Roshi and monks of Tokugenji temple in Nagoya, Japan, who believed enough in the integrity of Zen to open their monastery to me as both a lay practitioner and a non-Japanese to attend those Saturday evening (and occasional Monday morning) Zazen sessions and week-long sesshins before I left; and to have allowed me on those occasions that I have returned to Nagoya to find my way to sit in your zendo and on the temple steps in contemplation. Thank you.

To J. Kirkendall, who spoke those immortal words in the summer of 1988 as we languished in the heat of China, "There's this island in Thailand called Samui. The beaches are perfect and they barbeque looooong skewers of shrimp"; I would never have found Samui without you, and finding you again in Kathmandu as serendipity played out its game was to see the eyes of god in yours. It has been too many years my friend: it hasn't been a day. I love you brother. Thank you.

To my friends and colleagues from Nagoya: Jim Goater, David Dycus, Peter McFarlane, Tim Davis, Sabine Rockett, Chris Bond, Michael Kruse, David Kestenbaum; the late Gary Wood, the late Susan Griffiths; to Greg Ellis, my soul's true brother in a world where I have no biological sibling; to the others whose names I have forgotten, but not your faces or your influence. You made Japan the joy and learning experience it was for me. Every day in my life since I arrived on that March Sunday in 1986 has been informed by those months and years. For the better, I would not be the man I am today without Japan, and Japan would not be what it was without you. Thank you.

To my parents, Marvyn Boyter and Marion Boyter, who love me and have loved me and will love me, and whom I love, have loved, will love. MB^3. Thank you for you support, your love, your caring. Thank you for being here, still, to be able to share this with. For all my waiting, I have not waited too long. It would be a hollow victory for this to happen and you both not to be a part of it. I love you. Thank you.

To Iris Switzer, my companion in life, my love, my partner; who has put up with me, and loved me in spite of myself (and even sometimes because of my self) for too many years to count now, loving me so much that she didn't even need me around to do it. Now that I have stopped to breathe—to finally, truly breathe—I see that what I have searched for around me I had standing next to me. Love. Thank you. After so many years together, to say that this is the start of something big seems out of sync, but indeed, this *is* the start of something big. You once said that life with me wasn't always easy, but it was never boring. Let's make the rest easier, and even more exciting. I love you. Thank you.

To the people of Laos, and the monks of Wat Impaeng, Wat Sisaket, Wat Ongtue, Wat Chantabury, Wat Mai Shuvan na Phuma Ram, and the wats whose names are lost to me. Your curiosity, your welcoming, your hospitality, your kindness, your deep sense of place made my short time in Laos perhaps the most memorable days of my life. I could not have written *Crescent Moon Over Laos* without you. Thank you, with a bow and deeply offered *wai*. Thank you.

To Glenn Chatten for writing a "soundtrack" for *Crescent Moon*. It is an astonishing piece of music, and it is such a thrill to hear it performed, to hear my world conveyed to me in a way that resonates at the deepest levels. You put sounds to my heart, sounds to my life. They are beautiful sounds, and so it is that I come to understand that beauty begets beauty. Thank you.

To Anthony Robbins, whose late-night infomercial all those years ago changed my life in every way, in every shape, for every day since. "My new best friend" I called you until friends pointed out that it had been years already, and you became simply "Tony" in conversation. Thank you for the love, the support; the questions, the avenues to finding answers; the events where I have been invigorated, rejuvenated; where I have met dear, dear wonderful people; thank you for helping both Iris and myself to find our way out and back, to find those 2mm, and thank you for the joy and the passion. My world, our world, is better for having you in it. I love you. Thank you.

To all my friends at Anthony Robbins and at Anthony Robbins Leadership who proved conclusively that the best way to change NOW is to confide in your lead trainer that "I need to change". You are an astonishing group of people that I am honoured to know, honoured to be a part of. Thank you.

To those many others that have touched my life and shaped it by being a part of it, whether long or short, thank you.

To all those on the path: travelling, spiritual, self-discovery. Blessings, support, love. Be strong. Be happy. Be bold, and mighty forces will come to your aid. Life is good.

Last, but by no means least, to all the fine people at Promontory Press who have helped me and *Crescent Moon* get through this final stage of its gestation: Ben Coles, Lisa, Candace, and all the others behind the scene whose names I do not know, but whose efforts are indispensable; and to Iryna at SpicaBookDesign. Your support, encouragement and professionalism have been a Godsend and are greatly appreciated. Thank you.

Finally, all the people in this book are real. I have changed some of the names and some of the characteristics to allow them their privacy.

Crescent Moon Over Laos
by Mark Boyter

Table of Contents

North

Louangphrabang

To Thailand

Introduction

*C*rescent *Moon Over Laos* is about Laos. *Crescent Moon Over Laos* is about me. *Crescent Moon* started out as simply a book describing the events that transpired during a seventeen-day journey through Laos. When I arrived in Laos in February 1990, the country had only been reopened to independent Western travel for six months after being closed for ten years. There was little in the way of travel infrastructure, few Western travellers, no guidebooks, and what out-of-Laos information was available was based almost wholly on rumour, second-hand anecdotes and supposition; stories of guerrilla attacks, of disabled buses, that entry at the Laotian border was even possible.

The more I wrote though, and the more I thought about what actually had happened during those seventeen days, the more I found the thoughts and images that Laos had evoked in me crossing over into the book until it became apparent that the story of Laos and the story of me were inextricably meshed. *Crescent Moon* is about a country and it is about a traveller. It is about Laos being travelled in by Mark Boyter. It is about Mark Boyter travelling in Laos.

In the winter 1990, there was an "old" Southeast Asia and a "new" Southeast Asia. Neither designation had anything to do with age. "Old" and "new" was about the "Been there. Done that" factor. Did the country have a travel history? Was it open? Thailand, the Philippines, Indonesia, Malaysia and Hong Kong were "old". Laos, Cambodia, Burma and Vietnam were "new". In the late 1980s, Vietnam was just opening up to travellers and Cambodia and Burma were "difficult". Sometimes they were open, sometimes they were closed, all the time they were dangerous. But Vietnam, Cambodia and Burma were a familiar new. They had history, a substance—places, images, words. Vietnam is Saigon and Hanoi and Hô Chí Mihn. It is *Apocalypse Now* and *Platoon* and *Good Morning Vietnam*, John Wayne and Sgt. Barry Sandler, *Fortunate Son* and *Run Through the Jungle*, and Kent State and draft cards and draft dodgers and Jane Fonda. Burma is the Jewel in the British Crown, teakwood and rubies. It is Lon Chaney's *The Road to Mandalay*, Goenka-ji's Vipassana and more esoterically, shaves, road signs and Seinfeld. Cambodia is Angkor Wat, the Khmer Rouge, Pol Pot and *The Killing Fields*. Like Vietnam, Laos was just opening up too, but its "new" was unknown, unfamiliar. Laos is . . . Indeed. That is the question. What *is* Laos? Where does Laos fit in? The answer is it doesn't. Laos just is.

Unknown. It is Laos' defining characteristic.

My characteristics are much less elusive, although perhaps as equally defining. I graduated in 1981 with a Business and Economics degree, bought a blue pin-stripe suit and a Japanese sports car and started working in the same Vancouver company as my father. I was disillusioned almost immediately. A BA was supposed to have made me educated, which in my world meant well read, worldly and sophisticated. What it made me was a low-level manager in a redundant branch plant office, culturally and spiritually ignorant, and adrift. The gulf between who I was and who I wanted to be was enormous, and the path I was on was not going to get me there any time soon. I saw my life as a tower, but my foundation was so small, a tower of any height would topple. How could I build so high on so little? Unburdened by academia, I began to read: Kafka, Camus, Hesse, Richard Bach. I loved Richard Bach. I read *Siddhartha* over and over, *Illusions: The Adventures of a Reluctant Messiah* even more, *The Castle, The Trial, The Stranger, The Fall*. And I wrote. Mostly reflective diary stuff, but given my lacking literary education, anything was impressive. In the spring of 1984 I quit my job, sold my car, traded my stereo for a Nikon FM camera, bought a one-year open ticket to Europe, said good-bye to friends and began a year of travel that grew into a life of discovery and experience; nine months in Europe and the Middle East; five months travelling across Canada; twenty-seven months living and working in Japan; three months living and working in Ontario (on the tobacco harvest no less); and on two separate occasions, six months travelling in Asia. Over a period of 72 months, I spent 56 of them away from Vancouver. Travel became a drug.

The more I travelled, I move I lived. I spent as long as possible in each place, trying to understand, not what it was like to be there, but what it was like to live there, to be *of* that place and not simply *in* that place.

In Japan I became a language teacher, which is to say I found a new way to learn and experience life, because as a teacher I was sorely lacking. What I knew of teaching came from having been a student. What I discovered in Japan was that what I had learned best—spirituality, culture, art, literature, history, self—was what I had experienced travelling. In Japan I discovered Mishima and Dostoevsky and Zen and Vipassana meditation. As well, I began to discover, or at least to understand, this thing I and others called "me". I left Japan promising never to teach English again, as much then a statement about my life teaching as it was about the new experiences I wanted to have. I wanted to write more, to travel more, to experience life more. After all this time, I felt my base solid. It was time to build upwards, not outward. Ultimately, I broke my promise about teaching. I still teach today; the job that I originally chose so I *could* experience became a profession *through* experience. In 1997, I went back to school to get a graduate degree in teaching languages from The School of International Training, SIT, a New England school whose educational philosophy of Experiential Learning matched what I had found through travel; that to experience was to know, and to know was to have experienced. There was no disillusionment. I had always been right; from a broad base, you could build very high.

In late fall of 1988, after thirty-three months in Asia, I returned to Canada and almost immediately made plans to go back the following September. On the eve of my departure, I met a woman named Cassie. Life. Together we travelled through Asia for five months, and when she had to return to Canada to resume the life she had put on hold, I stayed behind not ready to let go. I knew that what I had returned to Asia to do wasn't finished, but how and what that was I had only vague ideas. And then, alone in

Bangkok, Laos presented itself to me. The art of serendipity is being unattached and being open.

And so in February 1990, I arrived in Laos, quite by accident, except that there are few real accidents in life.

Introduction 2013

September 2013. San Diego, California. I'm at the Anthony Robbins Leadership Academy. It's not my first Robbins event. It's my 6th. I've made monumental changes since I discovered Tony on late night TV way back when, but for all those monumental changes, there are still hurdles, still fears, still ... walls. I know that I *must* change in the four days of this academy. I *know* that whatever walls still exist, they *have* to come down. And not soon. Not in the future. Now. Right now. As in, "I've got four days. I'm not getting back on that plane the same Mark that got off it. There are no second options now." I confide in my lead trainer, Gina. "I never finish anything," I tell her. "I start things, and then ... I get stuck."

"Never?" she asks. "Anything?" The accompanying look does not suggest gentle acceptance.

"OK. Not never, and not anything, but it's my book. I wrote it ... I'm embarrassed to say. I finished it—last final draft—in 2002 (see? I can't even say 10 years ago when I write. Looking someone in the eyes? Forget about it. To tell you when I started it just compounds the embarrassment). Back then, the last time, I thought I had an agent lined up, solid support in the industry, solid editorial input. And it was good. The book was good. Really good. At least I thought so. And so did my editor. And then ... then it turned out that I had no publishing history, which apparently was very important to the agent. I put the book away."

"Away?"

"The top drawer of my filing cabinet at work. It's sat there a while. A few people have read it, but not many."

"Does this book have a name?"

"*Crescent Moon Over Laos.*"

"Nice. So, why can't you publish it?"

"Too many obstacles out there." To the story of my last submission I add the submissions before that were unsuccessful, the sexually-ambiguous rejection letters ('Dear Madam or Sir', as though 'Mark' is one of those names where people just aren't quite sure if it's male or female.) What I don't say—what I really mean—is that I was discouraged, that I was afraid. That locking the book away was less painful than being told "no" again. Gina knows this though. This isn't her first Robbins event either.

"But the rules have changed now, you know," she says. "You can e-publish. Kindle. Barnes & Noble. Apple. All of them. Is the manuscript on-line? Can you get access to it? Now, I mean. Like, tonight? There's a computer in the hotel lobby. In three hours, you can be on-line. No agent. No publisher. No mess. By breakfast you can be on-line. So, what's stopping you?" The accompanying look still did not suggest gentle acceptance.

Ouch. I hate it when their logic is better than my excuse.

She was right. Fears. Oh how insidiously they snuggle up inside us. Well, me at least. It's the obstacles in *here* that are the real problem.

And so here I am, so here it is. *Crescent Moon Over Laos.* I'm so excited that it's finally arrived. What's the adage? When the student is ready, the teacher will appear? I may have written *Crescent Moon Over Laos* years ago, but the student wasn't ready. There were many many more hoops I had to jump through—or walk through, or come to realize that they weren't really there in the first place—than simply getting an agent's or a publisher's attention. One hoop was actually understanding what it was I had written. I kept calling it a travel book, because that's what I had done. Travel. And written about it. So, logically, it was a travel book. Except when you say "travel book", too many people immediately assume that it has hotel information, costs, itineraries. Or worse. And I always thought it was more than that, but coming from a not-formal-literary background, what did I know? It wasn't a play, that was for sure. And how do you sell something to someone when you can't really describe it to them. But now I see. Now I know. It's a voyage of discovery. Of a place, of a person, of a soul. The questions I asked are universal: Why do I do this? Who am I? Where do I come from? What do I believe? Why do I believe this? And so it is a travel book, but not simply about travelling. It's about the journey of a human, through a country.

Another hoop was being perfect, or rather the need to be perfect. I kept thinking that as soon as *Crescent Moon Over Laos* was perfect, I would send it out, it would get accepted.

Problem.

Nothing is perfect. At least nothing man-made (Michelangelo's "David" comes close though, I have to admit). I was waiting on an impossibility. Or perhaps "fiddling" is a better word. And so it goes. Life. Mine, at least.

But back to the book; *Crescent Moon Over Laos* is about the unknown, about serendipity, about being open to the world, and for that openness gaining astonishment. But *Crescent Moon Over Laos* is about being honest too. Honest in the face of desire, honest in the face of that unknown, honest in the face of myself. There are a couple of passages in the book that I might not write that way now, but they were me then, and to take them out, to re-write, to amend, wouldn't be honest. This introduction is honest. At least it's supposed to be. Sometimes it's easier to be honest alone on a page than face-to-face. Sometimes it just allows a more formal elegance to the deceit. But if I can admit that it's been 10 years since I last sent *Crescent Moon* out, if I can admit that I started a decade earlier, then I guess I can admit anything. Ok, most things. Up until two years ago, I was still buying waist 32 pants.

I feel like the world's longest gestation has finally ended, and I am thrilled for it. It's a new world out there for me. For all of us. Everyday, another chance.

And so full of joy, full of eagerness, full of strength, I present to the world my book. My first book. *Crescent Moon Over Laos*. I hope you like it. I hope you find something in it that moves you, that says, "Yes. I can relate. That's not just the human condition he's talking about. That's *my* human condition in there."

Blessings,
Thank you.
Mark Boyter
Vancouver, British Columbia
May 8, 2013
In the sunshine
And the perfume scent of spring
Which *is* perfect

Prologue

Monday, February 26, 1990

W ho would want to shoot us?
Who would want to shoot me?

Indeed, it isn't *us* I am worried about. It is *me*. "Us" is too abstract, too artificial, too impersonal. Like an evening news story about a Nepalese bus sliding over a cliff on the mountain road you travelled last year, or a Bangladeshi ferry capsizing in monsoon flood waters drowning hundreds at a place you debated over and rejected, "us" creates interest and no more. This time it *is* me and it is *here* and it is *now*, and in this solitude, the solitary foreigner on the Vangviang bus heading north out of Vientiane on the first leg of the journey to Louangphrabang, I am scared. Not by what I see around me. Not by the other passengers on the bus. Scared by the marriage of logic and rumour. Scared by what I can't see around me.

In Nong Khai I had heard the rumours of guerrilla attacks in Laos; of trucks and buses left disabled in the mountains by sniper attacks; of bodies lining the road's edge. I had read the stories left behind by Laos-travellers before me in the loose-leaf binder at the Mee-Krabe Guesthouse in Nong Khai. Stories that stopped when the Mee-Krabe lost its status as the sole agent for Laotian visas in Nong Khai. Stories that stopped when the Mekong River View Guesthouse became the sole Laotian-visa agent. Scribbled comments written quickly and left too full of gaps; scribbled comments offered in English by someone whose first language was too often something else; scribbled comments imprecise and yet clear. Scribbled comments that both lost and gained their impact without the first-hand knowledge of experience.

When I arrived in Laos nine days ago, the locus of danger was as imprecise as its nature: the south? The north? Vientiane itself? Now I know. The danger is in the north. The danger is what I am travelling into. At least I think I know. To experience is to know, and I haven't experienced the north yet. What I "know" is a very short history and intuition. I *have* experienced the south. I *have* experienced Vientiane. They were both safe. There was no danger. There was no military. The north is the only other option.

No traveller I know *wants* to be attacked from some unseen gun emplacement, to die in the anonymity and cultural seclusion of another's battle. Unlike the capsized ferry or the rolled bus, this danger is too immediate, too arbitrary, and at its core, too unknown. Heroic and clouded in its own legend, it is also too probable and at least in this case, too personal. The rolled bus has a validity accepted as an inherent quality of travel, a validity of probabilities and realities that can be rationalized and accepted. Until now, it had always been someone else. Someone else's danger. Somebody else's story.

Who would want to shoot me?

1
Vientiane

W e crossed the Mekong on the 8:45 A.M. launch. Launches
cross the river continuously from early morning to sunset from Nong Khai, the Thai exit point, to Thaduea, the Laotian
entry point thirty kilometres east of Vientiane, Monday through
Saturday. This was Saturday, February 17. Sundays, the only
boats on the Mekong are military patrol cruisers. The river is
quiet. The border is closed.

There were five of us: myself, an Englishman—David, who
had been staying down the road at the Mee-Krabe Guesthouse—
Andy and Laura, also English, and our visa-procurer, the owner
of the Mekong River View Guesthouse. I didn't know David.
Before this morning, I'd met him only once. Andy and Laura and
I have been staying at the Mekong River View Guesthouse. Laura
and I even taught English together one morning to a group from
the local police force on the river balcony of the guesthouse. She
had enjoyed the experience more than I did. For her it was all new.

A ten minute trip. On the Laotian bank of the river, a long, rickety, rusting staircase rose up from the river's edge to the top of the
embankment and Lao immigration. The staircase reminded me of
my childhood, of the steps up the clay bank at my grandmother's
cottage at Port Dover on Lake Erie in Ontario. That staircase was
rusted and rickety too, the wooden steps painted green, the iron
railing painted black, the paint from both flaking off on your feet
or in your hands, the exposed iron-rail tubing pitted and smooth
and weathered. Lao immigration even looked like a lake cottage:

a small wooden hut surrounded outside by a narrow garden of powder blue and white rose trellises, grass and flowering trees. The path from the steps took us under the roses. The yard felt cramped, as though before it became an immigration centre, the building was just a weekend cottage, far enough from Vientiane to not see house guests, small enough to be cosy but not claustrophobic. Inside, Lao immigration was a confusion of uniformed and civilian bodies and shouting to be heard in a small, overcrowded waiting room. Our Thai handler huddled us to one side while his Laotian counterpart, our "tour guide," collected our passports and pushed them through the formalities.

I had sat in Nong Khai for over a week waiting for this morning, reacquainting myself to morning cups of coffee and breakfasts of ham, sausage and eggs taken with *Bangkok Post* crossword puzzles, waiting for my passport, which allegedly sat in the Laotian embassy in Bangkok. I'd been in Asia since October. In Asia with Cassie. I wanted to show her the most beautiful places in my world: Nepal, Thailand. For many reasons, Cassie had gone home from Bangkok: there were divorce papers waiting for her to sign in Toronto, with a deadline; she needed to get back for the new job she had already postponed twice; the intensity of travelling together, of us being us—so much, so soon—was proving too much and too soon. At Don Muang International Airport in Bangkok the morning she flew home, she said she'd wait for me: not forever, but for a while. She didn't know how long "a while" was. I still had some travelling to do. It wasn't time yet. When it would be time, I wasn't sure. "A while," I said. I took a taxi back into the city. For the first time in many months, I felt very, very alone.

Nong Khai is a small, noisy, nondescript frontier town at the end of the northeastern branch of the Thai rail line. For Western travellers, its *raison d'être* is its magical proximity to Laos and to the Mekong. Mekong. Just the name stokes the Asia of my imagination and desire; of sweltering days and yoked water buffalo breast deep in flooded rice paddies; of the whine of cicadas in a stifling dripping heat; of tangerine robed monks glowing through the evaporating mist of an early morning alms procession; of sensuality and desire and lust. I, me, mine.

In Thai guesthouse conversations, the Mekong River means only two things: Golden Triangle opium, and Vietnam. "War" doesn't even need to be mentioned. It is a given, an obvious. For adventure seekers and romantics all, Vietnam means war and Mekong means Vietnam.

For adventure seekers and romantics, the need to search for the war is almost obsessive. Surrounded by centuries of archaeology, beaches, jungles and forest monasteries, they come to buy souvenirs and trinkets before it is too late, to ask the journalist-questions *what, where, who, why, tell me, when, tell me.* Questions I could never ask. They are too personal, too close to wounds I feel neither the courage nor the right to re-expose. Touristic inquisitiveness. Historical voyeurism. Touristic voyeurism. By any other name, it smells as sweet. It is not my indulgence.

Nong Khai itself has little to offer. Its best attraction, next to the Mekong, is Wat (rhymes with thought) Kaek, a strange hybrid temple of Buddhism and Hinduism realized in concrete statues of laughing, walk-through dentures, and packs of ravenous, gun-toting, sports-car-driving, screamingly erect dogs. Nothing says God quite like the images of mechanical chattering teeth or a puppy with a hard-on. Is that religion in your pants or are you just happy to see me? Whether the statues are grotesque, comical or religious is, for non-believers at least, an individual matter. Among travellers, Kaek is known as Wat Disney.

For me, the problem with getting into Laos had been the waiting. For others, the problem with getting into Laos was just that: the problem of getting into Laos. The country has been reopened to Western tourism for six months, since August of 1989. Government visa policy seems to change weekly. At the Laotian embassy in Bangkok a sign stated tourist visas were available for 300 Thai baht, about $12 US. Approaching the counter gained you a brochure on Lao Tourism travel packages and a bureaucratic shrug over the 300 baht. My friend Paul had tried that, just to prove that everyone else and what they were telling him was right. They were. It was. Tour agents offering visa services to Laos, Burma, Vietnam and Nepal returned Laos-bound passports with their regrets and the exorbitant advance fee intact. Paul tried that too. The acknowledged best approach was also the option of last resort. Go to the Laotian border entry point, Thaduea, and in person, try. Paul decided to try that too, but I haven't seen him since the day he left Bangkok. Would going to Thaduea work? I didn't know. No one I met knew. To experience is to know. I knew hearsay.

Arriving in Nong Khai on the overnight train, I stumbled half-asleep into the Mekong River View Guesthouse. The Mekong's owner assured me in emphatic English my only option was to join the "group tour" he was organizing. Thaduea was impossible. Thai customs in Nong Khai wouldn't let me on the boat without a valid Laotian visa. He was the agent for Laotian visas in Nong Khai. The sole agent. Success, he promised, was guaranteed. It was, he insisted, the only way.

He already had Andy and Laura waiting to go, and with three people, it would be, he said, cheaper. Once in Laos, we would be on our own to travel as we wished, our bureaucratically convenient tour over. If I gave the Mekong's owner my passport today, Thursday, February 8, I would have it back, visa in hand, the following Thursday, February 15. Guaranteed. The cost was 3600 baht, about $145 US. For a three-day visa that he promised was easily and cheaply extendable in Vientiane for an additional fourteen days. For my 3600 baht, I would also get two nights accommodation in the Hotel Ekalath Metropole, and all my meals for the first three days. David joined the tour a few days later. The Mekong's owner made no mention of a fourth person making the tour price cheaper.

Just like that, after ten days in Nong Khai waiting, we are in. Welcome to Laos. A three-day visa. Our visa man was right. So far, so good. And then we are in a mini-van, racing along an undivided two-lane highway, deep ditches on either side, rice paddies beyond them, into Vientiane, Our Man in Thailand long gone back to Nong Khai on the first available boat. On the roadway, we pass a large billboard for Pepsi. It is the number one soft drink in Laos.

The Hotel Ekalath Metropole on Samsen Thai Road is near Tat (rhymes with fat) Dam. The Mekong's owner told us this when we booked on the tour, a selling point meant to impress the convinced and sway the undecided. None of us had any idea what a Tat Dam was, but between the four of us, there was general consensus: only the worst of frauds feels obliged to justify their fees through embellishment and description. The gulf coast of Thailand or Mexico, in the bleakness of a Vancouver winter, does not need the adjectival tag "exotic" to be alluring; by the fifteenth day of rain, "not" and "Vancouver" in the same phrase is alluring. That Tat Dam, which means "the black stupa," turns out to be exactly that, a small crumbling black stupa in the centre of Thanon Bartoloni Street, was never offered. Maybe there'd be more of us on his "tour" if he'd said exotic.

At the hotel front desk, our Laotian "guide" checks us in, speaking English with the English-speaking front desk clerk, and leaves. We have twin rooms. I am sharing a room with David. On the counter, our room is rack-rated at 900 baht, or $37 US, per person per night. There is no mention of price in Laotian kip. Travellers are expected to be rich, to have foreign currency, and to want to spend it. Or perhaps not want to, but at least to be resigned to. "Foreign" means American dollars or Thai baht. There are no listings for English pounds, Japanese yen or Russian roubles. Less surprising is the absence of Polish zlotys or Canadian dollars. The Ekalath is luxurious in a one-star concrete box manner—three front-desk clerks behind a counter large enough only for one, air-conditioning and a lobby fountain that splashes over a dish of coloured pebbles, nylon-pile wall-to-wall carpet, Best Western-style beds, quilts that match the wall paint—as opposed to luxurious in the manner of the Raffles in Singapore or the Oriental in Bangkok or the Peninsula in Hong Kong—high stucco ceilings, ceiling fans, teakwood walls, Persian carpets, polished brass railings, glass skylights, the creak of white rattan furniture, bellboys in red caps and starched-white waistcoats and guests in teak panel rooms who dress formally because that is, old chap, how one dresses when one travels. How many writers wouldn't be if W. Somerset

Maugham had written of Asia while under the rumble of an air conditioning unit?

The Ekalath's luxury notwithstanding, 900 baht for a room in Laos, even in Vientiane, is absurd. The clerks at the front desk know. The Ekalath is almost empty, and at reception, after our "guide" has left, it is suggested in hushed tones that perhaps a "discount" can be arranged if any of us wish to stay on after the "tour" expires.

Andy and Laura take up the suggestion and after some discussion a price is arrived at. 250 baht per night, for the both of them. About $10. So, if the counter-negotiated market rate for the Ekalath for two persons is $10 for one night—$5 per person per night—then my hotel bill, one person for two nights, should be $10 as well. Out of the $145 US our "visa/tour" cost. That leaves $135 for food, the visa and the "tour". (It was all our "guide" could do to not laugh out loud when Laura asked him when our tour started.) Neither David nor I want to stay on in the Ekalath. I'm just thinking out loud, that's all: an exercise in seeing how badly we were ripped off by the Mekong River View Guesthouse.

The Ekalath restaurant offers an unlimited, all-you-can-eat French gourmet menu: escargots, crêpes, pork, fish and water buffalo steak. The dining room sits a hundred. At each of our six sittings, we are the only diners. The steak is good, the fish adequate, and everything else unavailable. I have two steak lunches, one steak dinner, one fish dinner and two breakfasts of Laotian coffee and baguettes with butter and a plate of sugar. How much all of this would have cost had we been "regular" guests I don't know. The menu has no prices. If you have to ask . . . and luxury is never cheap. At the Santiouk restaurant in the centre of Vientiane though, where I ate one night by myself, the only customer in the restaurant, I had a Chateaubriand on a sizzling cast iron plate, a basket of fresh French loaf, Campbell's Cream of Mushroom soup, a salad and a bottle of drinking water for 1800 kip, about $2.35. At the bakery next to the Sailom Guesthouse, where David and I will move after our two nights' accommodation at the Ekalath, that same *petit déjeuner* of a morning baguette, butter, sugar and coffee costs 150 kip, about 20¢. For two breakfasts and four dinners, that's $9.80. Plus $10 for the hotel. $19.80 total. So, my Laotian land-entry visa cost $125.20. For three days. In Vientiane, the fourteen-day visa extension, that was in fact as easily and cheaply obtained as the Mekong owner/agent promised, cost 400 kip, *local* currency. About 50¢. In retrospect, the Mekong owner never mentioned how cheap "cheaply" might be.

Two months earlier, this same $145 visa "package" to Laos had been available in Nong Khai for $50. I found that out in Nong Khai after Laos. Maybe that's why the Mee-Krabe lost their Laos-visa-agent status. Maybe $95 greases a lot of palms and still makes the entrepreneur money. Nong Khai is full of excellent questions.

Still, for the money, we got in. At Thaduea when we arrived, two American women I had not noticed in Nong Khai were standing at the customs desk pleading with the starched and pressed olive-green official to let them enter. Against all odds, they had obtained a tourist visa from the embassy in Bangkok, discovering too late they had been issued "air arrival only" visas. They had seen the stamps immediately, but the fee paid and the visa obtained, there was nothing they could do. Expecting an overland entry visa, they had no flight booked and no time available to arrange one. They would try Thaduea. They had no other recourse. I sympathized with their predicament, with their having waited for the visa, anticipating Laos, only to be cruelly denied at the last moment. If I had been the border guard I would have let them in, but I wasn't, and I never saw them in Vientiane.

2

Vientiane

We need Laotian kip and what we have is Thai baht. The man at the front desk is more than happy to change currency for us. "It is a good rate," he promises, but we have no idea what a "bad rate" is, and after all, how expensive can Laos be? All our meals are paid for, and our hotel. First Andy changes money, then Laura, then David. By my turn, the desk manager has run out of 500-kip notes. I change two 100-baht notes for the 72 notes that make up my 6150 kip. Who wouldn't feel rich when you can't close your wallet? I'm carrying almost $8.45. It is a mistake I will make again and again in Laos: carrying a wad of money instead of a lot of money.

Left unguided and alone in Vientiane, David and I have no maps, no information and no idea. Andy and Laura do: they were given a "tour packet" in Nong Khai by the Mekong River View Guesthouse, including, among other things, what seem to be tenth-generation photocopies of a badly hand-drawn city map, a badly hand-drawn country map and a list of restaurants. They are almost illegible.

Saturday afternoon and all the stores and shops that line the main street off Samsen Thai Road are all closed behind padlocked rolling metal shutter-fronts. Wide dirt-gutters separate the greying road pavement from cracked and broken concrete sidewalks. There is nothing. The only sign of life, far down the road, is red and says Canon Copiers. There are no pedestrians, no cars, no bicycles, no travellers. No nothing. David goes off in search of both the guesthouse listed on Andy and Laura's map— the Sailom—and the possibility of other travellers. After ten days waiting, other travellers is not what I have come here to find. What I *have* come here to find I'm not sure. I have three, and hopefully seventeen, days to figure it out.

And so from out of nothing come the simplest questions: Where? What? Who? There is no obvious direction here, no obvious landmark, and no known history to search out, no familiarity to confront. Andy and Laura's cartoonish map notwithstanding, how big is this city? Where, exactly, am I? How far is it to the centre? How far to the edges? Standing here, the three of us alone, Vientiane is without dimension. Andy and Laura turn left, away from the sun. I turn right, into the sun, and then I *am* alone.

Across a tree-lined boulevard, Wat Impaeng rises up through a grove of psilocybic palms. Persimmon and palm-leaf green, three terraced roofs of ceramic tiles glint in their sweep against a cloudless sky, each roof nestling into the previous, growing organically into a gentle cradle curving into flames at either end.

Inside the wrought-iron and plaster perimeter wall, rows of small white funeral stupas unseen from the street fill the gaps between the palm trunks. Dry, fallen palm fronds and pieces of branch and twig litter the ground. A small breeze catches the living fronds overhead, rustling them. Cicadas sing, and the oppressive heat from the street turns cool in the shade. Past the palm grove, a large teak building teeters on crumbling brick pillars and wooden scaffolding and posts. Underneath the building, hollowed into the earth, is a classroom. Six large wooden worktables crowd together in the cramped space in front of the chalkboard. The table tops are each a single, thick wooden plank worn polished and smooth—maybe three inches thick, three feet wide, five feet long. A single slab of wood—no joins, no cuts. The tree must have been enormous.

Stones and chunks of broken plaster under the legs prop the work surfaces level. The illusion is control, the surface calm against the makeshift confusion on the ground. You make the best of what you have in the third world: whoever has created this has made very good.

On one side of the classroom a brick wall has been built, filling the spaces between the brick support pillars. The mortar is disintegrating, crumbling away in the humidity. Behind the chalkboard is a peeling, yellow-washed plaster-of-Paris wall. Scabs of the exposed powdery white plaster connect with each other by meandering fingers of water damage and pressure cracks as though God were creating Adam in Wat Impaeng. The outline of an old doorway in the pockmarked plaster is clear, the lintel and heavy wooden frame unhidden by the thin coats of orchid yellow wash. Old plaster flakes lie swept in the corner, fresh flakes scattered along the gutter where the wall touches the earth.

The last lesson is still on the board, the Roman chalk letters sweeping along the board's faint green guidelines in the graceful manner of Laotian script. The individual characters are beautiful, if not inherently un-Western in their creation, in the same way that Japanese characters drawn by a hand educated in the juxtapositions of English letters remain awkward and childlike long past the threshold of understanding.

The lesson is grammar—Present Perfect—and not a very good one at that.

Present Perfect Tense
1/..ex "He has lived here for three years",
"They have lived here for years",
2/ ex. "the train has just arrived",
"the train has already arrived",
"they have gone already"
OR
"they have already gone"
"he hasn't finished it yet"
OR
"he hasn't yet finished it".
See, saw, seen . . . finish, finished, finished . . .
I have, you have, he has . . .

There is too much going on for a structure that doesn't need help being complicated. Present Perfect describes an action that started in the past and continues till now, but hasn't finished. Just like Present Perfect Progressive, except that Present Perfect Progressive uses a present participle instead of a past participle. The two tenses mean exactly the same thing, except when they don't. There are rules explaining when and why they act the same—or don't—plus the exceptions. Native speakers seldom make mistakes because in the end it comes down to context and we *just know*. Or, Present Perfect describes an action that has finished, just like Simple Past, except that for Present Perfect, we don't know, or don't care, *when* the event happened and in Simple Past, we do. That's the key: Simple Past always has a time clause, and Present Perfect never does. Except, English often allows Simple Past statements to drop the adverbial time clause (I slept like a baby doesn't need *last night*) because it's all about context and native speakers *just know*. Or, Present Perfect describes a recurring action that has occurred in the past but will repeat itself into the future—the event has finished, except it hasn't, if that makes any sense. For me, it's simple. I'm a native speaker. I understand the context. I *just know*.

Just to be on the safe side, the teacher is using both regular and irregular verbs, negatives, contractions, has added the adverbs *already*, *just* and *yet*, uses capitals on a whim, and quotation marks with incorrect punctuation: someone is *speaking* these phrases. Mercifully, he or she hasn't introduced the question form. That's the problem with teaching: if you're good and the students learn quickly, you're out of a job that much faster. Better to be indispensable than good.

Less really is more.

I guess you had to be there.

And then, in this quiet, a voice.

"Hello. How are you? I am . . . " He clears his throat. "My name . . . " He clears his throat again. "My name is Monk Thong Liam Inthvong. Who are you?" His throat is clear.

Monk Thong Liam Inthvong is young, a pie-faced monk with full jowls and his shaven head dark in a Fred Flintstone five o'clock shadow, a thick, stocky Buddhist monk in a brilliant rust-coloured uttarãsanga robe and black plastic sandals. His real title is bhikkhu, the word for monk in Pali, the language of the historical Buddha—Bhikkhu Thong Liam Inthvong—but bhikkhu has become lost in even the most simple of conversations with foreigners. Life.

"Stocky" and "Buddhist monk" don't belong together, but then neither do "Fred Flintstone five o'clock shadow" and "head". Maybe there are more like Monk Inthvong. Maybe if I'd met him first, I'd think that "thin" and "monk" didn't belong together. Maybe I have too many preconceived ideas. After all, "flying" and "nun" belong together.

Even within the confines of Wat Impaeng speaking to another male he is modest, his uttarāsanga pulled high and tight up to his neck instead of loose and falling down across his chest exposing his right breast. Monks wear only three garments, called collectively the tricivara or ticivara, depending on whether one uses Sanskrit or Pali: the antaravāsaka, the undercloth, a sarong-like fabric; the uttarāsanga, the upper body covering; and the sanghāti, a shawl. Monks are obliged to cover up outside the wat, but inside, they are already, by definition, modest. Monk Thong Liam Inthvong's impression is of a strapless gown and 36D breasts stuffed into 36B cups. Jane Russell with no hair. "Bulges" and "monk" don't go together either.

I am Mark, I tell him. From Canada. I just arrived in Laos today.

He studies English every day, he says. Please, can I help him? Please, there is a page he does not understand. He lives "there" he says as we walk alongside the teak building, pointing upward at a shuttered wooden window above the dugout English classroom. All the monks and novices live here, he says. As he lifts his arm, there is a flash of yellow undershirt. He's wearing a fourth garment. Now I feel voyeuristic. *Am I trying to look down a monk's top?* Please, would I like to come inside his room? Please, there are separate rooms for each monk and novice he says. In his, he has a bed, a spare robe, his alms bowl and a dresser.

"Sit?" he orders, and there is only the dark, swept teak floor. He opens the shutters to light the room, and from a jug of water pours me a glass. I hesitate to accept, hesitate to refuse. How do you ask a monk befriending you if the kindness he is offering is clean? What questions does he ask before receiving his alms? Monk Inthvong is a better man than I. "It is rainwater," he says, intercepting my dilemma. "It is good. It is clean." He has a photograph in his bureau that another foreigner has sent him. "My old teacher," he says and I suspect that all the foreigners he has ever talked to are his "teachers". In the purest sense of the word, they are. Perhaps I would do better thinking the way his English does, seeing the truth of learning instead of the discrete point of profession. The problem with being a teacher. As a group, we take it all too personally. I am not a teacher because I am a teacher. I am a teacher because I am.

I am a teacher, too, because I am a traveller. I was a traveller before I was a teacher, in both senses of the word. Everyone, in their own way, is a teacher. Some people just chose it as their profession. Travelling is what I did when I went to sleep, when I opened up *National Geographic*, when I went to the movies. Travelling is where I learned to be me, where I learned to see what that me could be, and how to let go of the me that I had been becoming and embrace the one I was fulfilling. I am a traveller because I am.

"This is him," Monk Thong Liam Inthvong says, finding the photograph. "This is my teacher. He is from England."

It's a teacher all right. A white guy standing next to Monk Thong Liam Inthvong inside the wat.

From an undershirt pocket Monk Thong Liam Inthvong pulls his textbook, a small American English paperback grammar, the Statue of Liberty splashed across the cover in aluminium blue and silver. From at least the 1960s. It is an exercise in conditionals:

if I have . . . I will
if I had . . . I would
if I had had . . . I would have . . .

If I really had a grammar question, I would ask, but I don't. And he doesn't. Grammar questions in Southeast Asia are rarely about grammar. *If I talk with every foreigner that comes into the wat, I will speak better English.* There are no questions. None at least that he can articulate. Please, would I like to see the wat?

In the courtyard, the façade of the viharn bursts in painted murals of the Buddha's life. Rushing, full Himalayan rivers, deep blue with breaking white caps; deep vegetal greens against earth tones of sub-continental plains and the terai of the Nepal-India border area; Siddhartha preaching, disciples in step, a cascading, luminescent robe the colour of Indian saffron falling across his knees. Swirls and lotus flowers repeat against an image of the Buddha seated in meditation on a lotus. A vast carved door, eight feet high, surrounded by images of small Buddhas in swirling gold leaf against red against the wood grain below, rising like Buddha curls, swirling into the lintel, joining, and rising as one into a flame.

He is a lucky monk.

Both Monk Thong Liam Inthvong and his English are exhausted. I like him, I really like him, but there seems no point in acting out a friendship from curiosity. Please, he wishes me a deep-bowed good-bye and returns to his room.

I am alone all over again.

3
Vientiane

A dirt boulevard traces the northern bank of the Mekong, the forests of Thailand across the river straining backlit through the late-afternoon haze to make an impression. Opposite the dirt embankment a long, high white stucco wall defines the courtyard of a hotel complex, grime and algae bleeding from the top of the barrier through the whitewash, flowing across the plaster face like guano across rock. Held in the shadow of the wall, the flagstone sidewalk running alongside is surrounded by puddles and damp leaves. Ahead is a roadside bar, a huge purple canvas umbrella and three rickety unfinished picnic tables mismatched in green stripes, white flower-print and garbage-bag-green vinyl tablecloths. There are four men drinking, four bicycles parked off the road on either side of the table.

An inharmonious "Hello" comes from the group with a wave to join them. "Where are you come from?" is the question and laughter is their own response. My half of the conversation is strictly optional. They are well on their way to drunk.

"Do you want drink?" is the follow-up question but regardless, the answer remains laughter. "Where are you from? It is good! Whisky Lao!" and the drinker in the powder blue tracksuit top and over-sized aviator glasses holds up his glass in proof. "Please. It is good. Try."

The barmaid flirts with the moment, teasing both their questions and my stumbled answers. Across the breast of her baby-pink T-shirt is written BIG-JOHN, her hair pulled back into a ponytail that bounces in her flirtation. She must know them. Then again, sex is good business, and teasing is the best kind of sex. Perhaps this is their regular Saturday. Then again, perhaps I am just in the mood to see flirting. Desire is always about the body. The mistake is thinking the body is someone else's.

On the "bar", a line of Pepsi and Mirinda Orange bottles book-end two different local drinks in recycled Johnny Walker and Old Mac bottles. One is bright yellow, *laotho*, the other a cloudy white, *laokao*.

"They made from fruit!" the aviator says. "Please try," and the semen coloured fluid is spilled over the brim of a gritty plastic glass, puddling across the flower-print vinyl tablecloth.

"Good, yes!" asks the aviator. "Where do you staying?" and there is a smile in my response.

"I work at the Ekalath," he says. "At the front desk. I do the books, the numbers. Today is my vacation, but tomorrow I will be there. I am Vongthong. Please sit down."

The laokao smells heavy and bittersweet, like Ouzo or Sambuca. Substantial. Nepalese rackshi is what it tastes like. Burning and rough to swallow. Vongthong's breath has no discernible smell. He is smoking however, always a dangerous habit around unstable combustibles.

"You want girl?" the man in the white short-sleeved golf shirt and blue rubber flip-flops asks, tugging at my arm across the table. I have only been in Vientiane for four hours. Already "you want girl?"

"You come from Thailand. In Thailand, many girl. Cheap. You want girl?" Another laokao is poured and a single cigarette is offered for me to reject. Allergies are never convenient, especially when they get in the way of ritual. More so when I want a cigarette. In an instant, I am outside the moment. Three of the four can't speak English that well, and the fourth, Vongthong, I suspect has exhausted most of his. I can't even smoke with them, communication reduced to grunts and smiles and the thought of a woman.

Part of me longs for a woman, to hold, to caress, to . . . It is the same part so susceptible to the laokao, gaining warmth and desire in the effort to drink the rough liquor. How easy the warmth comes: *want girl? Cheap.* How easy the warmth answers: *Yes.* I hoped Laos would be different. I hoped I would.

But still, a woman.

And I would only be satisfying desire and lust over desire and love. It is not an anonymous love I want. My craving is out of absence from the woman that I love, the woman that I long for, the woman that is my destiny. Not the absence of sex. The craving is for sex, but not inarticulate, anonymous sex. The craving is for Cassie. That's what I keep telling myself at least. Or at least what I keep telling the warm part of myself.

Words in Laotian are spoken to the pink-chested barmaid and there is more laughter that I am not a part of except as catalyst. I feel embarrassed for her and for me, my assumption that she is my "want girl," that they can read my mind. The bottle of laokao emptied, a second one is opened with the promise to spill more into the glasses than onto the tabletop. I suspect it is second only since I started counting. The barmaid blushes under her freckles, brushing her hair from her forehead, concentrating on the bottles and not the client.

A bar snack of root vegetables appears. They have the size of a small beet, skin dirty like a potato's, and creamy white flesh. The others dive into them. The white-shirt golfer pushes the bunch towards me.

"*Man pau,*" Vongthong spits. "Radishes." *Radishes? He knows radishes?* They are jicama, Mexican yambean: crisp and starchy and sweet. The texture is lychee nut/raw potato. The shape is testicle. The lumberjack grabs a handful.

The second bottle of laokao is gone, the liquid spilling over the brim onto the table in the filling of glasses, the promise broken. With a rag my BIG-JOHN pink want-girl wipes the table clean, the fluid beading across the vinyl in a wave, refusing to evaporate and unable to quietly soak away.

"You okay? You want girl?" the stylish drinker in the red and brown patterned dress shirt, black slacks and black belt asks, the repeated question more slurred, the dulled demand less urgent and more pleading. Already three laokaos for me. They drink easily, especially when they're poured badly. *You want girl?* I roll the question over in my mind and it drifts to the freckled barmaid and the warm flesh hiding behind BIG-JOHN, no longer the publican but just cute and pink. *Do I want girl?*

The drinker in the red flannel lumberjack shirt with tartan lining and his sleeves rolled up wants to talk, but he knows no English, tugging at my sleeve and sculpting in the air to explain his point, wasting both of our times. He pulls Vongthong into the helpless conversation to be his voice, but Vongthong's English isn't good enough to translate the muddled alcoholic ideas formed in a native complexity by a man unfamiliar with the juggling of languages and in the unfamiliarity assuming ease.

"We go to a different bar, yes?" and the four mount their bicycles to leave. The Scottish lumberjack offers me a ride, but there is no seat, the tire is flat and he is drunk. A pedal rickshaw is flagged down and all four shout confused directions at the driver.

The bar is only up the road. I could have walked. I pay the rickshaw and watch the four bicyclists fall over their attempt at parking. With our arrival, the number in the bar jumps to seven, not counting the two servers. Saturdays start late in Vientiane. We grab a booth and five large beers and five bowls of appetizers are ordered. No one is hungry, and one beer would have been enough. Still, it is a party. There is music, and for patrons unable to hear through the alcohol, the volume is blasted in painful reverberations into the confines of the cement pillbox masquerading as a nightclub. Our voices are lost in the pounding bass line until even the pretence of conversation over this distortion is dropped. Two of the men sway in their seats to the beat, thumping and sliding their hands on the tabletop, trying in drunken awkwardness to capture the rhythm and make it their own in this heightened participation. Two young girls sit at a table across the room, tight against the far wall under a soft-focus sunburst poster of a boy and girl holding hands. The drinker in the brown-and-red-print short-sleeve dress shirt, the only one of us wearing socks, bobs over to the targettes, shouting something and pointing. They look away, trying to ignore the brutality of his introduction and attempted sophistication, but again he shouts until they can no longer feign ignorance. They shake their heads no, but he has gained their attention and I am afraid through force and persistence we will soon find ourselves with two "want girls". The negotiation continues, but in drunkenness, his rambling loses the argument. To his dismay the targettes stand up leaving—far earlier, I sense, than they had intended. He turns and throws his hands up in the air. The vibrato of a *khaen* free-reed mouth organ streams in staccato licks over the bass line; *brree – brree*, bum bum bum bum bum, *brree – brree* . . .

"We have no money," Vongthong blurts.

"What! What do you mean, you have no money?"

"We use all our money at the other bar. We are poor men. We not have much money."

"Why did you come here if you have no money? How much do you have all together? Show me."

"Nothing. We have nothing. We thought you pay." Across the table, vacant forlorn looks. They know the content without the language. There is no money.

It is an outrageous 800 kip per beer, a few hundred more for the food. 4800 kip in all. About 170 baht, about $6.60 US. Pathetically cheap, but cheap is not the point. Cheap is relative. Besides, I don't have that much kip left myself. A lot of baht, not a lot of kip.

"I have money for myself. I don't know what you four will do."

Vongthong looks trapped. The others look empty but for the one in socks, who looks for another "want girl". Too much beer. Too much laokao.

"I don't want to pay for you. I pay for me. You pay for you."

I want to get up and leave, to leave these four to make their own explanations to the girl at the counter. They have no money, they get a foreigner, buy him cheap drinks, go to a bar, drink expensive beer, plead poverty, go home. Drunk Laotian. Stupid tourist.

And what if the misunderstanding is genuine? What if they brought me here in the friendship of alcohol, got caught up in the camaraderie, and too late acknowledged they had no money? What do I do?

"Why should I pay for you? I pay for me."

"I am sorry. We have no money. All money is gone. We have no more until we get paid."

So I pay, rejecting Vongthong's thanks and remorse. Sigh. It's OK. Never mind. Drunk, dancing, singing, the others have no interest in the moment between Vongthong and myself.

At 11:30, as David and I sleep in our beds, the door to our hotel room opens. There is a voice thickened in the slur of drink, loud in a drunken whisper. Muffled sincerity. It is Vongthong. David doesn't know who Vongthong is. Someone is in our room, in the night. That's all David knows. Vongthong is sorry, his hands sliding all over my arms and hands in a grope for sympathy.

Didn't we lock the door? We can't remember. I try to explain to David that it is okay, but I only half believe it myself. "Tomorrow," I tell Vongthong. We will talk tomorrow.

In the morning, despite his promise, Vongthong isn't there.

4
Vientiane

The Laotian word for market is talàat. The morning market in Vientiane is the Talàat Sao. The last stall closes sometime after 4:00 P.M. "Morning" is somewhat of a misnomer, and the impression from the street is less market than shantytown. Individual wooden and corrugated sheet metal stalls sit crammed under haphazardly makeshift canopies of canvas and more rusting sheet metal in long muddied alleys covered over in alternating plywood sidewalks and 2x6s laid end to end through the puddles like duck-boards. The impression of walking on water is decidedly un-Christ like.

The market is filled with a wealth unjustified by the surrounding poverty. The currency, the kip, is worthless outside the country and so far worth very little inside. Yet in a city where pedal rickshaw men sell themselves as human engines ferrying passengers across town for 50¢, the stalls of the market are filled with gold and silver ingots and jewellery, authentic—as opposed to the cheap factory-made imitations sold in Thailand—hill tribe artefacts, semi-precious stones and the solid-silver Piastre de Commerce coins of 19th century French Indochina.

At one jewellery stall, a Thai woman holding at least forty bills counts out in methodical precision 500 baht notes in consideration of an entire counter-top piled with silver bracelets and necklaces. At 25 baht to the American dollar, that is $800 US. At 645 kip to the dollar, the figure is a staggering 516,000. Laos is classified by the United Nations Conference on Trade and Development

(UNCTAD) as an LDC, a Least Developed Country. To be considered an LDC, per capita GDP (Gross Domestic Product) has to be less than $200 US per annum. Laos's GDP is $190 US, ahead of only Chad and Bangladesh at $180. By comparison, US per capita GDP is $20,000 US. $190 US equals less than a quarter of that single jewellery stall transaction. She is trading four average annual Laotian incomes in one isolated business deal. In the US in 1990, it would be the equivalent of an $80,000 transaction: in 2000, $88,000. In the food stall at the rear of the market, a baguette is 50 kip, a Pepsi expensive at 200. Rumour has it that transport to Louangphrabang, a three-day journey, will be either *only* 2700 kip or 2700 kip! depending on whether it is a Westerner or a Laotian describing it. For me, 2700 kip is how much I can make in seven minutes teaching in Japan. For a Laotian, it is 2.3 percent of a year's income.

At the northern entrance to the Talàat Sao work the chief currency exchange dealers in the city: old women with hard, impassive looks, lost in conversations with each other until approached. Stacks of currency surround them, folded and wrapped into bundles of tens bound by rubber bands into exchangeable amounts of 1000 or 10,000 kip

They sit in the dirt and mud at the entrance to the rows of appliances and jewels and house wares, on up-turned packing crates and fruit baskets, some with small collapsible tables to work on, some with only cheap cellophane bags to work out of. In their laps, they have small Japanese calculators, still sealed in factory shrink-wrap.

In the economic chaos that is Laos, these are the people who administer the exchange rates. There is no barter, there is no fluctuation, there is no movement. There is a rate. It is understood. Thank you very much. These are not the parasitic traders in China that filled the streets in front of the youth hostels and Westerners' hotels, clustering in groups along the walls and under trees waiting to attack. Shiftless scalpers of currency, badgering each Westerner that went by with unsolicited demanding cries of *Haro! Chan-ji ma-nay?* that sees your way *Haro! Chan-ji ma-nay?* blocked and your footsteps *Haro! Chan-ji ma-nay?* followed after, offering rates that reflect as much your perceived *Haro! Chan-ji ma-nay?* gullibility and their desperation as any sense of a de facto standard, whose every move is counterpointed by a glance that simultaneously cowers in and challenges at the face of authority. They work for others, the middlemen to success, running the risks of imprisonment for those rich enough to wait and control. In Laos, the transaction is in the open. Banks can't do it, but old women do it, hotels do it, even educated fleas do it. In Cheng-du, China, it was in the stall of a restaurant washroom.

The Ekalath's desk clerk's rate was fair.

One woman approaches the changers holding a $100 US bill in her hand, walking away with six thick stacks of ten bound packets of ten 100 kip notes and four and a half loose packets, depositing the wad of cash into a cellophane bag. The moneychanger slips the American bill into her collection of baht, francs and dollars. It is business. That I can see in her pile of American currency, she has at least five more $100 notes.

The banks, on the other hand, are a complete confusion. Venturing in one finds all of the counter space and huge sections of the floor buried under squared blocks of bound currency, entire desk tops hidden under piles of kip, bundled together into foot-deep cubes. It looks like a recycling depot for newspapers and telephone books. On the street, the ones, fives and tens are useless, the tiny bills worn so soiled and tattered they threaten to fall apart at the touch. In front of the bank, three boys toss their rubber thongs at a stack of 10 kip notes tied in a thin red elastic band fifteen feet away in a game of horseshoes.

At a second jewellery stall, a boy carries an Adidas gym bag crammed full of kip, bursting its zipper. Turning it upside down he empties it, bundles of currency tumbling onto the glass countertop as if emptying loot from a satchel in tired film noire.

In a country so poor, where does this wealth come from, this wealth held in so few hands? The old women moneychangers sit with considerable amounts of cash, even by Western standards.

To change $100 US requires 64,500 kip. To be able to change only $100 would be a waste of time: unprofitable and useless. The day's first transaction could be that much. To do business in the market the changers would need the capacity for at least $1000 US and probably more. That is a minimum of 645,000 kip, or 64.5 three-quarter inch stacks of 100-kip notes: 290 cubic inches of currency. Moreover, the currency would be needed every day. Where does this foreign currency go? How is this financing achieved? Where do these women find $1000 US worth of kip each day?

Even more astounding are the gold and silver merchants. They hold enormous wealth in their stocks, a wealth tied up in an inventory with no intrinsic value but that which others are willing to place on it. Compared with the brushes and soap of the neighbouring stalls, this precious metals inventory demands an enormous up-front outlay of capital, with no guarantee for either price or a predictable, cyclical turnover. Even the poorest need to wash, but gold and silver depends too much on tourism, currency fluctuations and international commodities markets. Given the demand for foreign currency within the city, the assumption that most of the inventory was acquired with a hard foreign currency is reasonable. Where did that come from?

The people here are not rich. Vientiane is not Bangkok. The gold and silver dealers are out-dressed and out-conspicuously consumed by the overt claims to fashion of their Thai buyers. Laos's weaker sister status to the thriving economy of Thailand is obvious, and Thailand is not rich. There is great wealth in Thailand, but it is concentrated in the hands of a few in Bangkok and Chiang Mae. Even fleeting glances into the *klongs* and alleys belie the illusion of Mercedes and gold Rolexes as the norm and not the anomaly. In 1988–89, Thailand's GDP rose an astonishing 13.23 percent. In 1989–90, it "slowed" to a still astonishing 12.1 percent. At the same time US GDP rose 4.5%. Yet in absolute terms, Thailand's per capita GDP rose only two hundred dollars, from $1200 US to $1400 US. Two hundred dollars was one day's salary for me in Japan, and not a long day at that. In 1989, American per capita GDP was $22,188. In 1990, it was $23,215. That's a difference of $1027: 73% of Thailand's *total* GDP.

The Talàat Sao is full of excellent questions. The more I ask, the fewer answers I find.

Adjacent to the Talàat Sao is the new indoor market. Fashioned in North American department store style, it is spread out more like a trade fair display in an over-extended Quonset hut. Arena consumerism. Empty of both customers and almost of goods, the atmosphere is cavern-like and echoing. There are cleaned and polished floors, bright overhead fluorescent lights and well-dressed sales girls behind shining empty glass counters. Better-dressed floor managers are there to confirm the integrity of product displays. In the emptiness both stand awkward and unsure of what to do and how to act.

There are sections for freezers and refrigerators and tires and bicycles and stereos and household appliances, and huge end-aisle displays of Ovaltine and Pepsi. At the front, there is a small café, roped off in yellow nylon cord, furnished in white plastic patio tables and chairs under umbrellas arranged Parisian café style, in front of a sparkling glass display counter of cakes and coffee and breads. Hidden at the rear of the store is a small section of Laotian souvenirs.

The few things available in the new annex are all more expensive than in the Talàat Sao, with neither the inherent appeal nor familiarity that the neighbouring ritual carries. The fluorescent atmosphere is uninviting and thick with pretensions to class and exclusivity, pretensions the older market does not even attempt to engender. The Talàat Sao welcomes, in its crowds and its crowdedness, in the informality of its process and its obligation to bargain and socialize. It is, in fact, the removal of the obligation to socialize that at its core differentiates the two. Talàat Sao shopping is the means and the event. Annex shopping is the event, the roped off café just another consumable rather than an inherent characteristic. The Talàat Sao is Laotian, and in its essence belongs. The new market's sterility is uncompromised by either. The dysfunctional leap into a future out of an economically dysfunctional present.

5
Vientiane

N orth of the talàat along the Avenue Lane Xang, standing embarrassingly alone commanding the centre of the avenue, is the Anousavari Monument, the monument to the dead, a huge clay-grey Arc de Triomphe hybrid of classical Laotian Buddhist architecture, French Revolutionary heroism and Stalinist Russian propaganda. It must have sounded better conceptually to the architects sitting around the design table over a glass of wine than it looks actualised in this un-liquored midday; this is the monument Donald Trump would build if he were Laotian. French heroism is symbolized by the basic Arc itself: there is no mistaking where this monument comes from, and like French Colonial thinking, all things emanate from that shape. Whatever else the Anousavari is, French is what it comes from. Buddhism is symbolized in the top of the Arc, the turrets rising up into an ushnīsha, the Buddhist crown. It is the same design as for all door lintels in wat façades: the Monument is like an enormous wat door. The homage to Soviet Communism is much less elaborate and decidedly less permanent: a wooden star, outlined in a string of red Christmas lights, is barely visible over the centre of the Arc, just below the turrets of the ushnīsha. Perhaps when lit it inspires, but on this February day of summer-like heat, it says more derelict trailer park Christmas than Mother Russia.

In a grassy corner park across the avenue from the monument, four small political billboards peek out from underneath a grove of broad-leafed trees. These are neither the side-of-the-wall billboards propagandizing in Xian and Beijing for the twin *C*'s of Communism and copulation nor the sermonizing placards for Motherhood and the Kingdom in Kathmandu. These four neither dominate nor intimidate, their messages quiet and naïve: political equality between sexes and for minorities; the promise of a prosperous future; the continuum of Laotian history from the Kingdom of Lan Xang—the Land of a Million Elephants—to now; and the divine benevolence of the party. Protecting the grass and trees and signs is a white picket fence. Without pictures or text, the message of the white picket fence is more abstract. To me it says Iowa, cornfields and baseball. But this isn't heaven either.

In the vast emptiness under the mortal arch, a lone soda pop peddler waits for the crowd of visitors he has anticipated but who have not yet arrived. It is just him, me, and six empty tables. Clearly, "if you build it, they will come" is a faith, not a guarantee. I circle him and his uninhabited tables, looking for the entrance to the monument I am sure must exist. There's an entrance to the Arc in Paris. Since he is the only person here, if indeed there is an entrance, it is he who would be the keeper of the tickets. The only obvious doorway is padlocked and the interest my blatant circumnavigation should suggest falls on blind, indifferent eyes. I buy a warm Pepsi to justify having walked all this way. To do less would be to look lost and stupid. At least he'll have to notice me now. Without warning, from out of the padlocked door a group of blue-suited businessmen spill. The trick to magic, it is said, is knowing where to look: on second glance, the padlock is hanging un-locked in the hasp, the door closed to create the illusion of impassibility. Still feverishly ignoring me, the Pepsi vendor fawns over the well-dressed dearly departing, against the complete indifference he is returned. Turnabout is fair play. I walk towards the open door, letting the white shirts and neckties pass me by. The pop peddler's body language and facial expression at the blue-suit snub says dazed and confused: he speaks some words, his arms wave, he moves jerkedly back and forth following them as they walk away, he looks and searches for answers, and he speaks again. Profits be damned, maybe he should buy a Pepsi too. Nothing saves face like a tepid soda. His body language at me is less tangled in defeat:

You want what? Do you <u>know</u> who is ignoring me? Still, he can run but he can't hide, and now his cover is blown. There is no denying the open entrance I am standing beside. Tickets are 50 kip. Reluctantly, he takes my money.

The smell is of must and construction, of unfinished basements and underground car parks. Rusting rebar juts from concrete staircases that spiral either upwards, always upwards, or dead into concrete walls. It is like being trapped inside the world of M.C. Escher. The crunch of debris under my feet echoes off the walls and then flounders, muffled in the dust. The feeling is one of abandonment: *monumentus interruptus.*

The turreted panorama from the top proves two things: Vientiane is less a city of buildings than of trees, and it is empty. Avenue Lane Xang reeks of inactive desolation: colonial buildings grand in conception behind vast tracts of frontage left empty in architectural design, but in the unrealized skyline of cosmopolitan development, a mere acknowledgement of crumbling colonialism, of permeating neglect and poverty. The curbs and sidewalks that front the length of this architectural disintegration have fared no better. They too are empty, and while treeless, at least have given themselves back to nature and vegetation. Huge cracks and heaves break the surface, sporadic chunks of pavement lifted away and discarded, dirt and grass sprouting in reclamation through the neglect. Scars of exposed cement are covered with dead leaves and fallen tree branches. The roadway itself is a blotched patchwork of discoloured repair, six lanes of checkerboard road lying deserted but for a handful of bicycles and even fewer vehicles.

Nowhere is there the congestion and commotion of the rest of Asia. A similar ascent in Cheng-du *Haro! Chan-ji ma-nay?* proved with equal conclusiveness China's treelessness *and* overcrowding. Rivers of bicycles moved in continuous flows down either side of justifiably immense boulevards, each cyclist fighting for his or her own few feet of space against the surges and demands of a current that, acting independently of the individual, never allowed more than inches.

Deserted. Empty. For minutes huge sections of the road remain untouched by even the shadow of movement, a stillness broken

Fellini-like in slow motion surrealism by a solitary bicycler cutting across the patched pavement, a woman in green holding a red umbrella. Then a second bicycle, a man sweeping through the space, an un-umbrellaed woman slung side-saddle over the cross bar, balancing on her thighs between his hands and the seat. I feel like I'm watching Paul Newman and Katharine Ross listenin' to *Raindrops*.

My solitude is broken by the appearance of four children as startled at my presence as I am at theirs. They approach, straddling in taunts and dares the line between satisfying their curiosity and exposing their fear. A game played with an unknown adversary, defined by laughter and teasing and an exaggeration of voices too confident to be so.

As consideration to friendship, I offer them my camera to look at. They peer through it, a view they must have felt the exclusive domain of tourists. The opportunity to look becomes mesmerizing, and after waves of the camera towards the skyline, the view is turned towards each other. The commonality of faces, feet, friends—seen in a suddenly realized wonderment. They become models and photographer, posing and preening for each other. Even more anxious are they to pose for me. It was not the monument experience either of us had expected. Sing it, B.J. Soft trumpets.

Four Russian voices reverberate out of the stairwell, echoing against the cement. Two heavy-set caricatures of Soviet matronhood approach me up the stairs. Their cheeks are red as we pass, not from exertion but heavy make-up trying both to hide a pale complexion and to accent the *haute-couture* of proletarianism. One is clearly the other's elder, but the difference seems not so much youth versus age as cynicism versus resignation. The three of us pass each other on the narrow steps, myself smiling in anticipated acknowledgment. They pass me without notice and I feel my skin blush. At the bottom two equally heavy-set male caricatures wait clutching video cameras and sipping tepid Pepsi's through cellophane straws, their matching fire-engine-red Polo shirts pulled without satisfaction across their potbellies. Trips to Laos, so goes the rumour, are a reward for attaining factory production quotas. Red is a common signal in nature for danger.

At the opposite end of Avenue Lane Xang, south from the market towards the Mekong, are Wat Sisaket, the oldest existing wat in Vientiane, built in 1824, and Wat Pra Keo. Sisaket's viharn sits in the centre of a large, crumbling, yellow-wash stucco quadrangle under a thatch and wood-beam roof, the protected cloister lined with two tiers of life-sized Buddha images.

In Indian iconography—for the historical Buddha, Siddhartha Gautama, was an Indian—there are thirty-two "marks" which are common to all *mahāpurusha*, all "Great Persons". Great Persons can be either Universal Emperors or Buddhas. According to one legend, the infant Siddhartha was visited by the sage Asita, who saw the "Great Person" signs on the child's body. The *Dīgha Nikayā*, a sacred text in Theravada Buddhism, lists the thirty-two marks of the "Superman", the term used in the *Dīgha Nikayā* for Great Persons, including: 4) He is long in fingers and toes; 11) His complexion is like bronze, the colour of gold; 14) The down on his body turns upward, every hair of it in little curling rings to the right; 19) His proportions have the symmetry of the banyan-tree: the length of his body is equal to the compass of his arms, and the compass of his arms is equal to his height; 28) He has a divine voice like the karavīka bird's; 31) Between the eyebrows appears a hairy mole, an ūrnā, white and like soft cotton; 32) His head is like a royal turban, an ushnīsha.

Iconographically, some of these thirty-two marks are evident in Buddha images. Some, clearly, are not. In practice, sign eleven is depicted through gilding: worshippers buy small squares of gold leaf and rub it onto the surface of the images, eventually creating a solid gold façade. In the meantime, the statues are patched in confusions of squares more resembling neglect than adoration. Mark number four manifests itself iconographically by the fingers of Buddha images coming to be of equal length. Marks number thirty-one and thirty-two join to make the Buddha's hair. According to legend, when Siddhartha left home, he cut his hair with his own sword, and afterwards, it curled clockwise and never needed to be cut again. Iconographically, his scalp is covered in hundreds of tight, clockwise knots, sometimes simply following the shape of the skull, sometimes rising up into an ushnīsha.

The images in Wat Sisaket's cloister are identical, repeating Buddhas sitting cross-legged in the half-lotus bhumisparshmudrā, the "touching the earth" position, the feet crossed in the virāsana, or "hero," position, the right leg lying over the left thigh rather than both feet lying across opposite thighs. In the bhumisparshmudrā, which represents the Buddha's enlightenment, the left palm lies open across the lap, the right hand reaching down, touching the earth. Iconographically, the bhumisparshmudrā represents an event on the night of the Buddha's enlightenment and his passage from the of-this-world Siddhartha to the not-of-this-world Buddha. Touching the earth, Siddhartha summoned Thoranee, the earth goddess, to witness the merit he had accrued through many lifetimes to justify his passage into Buddhahood. The foreheads and breasts of the large images have been anointed with foil squares of gold leaf, fresh squares glittering and bright over older cracked and dusty blessings. Behind the images, in six tiers of votive niches, more identical bronze images meditate, two Buddhas to each niche. Behind a padlocked jail cell door in the portico, hundreds of mutilated Buddha images have been crammed into the space, the images piled one on top of another in a disembodied collage of shapes, across each image's base a hand painted white identity tattoo: D4299, 335, 389, 526, 377, 371. Some of the Buddhas have been decapitated, some simply disfigured with hands snapped off at the wrists and arms at the elbows. Many are missing their entire upper torsos, the metal eaten away, bronze chests reduced to formless blobs as though dissolved by acid, leaving disassociated virāsana legs and the crossed, palm in palm hands of dhyānamudrā meditators.

Three Laotian men arrive, and as we approach each other in the sanctuary, a clink, clink, clink, clinking of metal against metal becomes audible and grows louder. One of the men is holding his ring of keys, and as they circle the images, he taps it against the shoulders and head of each Buddha as though making sure they are not chocolate. With each clink I feel the slow, reactive building to anger. Not at the noise, which while annoying is really inconsequential, but at the apparent irreverence for the images, the disregard for the history, for the art, for the sanctuary. It is a dilemma, for this place is his history, this sanctuary is his religion. I am only a visitor here, and a convert of the most unapparent kind. Who am I to tell him how to act? Who am I to know? What is it that I do that without intent creates reactions in others? Perhaps the tapping is in reaction to me? What, after all, is some white guy doing in this wat? But this is my adopted religion, or at least as adopted as I can admit to. There is more, and less, to being religious than proclaiming it. Moreover, these Buddha images are part of the collective world culture, a collective I am as entitled to here as he is to old-growth Douglas Firs in Canada. These are my statues too.

A guided Western couple arrives and now I feel encroached upon. To enter an area already crowded is to notice and accept. To have the crowd arrive is to have acceptance forced upon you. That the end result remains the same is an unconvincing argument. The time to go is not always determined by a watch.

What was once Wat Pra Keo is now museum Pra Keo, the single viharn standing alone in an open grassed yard. Fumbling through my pockets for the 200 kip entrance fee, I have only 170 left. The third-poorest country in the world, and I *still* don't have enough money. The woman in the booth takes it anyway, smiling me inside. A forest of Buddha images crowd the small floor space, cluttering the room in a jumble of shapes and colours that blend and feed into each other, engulfing me and making me a part of the display, moving the experience from one of seeing to one of being. Outside, the portico is lined with bronze Buddha images, each meditating in bhumisparshmudrā, their eyes downturned and serene under gull-wing eyebrows, the deep brown of the bronze rich and deep held up against the gold-leaf of the wat's façade. In a single open palm in a single image there is a solitary marigold. Withered in the heat, the petals have dried and fallen off the bud, collapsing into a halo around the stem. Thoranee's answer.

6
Vientiane

In our last night at the Ekalath, an Englishman that neither myself, David, Andy nor Laura has seen before walks alone into the dining room just as we are starting our after-dinner coffees. He is an old Mekong River View Guesthouse Tour-ist, which makes him an ex-Ekalath Hotel guest too. Now he is a Sailom Guesthouse guest. Tonight is his last night in Laos, the Ekalath a final reminiscence. Tomorrow David and I will leave the Ekalath, becoming ex-Ekalath Hotel guests and new Sailom Guesthouse guests. Andy and Laura chose the 250 baht offer. They will become ex-Ekalath Hotel guests as well, but not tomorrow. There is nothing the Englishman wants at the Sailom, no one he wants to talk to. Tomorrow he will be an ex-Laos-traveller.

At the Sailom there were too many telling stories, too many searching for information: Vietnam, Thailand, China, my story is better than your story. Travel one-upmanship for the sake of ego over experience. He felt alone, reflective; looking for completion, an ending justified, an ending worthy of this experience. There is a time for information during travel, a time when where you are going tomorrow is more important than where you have been. But not tonight. Not now. After the long wait in Nong Khai, after the struggles and fears and events, it was over. Tomorrow Thailand. Just like that. Thailand. It rang hollow, like an evening of beer drunk alone by circumstance instead of choice.

Can he join us?

"Look," Andy says. "I was in the hospital sick. I should have died. I was operated on. Everyone thought I would die. And I recovered. They even brought the priest in. But I recovered. My mother was sure it was the hand of God, sure that I was blessed. Sure it was her prayers. Sure it was something. So I took her to my doctor and I sat her down in his office and I looked at him, and in front of her, I asked him, 'Did God save me? Am I alive because of the hand of God?' And he said 'No. We saved you. You and me. My skill as a surgeon, your desire to live. I looked down on that table,' he said, 'and I knew you were a fighter. I knew you would live. It wasn't God. It wasn't Divine Providence. It was you and me. Us. That's all'."

"But lots of people want to live," David says, "Want to . . ."

"Look. No hand of God. No miracles. Him and me. Not him and me and Him. Just the two of us. That's all. This is the real world here. That's all there is. Start living in it. Stop wasting your time worrying about God or enlightenment and start living in the world because it's not going to wait around for you."

"What about love?" I say. "What about falling in love? Is that 'the real world'? Falling in love with someone that 'the real world' tells you is wrong? Or at a time when you don't want to fall in love? What about love at first sight? What about all the things we know ourselves, but we can't explain away with any kind of logic that a non-believer would accept? When I met Cassie, I fell down in front of her on my knees and said *Who are you?* and I felt neither embarrassment nor surprise because I knew, somewhere inside *we* knew, we had been together before. It was all too familiar, all too right."

"Maybe you know then," Andy says, "but I don't. This is the real world. Trees. Sky. This table. It's real, it's not some feeling. The real world. Start living in it. I believe in love because love is real. It's not some concoction someone's trying to sell you. It's not some religion. It's not some God. It's real. I can see it. I can feel it. It's part of the world. I know it's real. I know it exists."

"But how do you know it exists?" the Englishman says. "You can't see it. You can't put it in your pocket. Show me love. You can't, can you. You're married because you love each other, but that's not love, that's an action you took *because* of love. That's all you can do; show me actions, show me reactions. Events. Causes and effects. That's the same logic people use to explain God, but you say God doesn't exist."

"Look. You're just playing games now," Andy says. "You know love exists. I know love exists. Our love *scares* people at home, doesn't it? They think I'm too old, that she's too young. That we can't really love each other. Right? But we do. It's real. I know it exists. She knows it exists. Love is real, mate, it's not some dream, it's not some cosmic association."

"What about déjà-vu," I say. "About precognitions to events, that as they happen, I can see before my eyes as already having been? I have them all the time. Little ones. Flashes that say *I know this*. All the déjà-vu I had when I met Cassie, that I experienced when we were together? Overwhelming my logic, telling me *this is the one, this is your partner*. Flooding over me in relentless waves until I was forced to concede to something I had no real understanding of?"

"Look mate. I don't know what your déjà-vu are, but they aren't God, I know that. You want to make them God, fair enough. But don't sell it here. I don't believe."

"But," the Englishman says, "can you really understand something if you haven't experienced it yet? So the understanding of God and love becomes the same. If you've experienced love, then you believe in it, you understand it, how it works. If you've experienced God, *whatever* that is, then you believe in it too, you understand it. To know life, to know the world, you have to experience it. In Indonesia I was thrown in jail. I was stabbed with a knife. Now I understand what they mean and what they don't mean. It is a way of finding truth. To experience it. So you've experienced love and know it exists. Why not God? Why can't you experience God, whatever it may be, and know that it exists? Why are you so adamant?"

"Truth isn't getting stabbed in some jail. Truth is here and now. Truth is reality. This is reality. There is no searching for truth because it's here. You can't tell me that this isn't reality. This is real. The real world. Start living in it."

And of course he is right. Reality is truth, and reality is here and now. What else is Zen and Vipassana if not here and now. The moment. The reality of the moment, unadulterated, unconcocted. Goenka-ji taught us to learn to see the moment *As it is. As it is.* Not the *is* I wanted it to be, not the *is* I desired. Knowledge of Self and others and the world gained simply by seeing the moment in all its simplicity and complexity for what it is. And yet inside me there is still this conflict, this incompatibility of thought. I believe in the truth of the moment. I know I can't experience the future. I know I can't re-experience the past. They don't exist now. Only the moment. Only now. Yet in this moment, I have déjà-vus that tell me I have had these moments already, confirming inside me that I am where I should be, following my true destiny and not some contrived destiny of an intellectual determinism. Is it no more than an inadequate vocabulary? An inability to express myself through the limitations of my language?

"What are you going to do after this, when you get home?" David asks me. "After all this time. After everything done and experienced?"

"Act on my dreams. Make them work. From dreams to reality. What else can I do? A suit and tie? Nine to five?"

"But to follow your dreams is to face the possibility, if not the probability, of failure, and if you fail at your dreams, it's you that fails. It isn't some job where you can point to the product, or at the boss, or at the system. It's you."

"But how else can I live? I put myself on the line and I try to succeed. Which is better? Put myself on the line and fail, or never put myself on the line and compromise my dreams and goals to fear. I have to attempt my dreams. I can't simply exist. If I could just exist, I would still be at home now, instead of here. It's just existing I've run away from.

"I've already compromised enough in my life. I can't compromise any more. If you never open windows to look out, if you live behind your walls of safety and that's all you know, then okay. But if you open those windows, if you walk out from behind those walls, then how can you turn back to the life you had before, inside the walls? You can't. How could I look at myself as an old man and know that I looked life in the eyes and said 'No'? Some people do.

Some people look out of the windows and say 'Thank you very much, but it's not for me'. Fair enough. They made a decision. But I look out of the window and see life. In all its glorious possibilities, life. And for me to say 'No' is to betray myself and to betray my life. I can't do that."

"Yes, but fear. A lot of people are afraid," says David. "Scared. A job is a game. If you fail it's only a lost game. No more. But your dreams. To fail is to have nothing to turn back to. There is nothing else after your dreams. Do you have the strength to fight for your dreams? Do you have the strength to succeed? The courage?"

"The strength to succeed? I don't know. I hope so. Do I have the strength and courage to fail? I don't know. But I do know that I don't have the courage and the strength to not try, to acquiesce to the fears and to lose the knowledge of these years. There can be no more 'what ifs'."

At 2:30 it is time to go to bed. Andy and Laura wish us good-night and leave, followed soon after by David. The Englishman can't find his wallet. It has gone missing since he came into the hotel. He can remember taking it out to pay for a round of beers, but after that nothing. There were no other guests. Only the five of us. Only three staff on duty. No one has found the wallet, and a search in the dining room with all the lights turned on produces nothing.

Out loud we both wonder if the small staff knows he is both not a guest and is leaving tomorrow and that as a result, there is nothing he can do? That time was the only thing he really had here, and now, even that is over?

7
Vientiane

W at Ongtue's inner courtyard is a large grassy square defined by a quadrangle of weathered yellow stucco buildings and criss-crossed by flagstone walkways. Bobbing flashes of brilliant orange zigzag back and forth through the space, the draught of a novice's robe caught in the movement of step: a pleat, a fold, the shade of fabric deepening the oranges into undulations of waves as if ripples on a evening shoreline. From a second-storey window, a tangerine robe hangs across a windowless sill drying, a brass alms bowl anchoring it from the non-existent breeze.

"Sabadee," a voice says.

His arms are folded across his chest, the brim of a green baseball cap pulled low hiding his eyes. A layman. Where I am from, he wants to know. When did I come to Laos? Why am I here? What do I want to see? What am I looking for? What is my job? Am I really a brunette? His interest is questions, his approach abrupt and rapid-fire. Rapid-fire questions aren't really about information: they're about keeping power.

What *do* I want here?

A second voice, a directionless "Hello" interrupts the interrogation. I turn towards the voice, searching for it but not finding it. And again it comes. "Hello."

"You!" The voice is louder, no longer directionless. It is Monk Thong Liam Inthvong. "This is my teacher," he says.

"Yes," the man in the green baseball cap says. "Three times a week I teach the monks. But I get no money. I am not a teacher. I am a student to be a teacher. I go to the Training Teachers School College in Vientiane. I am in my third year. Class A. Next year I will finish and then I will be a teacher. Now I am a student."

More novices gather around us, crowding close to their teacher. Their robes catch the light, radiating the colour of the late afternoon sun into their faces.

"Do you like to see our school?" Monk Inthvong says. "Do you teach the monks? It is almost time to begin the class. I must to go. Do you teach the monks?"

Is all he knows questions too? Monk Inthvong's apple has not fallen far from the green baseball cap's tree of knowledge. At least I know his name now. My Class A interrogator is Mr. Pradith Souvanxay.

The classroom breathes colonialism. The yellow stucco walls that used to be white are like all the walls of Vientiane, streaked in the sweat and oppressiveness of age and humidity. High, heavy wood shutters fill the windows. Oblique planes of light filter through the louvres into the back of the room. Dust and chalk on the leading edges of the slats catch the sun and glow hot white, the brightness taking away the definition. The light strikes the worn dull ceramic floor-tiles hard, bouncing diffused back into itself, leaving the floor hazy, as if in a fog. The two-seat wood desks, grey and smooth with age, line up straight facing the front. The single overhead light is turned off.

The lesson is a series of elaborately complex "cloze passage" structures about *which, what* and *whose*: a grammar structure is written with a blank left, the student's job being to fill the blank with the correct noun or verb. The handwriting is delicate and precise, the chalk forms covering the entire green slate board from edge to edge, the letters crafted instead of written, with a resoluteness of style that says the teacher is a non-native English speaker. I've seen this chalkmanship before. For all its beauty, the lesson is burdened by vocabulary contrived and overwhelming for the target structure. At least Mr. Pradith Souvanxay is consistent. Question: "Whose wrought-iron gate is this?" doesn't ring quite like "Whose pencil is this?" especially when the full object pronoun is Monk Thong Liam Inthvong. Besides, "whose" is possessive. The students are Buddhist bhikkhus: they don't own anything. "Question: Whose pencil is this?" Answer: "It's no one's."

The green baseball capped teacher introduces the topic and me. I recognize Canada and a gesture of his hand, but nothing else. I let it go. This communication is about essence and not specifics, and I understand it completely. It is all too familiar: an older Asian male with a competent smattering of English introducing me to younger Asian males less competently smattered. The monks peer at me through the explanation, whispering among themselves, nudging each other. To see them singularly in the context of their robes is to lose sight of their youth. They are just teenagers, the bonding through religion left wanting by the bonding of their age and friendship. The dual nature of their reality too often eludes me. It is the uttarāsanga robe I see first: grey means Korean Mahayana, black Japanese Zen, burgundy Tibetan Vajrayana, the flavours of orange from saffron to pumpkin to rust, Thai or Laotian Theravada. It is the robe that I see first, not that the wearer is eighteen. Monks have no age.

The moment is my life in Japan revisited, the descriptors familiar: control, celebrity, Westerner, native speaker, dancing bear. There is no question of authority, no question of discipline or one-upmanship. No question that this is entertainment and not education. No question that this is not Japan: the nudging and joking I see here would have waited till break and me safely out of the way. Honour, you know. At least that's what they call it.

Whatever I am, what I am not is their "real" teacher. That I *am* a teacher is merely coincidence, and while it may be a meaningful, directed coincidence for me, it is unimportant to the man in the green baseball cap or the larger game as a whole. I am just another tourist pulled in off the street in a game of mutual curiosity and exchange. It's a game all too common in Asia: fifteen minutes of celebrity through the birthright of language. That night's hotel guest becomes "the foreign teacher" cajoled into teaching for free: good business masquerading as friendship, accepted in ego gratification masquerading as goodwill. Sometimes, the fifteen minutes lasts years. The teacher under the green cap stands calm and coy at the front introducing me. He is far too smooth for me to have been his first "guest".

Monk by monk I go through the class for introductions until after only a few it is obvious I will never remember even one name let alone twenty. Monk Thong Liam Inthvong beams in teacher's-pet pride, describing to all around him that I was to his wat earlier, that he gave me water. We are friends. I remember him, and in the remembering, everything is proven valid. And he does it in English too. For forty-five minutes I teach, moving the boys in and out of *which* and *what* and *whose*, applauding correct answers and slapping my forehead in feigned exasperation for the less correct answers, moving quickly, until the monks themselves initiate the applause, until they laugh and shout and smile.

And then it is over. "Please come back tomorrow. Or anytime," Mr. Baseball says. *I don't get paid whether you come or not.*

Two of the monks want to take me to their wat. "It is near," they tell me. The lessons, they tell me, are for monks at all the wats in the area, not just Wat Ongtue. Outside the complex walls, we turn away from the others and head down a dirt alley littered in rusting machine parts and papers, walled off from the outside by a high thatch bamboo-strip fence.

Wat Chantabury has no wall. There is a small hedge and a few large trees. There is no grass, no pavement, no stone paths. There is only an earthen courtyard with tufts of grass burnt brown and worn. At the rear under a Bodhi tree, there is a swing set and a jungle gym. Monasteries in Thailand and Laos often take in orphans.

Under the tree stands an old monk dressed only in his antaravāsaka smoking the stub of a cigarette. His skin hangs shrivelled and prune-like, the once-proud indigo tattoos that cover his chest and upper arms prophylactically, devoid of their youthful sleekness, relegated in age to discoloured scar tissue. A lifetime as a monk and he has progressed to no other wat, no other place but this poor temple, defiantly stealing drags from clandestine cigarettes in the fading dusk, an addict forced into the solitude of a back alley or building entranceway because the office has become non-smoking. The look of a wino in a soiled suit; wizened whiskers on a face that doesn't have to be that old; an opportunity lost and squandered. In the fading dusk he stands, old in a garb that is ageless, without the vigour to sustain it. Buddhadāsa was old, but he never looked old. Not to me at least. It was not the age I saw first anyway. It is not the age that sustains the robe. It is the Self.

The two monks who brought me here are Monk Sou-A and Monk Kanya Sanaxay. They have been studying English for two years now at Ongtue. It is a good education, they say. We climb a tree ladder into Monk Sou-A's khuti, the small square hut where he lives. He pulls a large green coconut from under his bed and from a side table, two clean tumblers. On the table there is a small machete, and he hacks at the crown of the nut until it breaks open. He fills one of the glasses with the milk and a slice of meat from the crown and hands it to me. He and Monk Kanya Sanaxay will share a drink water. It is long past noon. Their vows will not allow the milk. Monk Sou-A will eat the remaining flesh tomorrow. For now he and Monk Sanaxay will be satisfied with water. Monk Sou-A removes the robe from his shoulders and sits in his thin yellow undershirt.

Monk Sou-A loves English, he tells me. Green-capped teacher Souvanxay is good. He studies very hard, he says, but it is expensive. He must pay 2000 kip per month to take lessons at Ongtue, about $3.50 US. He has no money. His mother sends him the kip he needs each month. I keep waiting for him to ask for money, for him to add a *so* and extend his hand. He never does.

On the wall against the unfinished wooden slats is a huge photo of the golden Chinnarat Buddha image in Phitsanulok, in Northern Thailand: the Buddha sitting in the bhumis-parsh-mudrā position, left hand across his lap, right hand lowered touching the earth summoning Thoranee, the filial flame rising into an ushnīsha, a halo of brilliance and leaping fire licks that encircle the image's head. From the Talàat Sao, he says. The rest is Spartan, the expectation of a monk's residence: a dresser, his begging bowl, a window, a clothesline strung across the room, a second robe draped above his bed. In the outer room, the walls are covered in magazine pictures of models unprovocative in both posture and clothing. He is an eighteen-year-old monk, not a monk eighteen years old.

There is, he says, a monastery on the road to Thaduea. It is very good. I must go. He tells me the name, but it is lost to me in the unfamiliarity of the sounds, even in repetition. He draws the name on my book in delicate, reverent pencil strokes:

WAT XIANG KOUN

Monk Sou-A is delicate and serene, lulling me to calmness. His English is all but gone, used up in his name, his age, his need for money. Twilight. Shadows disappear in the quickening darkness. Crickets.

In the stillness under the Bodhi tree, the old monk lights another cigarette. So close to Buddha. Another defiance to overcome.

8

Vientiane

A ndy and Laura's map lists a night market only a few blocks from the Santiouk steak restaurant. The four of us—Andy, Laura, David and myself—make our way there; the promised market proves to be only a muddy street of two café patisseries, a "five and dime" store of children's plastic seaside toys, a Vietnamese restaurant and the city's only movie cinema. Life. There is no reason to believe the integrity of the experience to be in question. There is no reason to believe it isn't. Maybe there's just no reason to believe.

Pastry is one of the only vestiges of the French that seemed neither decrepit, crumbling nor unwanted. Rectangles of white cake with white icing and green leaves and syrupy yellow flowers; dark brown chocolate lines of coffee icing over cappuccino cake; circles of fruit in tart pastry shells and cream custard. Unquestionably French, unquestionably delicious, unquestionably questionable. As good as they looked or yet another mimicked reality, like the Shakey's Pizza in Nagoya? Shakey's (letting aside for the moment the oddness in general of a Sacramento, CA, pizza parlour designed around Barbershop Quartet music in Nagoya, the home of Shogun Tokugawa Ieasu, the inspiration for James Clavell's *Shōgun* and the first Japanese Shōgun) offered a Tuesday all-you-can-eat lunch. The toppings on offer included canned tuna, canned corn nibblets with *nori* (dried, shredded seaweed. It's the pizza seaweed of choice in Napoli, they say), and for true connoisseurs, canned corn *and* nori. Besides, cake has not always been kind to me, and fooled once, shame on you, but fooled twice, shame on me.

And so: Kunming, Sichuan province, China. Home of the wild Giant Panda. Home of the Kunming Zoo. There are an estimated 1,600 Giant Pandas left living in the wild. There are exactly 266 Pandas in captivity worldwide, although whether this is in fact "living" or not is a separate discussion. Kunming Zoo has five of them. In captivity, the oldest Giant Pandas lived to be thirty-four years old. The wild is much less forgiving. The exchange for this longevity is simple: instead of a dignified, although shortened existence eating bamboo in the forest, these pandas, at least, get to live a quarter of a century dirty and scrawny, held behind rusting steel bars in huge concrete boxes neatly devoid of even a single natural or man-made object that might detract from the large mounds of steaming panda shit produced from eating all that fibre. In front of the cage looking at the huge soiled animals, an old Chinese woman with bound feet; stubs of appendages in impossibly tiny, delicate silk booties. (The desired dimension was no more than three inches, although the average was closer to 3.9 inches. Size rears it's ugly head again. Despite claims to the contrary—that it wasn't the size of the stub that mattered, but what you did with it— size really did matter. That here smaller is better is not the point. It is all shit.) Two others helped the old woman along as she mimicked walking. Unlike the panda, Chinese women with bound feet are extinct in the wild, with few remaining in captivity. There are no accurate statistics for the remaining number, but it is thought that with proper care, they could live to be ninety-plus years old. Unlike the pandered to pandas, their cages are relatively gilded, and to my knowledge, they are not fed bamboo. Like the Pandas, these small-footed beauties also produce steaming piles of shit, but this is administered with much more discretion and much less fanfare. Only the finest women were considered important enough to deform in the name of beauty and eroticism, a truism that no amount of conciliatory bamboo offered the large-footed would change, although given their more peripatetic lifestyle, one would assume more food intake and larger piles of steaming shit, vis-à-vis the deformed beauties at least. Life for the poor is never about fair. But I digress. Next to the panda and the puss-in-booties was a full-footed cake vendor. The cake in question was a large slab-cake cut into squares, covered in a thick yellow swirling frosting that crested in peaks, dabbled with pink rosebuds and cream-lined edges, each square pricked with a toothpick for clean, no-fuss eating. After twenty-nine months away from home, hidden in the depths of China, I saw it. Western baking. The dive into my nostalgia was headfirst.

My mother, who bought those sugary Safeway cakes, taught me to wait an hour after eating before swimming. My friend's mother, who bought him similarly sugary Safeway cakes, taught him to look before he leapt. That is the problem with mothers and analogies. Sometimes, one isn't enough, and they're never there when you really need them. It wasn't cake. It wasn't icing. It wasn't fair. Cornbread smothered in food colour dyed butter was not the taste of my childhood. Cornbread was not what my mother had bought on my birthday. Unable to shake the remembrance of those Safeway birthday cakes, I carried my desire unrequited for days. It is not the shape of the cages that defines us, but the presence of the cage that connects us.

The cakes in Vientiane taste just as the cakes I remember. There are no false idols. Cake and coffee for 350 kip. My mother would be proud.

At ten o'clock, it is time to close up the street. How much cake can one man eat anyway? Andy and Laura make their way back to the Ekalath, David and I to the Sailom. We all got our visas extended today. There's nothing to keep us here but the time it takes to make plans. No one says it out loud, but we all know: it's time to go. This is probably our last night together.

9
Vientiane

I t's Tuesday. It's clear. David and I have decided. Today will be our last day at the Sailom, our last day in Vientiane. We are going south, overland, to Pakxé and Wat Phu, a Khmer temple in Champasak Province. Tomorrow. It sounds so easy: "David and I have decided." In Laos, nothing is as easy as simply deciding and then doing. "David and I have decided. We are going south." If we can: if they let us.

In Laos, there are only four travel options, and one of those is to leave the country. Since we are already in Vientiane, north or south are our choices. According to information at the Sailom, there is daily bus service to Pakxé. There is, as well, Lao Aviation.

Officially, travelling south is impossible. Although not explicitly stated at the Thaduea immigration, it was explicitly stated by Our Man in the Mekong: All visas issued for independent travel in Laos are valid for Vientiane and only Vientiane. Unless I am booked on an "official" Lao Tourism package, whatever lies outside the city limits is off-limits. Wink. So help me God.

There is one "official" loophole. Independent travel by non-Laotians outside of Vientiane is permissible with an internal passport, a document that is, depending on which story you believe, either unavailable to foreigners or easily available for $200 US. This means that the Air Lao option from Vientiane to Pakxé is also impossible. I am a foreigner and I don't have $200 US to spare. There are daily flights to Pakxé on Lao Aviation. They are $85 US. Not the bargain that one expects in third-world

Southeast Asia, but time-wise, cheap compared to going overland. To acquire an outgoing internal ticket is as simple as paying cash, booking a date, and showing your official travel permission. In the form of an internal passport. Which is unavailable. Or available for $200 US. Depending on whom you talk to. But I haven't met anyone with an internal passport yet, and I haven't met anyone who has met anyone that has an internal passport. And I'm not going to.

In the late afternoon, we head for the bus station. At the Sailom we are told it is "not far," but "not far" is half an hour's walk away from the centre of Vientiane, and we both wonder aloud if we haven't actually broken our entry-visa restrictions just getting there. Bus tickets are 4000 kip each, about $6.20 US. The trip is two days. The good news is that there are still tickets for tomorrow. The better news is that overnight accommodation is included in the price. The best news is that the woman selling the tickets, who speaks English, either doesn't know, or doesn't care, about internal passports. We have money and desire: that is good enough. The bad news is that the bus leaves at 5:00 A.M. Sharp. We both agree: 4:00 A.M. in the Sailom's lobby. Better early than late. I'm tired already.

David and I walk most of the way back together, but we are both in the mood to be alone, and at the Talàat Sao, we break apart.

All over again, I am alone.

It is twilight, moving to darkness, a shifting lilac monochrome folding over into itself that sharpens sounds, suspending them in the moment. Shapes and dimensions fade, the texture and quality of the object lost to its essence. Across from the Talàat Sao, a narrow paved side street that leads back to the guesthouse breaks away from Avenue Lane Xang at right angles. Removed from the avenue, the road's edge changes from concrete sidewalk to earth shoulders to bamboo and weed ditches to finally a slough surrounding a cluster of grey wooden shanties on stilts. Creaky boardwalks join the fronts of the shanties, the slats fading into the puzzle of mismatched, rusting corrugated metal roof panels, discordant and impoverished.

Sudden strobes of metallic blue and grey break the mauve light, flickering like a moth against a flame. Here, gone. Here, gone, a staccato brilliance moving through amethyst sky: a television set, at the rear of one of the shanties. Black and white, sitting on an upturned wood-slat fruit crate in front of a single candy-apple vinyl stool, the only piece of furniture visible. There is no one there. I squint to focus through the twilight. More movement, more confusion. The screen shifts, bouncing, unsteady. The Mike Tyson vs. Buster Douglas fight. Jab, weave, jab, HIT, knockdown. I had heard the results in Nong Khai. Douglas by a tenth-round knockout. A fight for undisputed heavyweight champion. At least until the next dispute. It had been fought in Tokyo at the Tokyo Dome, and because I had lived in Japan I felt I should care. Again and again and again the tape plays. Jab, uppercut, HIT, knockdown. Jab, uppercut, HIT, knockdown. Jab, uppercut, HIT, knockdown. Each time, Tyson falls. Each time Douglas wins. Again and again. Time stands still.

Not amethyst anymore. Darker. Lavender. Deeper. Calmer. Enveloping, like an unbuttoned flannel shirt. Surrounding. Behind me a sāam láw tricycle rickshaw rings its bell.

"Your friend is here," the old lady behind the counter at the Sailom Guesthouse says. "He is in the dorm. It is on the second floor."

Paul. At the Sailom. It's funny. I wondered if I would see him. Over these past few months, our paths have crossed so often I wonder if there is not some sort of bizarre destiny at work, some lesson to be learned through the association. Now, my first night out of the Ekalath, and here he is.

I met Paul in Nagoya, Japan, on a mid-week afternoon in the spring of 1986 at Time T.I. Communications. Time T.I. was, and still is, an English conversation school, specializing in business clients: Toyota Motors, Honda Motors, Mitsubishi Bank, Mitsubishi Motors, Nippon Denso. I was there when Paul and his then-girlfriend carried in a four-pack of canned Guinness for Gordon, their new boss and my then-boss. Paul and his then-girlfriend had wanted Kyoto and settled for not-Kyoto, which was Nagoya. I wanted not-Vancouver and jumped at the not-Vancouver which was Nagoya. I had started on March 8, 1986, finding the job through the brother of the ex-neighbour of my ex-boss. Funny old world. It's never what you know. Only weeks before I started, Time T.I. Communications had had the much more impressive moniker of Time-Life Educational Systems, Japan, but through mergers and corporate moves, it was no more. The *T* stood for Tesco, another educational company, the *I* for Itoman, a trading company. Tesco later went bankrupt, and Itoman "had problems". It was too expensive to change the name again. Time Communications just kept the T.I. Still, it wasn't "The Cherry English School" or "The Pencil English School", or worse, "The Cherry English School T.I.".

Paul, his then-girlfriend and my then-self were teachers by birthright. English is an official language in Canada. In Japan, this qualified me to teach English. This also made me a French language teacher by birthright, since French is also an official language. Oddly, this also made me a champion field lacrosse player and an expert in hunting and trapping beavers. Birthright has a lot to answer for. That I knew nothing about English grammar was irrelevant. I knew only marginally more about beavers and nothing about lacrosse. Only one of my seventeen colleagues knew anything about English grammar—that as time progressed many of us did was beside the point; it wasn't so much about job fulfilment as it was classroom self-preservation. The Japanese we were teaching knew way more than we did. But again, I digress. The one teacher that did know was affectionately called "Mad Ed" in spite of his knowledge of the Present Perfect and Passive Voice. Perhaps he still is. A more newly-minted member of the Sokka Gakkai sect of Buddhism, he chanted every night for three hours and solicited new sect members from the Time T.I. staff. It was not a ringing endorsement for grammar.

For me Japan and Time T.I. was the beginning of the start of Asia. For Paul they were the beginning of the end. In retrospect, I suppose it was the beginning of the end of Asia for me as well, except that my end was much further away. Every beginning signals the end. It is never a matter of "if". Only when. He left Asia for the first time at Christmas, 1987. His now ex-girlfriend left two months later. I left Japan in the summer, on June 8, 1988. Exactly twenty-seven months. That's eleven in dog years.

Paul and I had re-united in Canada the following June in Minesing, Ontario, population 92. Minesing, population 92, was farm country, 90 kilometres north of Toronto, population 2,192,275. Minesing was cornfields and freshwater lakes and the smell of hay and the rustle of the wind through crop rows and perfect sunsets and good people. Paul was building a house for his brother, needed some help and was trying to hold on to what he'd found in Asia and himself. I was trying to hold on to what I'd found in Asia and myself, needed not-Vancouver and jumped at Minesing. If you build it, you can hang on to it.

Paul and I had done Zen together in Nagoya at Tokugenji temple. Tokugenji is a Rinzai Zen monastery on Chayagasaka Dori, about a forty minute walk from my apartment. Two major landmarks made Tokugenji easy to find. First, it was near Ginei, Nagoya's most expensive and exclusive strip joint. Nude dancers covered themselves in Saran Wrap so they could be touched all over without actually being touched. Or so I was told. Very Japanese. Or so I was told again. It was also across from one of Nagoya's two Denny's. Nothing there was covered in Saran Wrap. Everything was fresh. And there is nothing quite like a Denny's BLT and fries after a late night session of zazen. Not until far too late in my twenty-seven months in Nagoya did I realize the first landmark's existence. "*Shogunai, ne,*" as they say in Japanese, or as we say in English, "*c'est la vie.*"

Tokugenji was also a Zen training monastery under the head temple in Kyoto, Myoshinji. Tokugenji was one of seven Sect-sect Zen training monasteries in Japan. Tokugenji had lay zazen sessions Saturday evenings and Monday mornings. It was Paul who introduced me to the Saturday night zazen sessions.

Paul told me only two things about Zen: it had enabled him to become clear about what he wanted to do with his life, and the monks hit you if you moved. Akira-san, the lay monk who ran the Saturday sessions, told me that the most important thing to remember was how to sit: like a tripod with knees and bum planted on the floor, back straight, face held up and eyes down. It was easy, he said. And they never hit first-timers.

I owe Paul Cassie. I owe Japan even more. I owe Japan Zen. I owe Japan Paul. I owe Paul Zen, or at least Tokugenji. I guess I owe Japan Cassie too. I may well owe Tokugenji for Cassie as well, but that is much less obvious. But I owe Japan to my education, and my education to my parents, and, well, that's enough owing for anyone. Paul is an artist, a sculptor. He had studio space in a barn near the house he was building. It was late August. I had just come back from a Vipassana meditation retreat in Shelburne Falls, Massachusetts, population 2,046 and was preparing to return, first to Vancouver, population 1,100,000, then to Nepal and Kanchenjunga, the world's third highest peak, located on the Nepal-Sikkim border. Paul was going to meet me there. Nepal's population was 16,625,000. Nepal was a repeat, for both of us. Kanchenjunga, being a mountain, did not have a censusable population. Kanchenjunga was not a repeat. I had never been there.

Vipassana is a Pali word that means "insight". To achieve Vipassana is to understand experientially three concepts: *annicatta, annatta* and *dukkhatta*; impermanence, not-self, and the pain and suffering self-created and self-inflicted out of not understanding the first two. In the mountains of Kyoto I learned to understand the concepts intellectually, which is to say I was told about them and they registered in my brain. I tried to understand them experientially, to meld the two experiences together, but that was part of the problem. Trying. Intellectually was a start and fully intellectual still in my distance, but as a Vipassana friend wrote me once, intellectual understanding never freed anyone, and the truth of the truth that I was searching for was that more than anything else, I needed to be free.

Through serendipity I had found myself in Nepal the previous November. The combination of the Himalayas, the people, the physical demands, the spirituality and one book, Idris Shaw's *Thinkers of the East*, demanded that I return. I had bought *Thinkers* in a used bookstore in Pokhara at the foot of the Annapurna circuit trek thinking it would last me for the three weeks I was in the mountains. It did, but not in any way that I had imagined. A book of short Sufi teaching parables, I finished it in the first few days. So over and over I read it, and with each new reading, an amazing thing happened. Each time I saw the stories again, I saw them new. Each time I found more. Stories that I didn't think were about me I saw were. Stories that had made no sense, I saw I had misread through an inverted or confused word. Stories that I knew I knew I saw in ways and with implications I hadn't considered before, and so the story grew dimensions when before it had been a plane. I felt I had been close to something, close to myself, to finding an answer, the answer, and that by returning I wouldn't lose it, it would be real. It would be mine and not simply a memory. I had talked Paul into coming along as well. He would join me in Kathmandu in early October. He needed to reconnect too.

My first unconsciously aware experience with Vipassana was in Herman Hesse's *Siddhartha*. I didn't know it, and Hesse never wrote of it, but there it was, in translated-from-German black and white. Over and over I read *Siddhartha*, not even realizing it was the story of the Buddha (you can take the boy out of the suburbs, but at that point, I hadn't been taken anywhere yet). It just was. It spoke to me, and the peacefulness and serenity and strength of Self that I found just in the words took Me away. It was what I searched for from that moment on.

My first consciously aware experience with Vipassana was in the Time T.I. office in Nagoya. On my first visit to the office for that job that I got through a friend of a friend of a friend, the woman whom I was replacing was pinning a poster for an upcoming Vipassana retreat to the office corkboard. "Truth," she said. "It's about Truth." She was Parrot, American and her fingernails were painted different colours, although purple and black seemed to dominate the palette. Her first name was Samantha. Nobody called her Samantha. Strange old world. "Good," I replied. "Truth is why I came here." Not Time T.I. specifically, or even Japan necessarily, but Japan as in discovery and travel and Time T.I. as a means to Japan. Back then my ability to articulate was still developing. The truth I was searching for was not the *The names of the twelve disciples in Da Vinci's "Last Supper", from left to right are...* kind of truth, but the truth of Richard Bach's *Illusions* and Hesse's *Siddhartha*, the truth of being—of now, of what was left when what was wasn't anymore. Later, in a very different kind of truth, Parrot married Gordon, long after he had become my ex-boss and Paul's ex-boss and both her ex-boss and ex-boyfriend.

My first meditation experience with Vipassana was over my second Christmas in Japan, in Kyoto at the retreat Parrot had posted the year earlier. It was Vipassana as taught by S.N. Goenka, the same Vipassana I later practiced at Shelburne Falls just before I met Cassie. Goenka-ji wasn't there, but they had his videos. He was the most enlightened man I had ever seen on TV, or anywhere else for that matter. It was all just an experience until his first evening discourse. The references, the allegories, the allusions. I knew it with all my body. It was *Siddhartha* except instead of reading it in my one-bedroom apartment overlooking another block of one-bedroom apartments, I was living it. I knew it without even understanding what it was that I knew. I guess this means I owe Japan Vipassana too. But I owe Gordon Parrot, and I owe them both to my Canadian ex-boss, whom I owe to my father, a cookie salesman. I owe cookies for Cassie? There is a lot resting here on baked chocolate and coconut.

My second Vipassana experience was in southern Thailand, at Suan Mokkh, which translates to Garden of Liberation, under the teaching of the Venerable Ajaan Buddhadāsa Bhikkhu, which means Slave of the Buddha. Suan Mokkh was what I had been missing in the aftermath of Japan, the anchor to myself that my self needed. I felt it but I didn't know it. What I knew was that I wanted to be more intellectually and physically grounded in the meditation. What I felt was being almost there, and as close as "almost there" is, by definition it means not there. At least not yet. And how often do we think "almost there" when the reality is "we can still see the house"? Anchorless I fall into intellectualizing and talking about reality instead of living one. There are always more thinking reasons why "not to" than why "to". Finally, I understood annatta, annicatta and dukkhatta. Goenka-ji's image had instructed the meditators as to what those words meant, and I had meditated on them after the fact, reflecting on my accomplishments and his words, but since when did telling, or even thinking about, equal understanding. At Suan Mokkh I understood and it all seemed so simple.

I had to clean the toilets. Excrement is not personal. In spite of what bosses and new mothers say, it is neither provided in more quantities by some than others, nor is it a gift. No one shits more just to get back at someone. No one sane at least. Excrement simply is. How could Self, annatta, be an issue? And perhaps the issue is not one of substance but production, satisfaction and judgment. What might be satisfying for one is, well, a disappointment to another. Both are ego, both Self, and both are shit. The shit itself does not work to engender the like or the dislike. That is you. That is annatta. The "gift" of excrement (*Has my little precious got a gift for mommy?*) simply is. How long is long? How big is big? To return the gift, do you need a receipt? And then, it is gone. The job does not remain, nor does the un-cleanliness. Nor does the shit. Regardless of one's misplaced pride over size (because unlike penises, with shit size does matter. Bigger *is* better. No one bemoans the big ones that felt small, only the small ones that felt big), no one stuffs and mounts these "gifts" for their mantel (*Yeah, it's big. But you shoulda seen the one that got away. We thought about mounting it on pine, but trophy excrement is so Hemingway*). No one with friends anyway. And so all things being equal, we also have annicatta, impermanence. Even Montezuma's revenge ends. So does the unpleasantness, although again, it really depends on which side of the toilet seat you're on as to the nature of the pleasantry. But unpleasantness is dukkhatta, creating for oneself a resentment of not-wanting when none needed to exist. Who said that cleaning toilets was in and of itself an unpleasant experience? There was no need for resentment because there was no annatta. Resenting the job did not make it go faster. If anything, resenting made it go slower. And who did the resenting hurt anyway? Whom did it affect? How resentful do you need to be to make someone produce less waste? When was the last time you overheard someone proclaiming such love for their mate that they were producing less shit than ever and enjoying life more? (*Yep. I the day I met her, I stopped buying oat bran and started buying brick cheese.*) Even when they're mad, people say they couldn't give two shits about someone. Sure, the trinity of weight, length and fragrance are issues, but then aren't they for everyone? Nobody's getting any younger here. As Bob Hope said, "I used to be a boxer: hard chest, flat stomach. But that's all behind me now."

And so the tumblers fall. It was the same with the numbness I experienced sometimes in my legs when I sat in a lotus or half lotus position. There is no personal element to numbness, no annatta; numbness is what sometimes happened to human legs trained to play ice hockey and run, when placed in that unfortunate Vedic position. My body was not out to get me, and in spite of what some of the other meditators at Suan Mokkh felt, neither were the monks. If anyone was out to get me, it was an underfed Indian mendicant 4000-odd years ago, and even then, it was not me in particular he was getting, but rather all those who are well-fed and athleticized. Regardless, the pain always ended. Annicatta. The second I opened my legs it began to end, and in seconds it was gone, and without memory except for what I chose to give it. In fact, the pain often left during the sit. It just was. And so there was no need to be angry or resentful. Being resentful in fact, observing the pain and reacting, only made it worse. Instead of letting it be and doing what I was supposed to be doing, I watched it and reacted against it and made it much worse than it needed to be. And who did this to me? I did. And who is me? Me! And the pain would go when it went, as soon as I opened my legs. Why create resentment? Why create dukkhatta? It was all so clear.

10

Vientiane

I was all prepared to leave Minesing and Paul when an end-of-summer barn dance was announced and I put off leaving one more week. For the dance—a western theme—Paul invited another friend from Toronto, he invited a woman he knew, she invited her friend, and she invited Cassie. After watching the first five songs, I threw my public caution to the wind, asked Cassie to dance, threw my private caution to the wind, forgot who I was and that I couldn't dance, and we were inseparable the rest of the night. At the band's first break, we left the barn to get some fresh air. I drew a map of the Indian subcontinent in the dirt, pointed to Kangchenjunga, and asked her to come. Cassie's girlfriend said to be careful. She was talking to me.

After Cassie was back in Toronto, all I could think of was her, my longing, my fears and my truth. I ached for her. My body ached for her, my spirit ached for her, and my life ached for her. From the moment I saw her again I knew she was the one. I was flooded with signs, overwhelmed by déjà vu. That was my sign. That was the moment.

I know the theories that try to explain déjà vu: that it comes out of reincarnation, that it is related to temporal lobe epilepsy, that it is a delayed inter-hemisphere transmission, that it is an acid flash-back. They are all interesting, and none of them have anything to do with how I feel during the experience, what they mean to me at the moment of being, at the moment of impact.

Déjà vu is for me neither a new nor unique experience. Neither makes the point anyway. Everyone has déjà vu. I've had them all my life. Not always, not often, but sometimes. And then, in Thailand, I had them every day, all the time. They came in waves. Experience after experience after experience. As many as ten in a day. What they told me was that my life was on track, that I was accepting life rather than dictating it. Not a passive acceptance rather than an aggressive dictating, but an active acceptance instead of a resigned dictating. I was supposed to be there, supposed to have these moments. I wasn't fighting my destiny or my existence. I was fulfilling it. It's the difference between being in university and studying what you truly desire, what makes your heart sing, what represents your true Self, and being in university and studying what you think is "the right thing to study," or worse, what your friends or parents think is "the right thing to study." One choice accepts your Self. One choice denies it. The reasons why one would choose to deny one's Self are irrelevant: parental-driven or peer-driven or calculated and economically-driven, the result is identical. I studied business and economics. It was a mistake. A complete and total mistake. My old Economics 345 professor could confirm it empirically, but the academic mistake that he would see is not the reason studying business and economics was a mistake. I was an Economics and Business Administration major because I was weak and visionless. I was weak because I *did* know what I wanted to study and I didn't choose it. I wanted broadcasting, to be on the radio, to play songs and become a music expert and entertain. I was weak because broadcasting was already a compromise. I wanted to be an entertainer. A singer. An actor. A comedian. Famous. But growing up in the suburbs, watching my father be a salesman, TV and ice hockey was all I knew. My heroes were Bobby Orr, Johnny Carson, and George Harrison. I was nothing if not eclectic. What's the joke? Two guys are talking in a bar. The first guy says, "Only hookers and ice hockey players come from Minesing." The second guy says, "Hey! My wife comes from Minesing." The first guy says, "Really? What position does she play?" I didn't reject archaeology or art or anthropology or modern dance or English Literature or Religious Studies based on rational, lucid logic. I didn't reject them because I never considered them. What did I know about the world, life, living with ethics and integrity? I studied business administration because my father said that you never went wrong with a business degree, and I had no comeback. I studied economics because I thought that if you understood the economy, then it would make you a better businessman. Good logic, except I didn't want to be a businessman. I was trying to build a solid foundation for a lie, and solid foundations for lies are the worst kind, because how do you extricate yourself from something that to all outward appearances is logical and strong and full of promise?

Long before I met Cassie, déjà vu told me I was on track, that I was where I was supposed to be: that I wasn't denying my existence, I was achieving it.

And when I saw Cassie, déjà vu overwhelmed me.

Everywhere I looked, everywhere I turned, there was something telling me *This is the place, this is the time, this is the one.* I fell down on my knees and I said, "Who are you?" and she had no answers and neither did I and we both knew it didn't matter. Cassie asked me if I had ever seen *The Princess Bride.* "This doesn't happen every day," she kept repeating, her favourite line from the movie. Her movie. *This doesn't happen every day.* Indeed it doesn't. Not for me at least. Not even every decade.

I was driving across Canada. A navy blue Cadillac, to Paul's sister who lived on the outskirts of Vancouver. I telephoned Cassie every night: Sault Ste. Marie, Dryden, Thunder Bay, Brandon. After four days, standing at a pay phone outside a hotel in Moose Jaw, Saskatchewan, she asked me if I had really meant it, if I really wanted her to go with me. I was scared. Terrified. *Don't be afraid* I told myself. *Yes, I meant it. Yes, I mean it. Yes, Let's take the chance. Yes, Let's be spontaneous. Yes, Let's be free. Yes.*

So she postponed the new job she was to start in two weeks, the job they had already held for her through one postponement. She had no money. She was going through a divorce. "People ask me if this is the right thing to do, and I ask them 'What *is* the right thing to do when you're getting divorced?' This doesn't happen every day." All her rules were gone. All her knowns. Where did common sense fit into the moment? *Don't be afraid. Come with me.*

Paul still came along, surprised at meeting a Mark and Cassie "us" in Kathmandu in October instead of a solitary "me". After Nepal, Paul and I found each other again in Bangkok, and then again on Koh Samui, a perfect island in the perfect Gulf of Thailand. My first perfect experience with perfect Koh Samui came on the recommendation of an American traveller from Maryland who looked like Jesus. I met American Dan in Cheng-du *Haro! Chan-ji ma-nay?* We had both gone looking for the romantic "Middle Kingdom" and found instead a dictatorial Maoist bureaucracy. As appealing as pebbles in our rice and never-missed-a-meal para-military train matrons in starched white uniforms rousting us out of bed at 6:00 A.M. were for a summer vacation, Dan told me of the mythical island of Samui where they barbecued huge skewers of shrimp and grew magic mushrooms. The shrimps were everything American Dan promised, the magic mushroom omelettes more. In mushrooms I saw God in all our glory, but the mushrooms just confirmed the end I already knew. They were never even the means, or at least not long-term means. That's what meditation was supposed to accomplish. Two weeks later, American Dan left for the States and I left for Suan Mokkh. A year later in Kathmandu with Cassie, only weeks after that hot August night dance, the two of us turned a corner we didn't usually, an hour later than normal, and there was American Dan. Cassie, good Christian that she is, saw the Jesus resemblance immediately. Non-Buddhist that she is, she saw the resemblance between my eyes and the Buddha eyes of the Tibetan Stupas. Who was I to argue?

Cassie was with me on that second Koh Samui time, but not nearly as perfectly. Life. How easily the moment is lost. How easily thinking gets in the way of being.

I knew that Cassie was the one. I knew it with every inch of my flesh and every pore in my soul. I knew. This was who nature intended for me, who God had meant for me. But niggling away inside me was this theory about love and life. It wasn't a happy theory. It just rang true. That's my problem: what rings true is too often not happy, and I am nothing if not consumed by my want of happy. This was the theory: What if we had taken too long to find each other, if too many events had already gone by, if there was too much of a past to overcome. What if we were too late, and even in acknowledging the moment we saw that it was too much work, there was too much history? What if God and nature weren't enough? What if I ran out of "what ifs"?

Now here, again, in Vientiane. Paul.

In Nong Khai, Paul had been the trump card of proof thrown down whenever we questioned the Mekong River View Guesthouse owner about the integrity of our pending visas.

"Your friend Paul isn't back yet, is he? And he went over last week. So he must have been able to extend his visa, right?"

Or he was dead, or he had been thrown in jail, or he had bought an airplane ticket out of the country to Vietnam or Thailand or anywhere because there was nothing for him in Laos and what was the point in coming back to Nong Khai?

But he is here, in Vientiane. At the Sailom.

"Your friend is in the dorm. It is on the second floor."

When I walk in he is straddled over the buttocks of a woman giving her a back massage, her shirt pulled up to her neck, her olive skin shiny and sensual in the humidity. I know her too. Or should I say we both do, although on a participatory level, Paul more than me. She is Mera, the ex-girlfriend of our ex-Nagoya boss, Gordon. She came after Parrot-the-ex-girlfriend and before Parrot-Gordon's-now-wife. She seems a lot freer unburdened by Gordon and Japan. I guess we all are. Sexier too. At least she is. Paul has always looked good. It's the blond hair on the chest I think.

It is a small world.

"Boyter!" he shouts across the row of empty cots, but I sense more resignation than happiness in the reunion. *Friendus interruptus.*

The Mekong Restaurant is a greasy chopstick on the bank of its namesake, up in the direction of the centre of Vientiane. It was Paul's favourite, his local. With so much time on his hands, he went there often to write, usually in the afternoon. It was more of a half-built bamboo Tiki-hut than a building, but it had a concrete floor, a few under-wattage fluorescent light tubes, and a tiny, tinny cassette player. The fluorescent tubes gave a pale-green cast to the faces and attracted insects. The concrete floor gave the insects a place to die on. The cassette player was just annoying. There was a roof, and bamboo-slat waist-high walls. In daylight, I suppose there was a view of the river. At night, the view was swirling green clouds of bugs and darkness.

There are three others in the Mekong when we arrive. Their table is filled with empty Beer Lao bottles, their skin shimmering in sweat. I can't tell if it is from the languid heat in the restaurant or the aftermath of a day's work. From the cassette, playing to no one in particular, scratches out tired Thai pop music.

Paul has made the overland journey to Louangphrabang, but after only a few days in the city flew back to Vientiane, desperate for the adventure yet another destination had promised and left unfulfilled.

Now it is Kampuchea.

While all around him have failed in their attempts to get a visa, he has found a contact and is convinced success is possible, if not probable. The contact is somewhat dubious: a friend of the driver of the Kampuchean consul, or some such thing. Still, it is something. It is more than most have. It's never what you know.

Laos had been Paul's driving desire. He had made the trek to the embassy, the fruitless efforts with Bangkok travel agents, walking the streets searching for the moment of serendipity that would fulfil his quest.

In the desperation of last resort he came to Nong Khai and found success, only to discover in its achievement that his goal had been misunderstood and misstated. The desire had not been Laos at all, but rather adventure, and so re-defined, still languished unachieved and taunting in front of him.

Kampuchea.

There is fighting there. It is dangerous. It is difficult to get in. Adventure. The integrity of the true experience in an otherwise marginalized existence. A self-sustaining repetition of desire.

The problem now is money. The rehearsed stories we were offered in Nong Khai have proven unfortunately true across the board. Travellers' checks are unknown anywhere, and in spite of the large glossy advertisement for both VISA and VISA Travellers' Checks at the bank, credit cards are useless. The currency you carried into Laos is the currency that you have in Laos now. Simple. And what Paul has, after buying air tickets to either Phnom Pênh or Vietnam, his contingency plan in the hoped-against failure of Kampuchea, is $100 US, without having worked in the cost of the Kampuchean visa itself. Give or take. Maybe, he says, he can sell some of his clothes on the black market in Vietnam, or his watch. "It doesn't work anyway," he says. Even the $100 US speculation is an exercise in guesswork though. Through the Vientiane rumour mill, we have heard that there is an "entrance visa" requirement for Hô Chi Mihn City. It could be as little as $10 or as much as $80. US. Or it could be just a story. Flip a coin.

So, to borrow money came the conclusion, but who has cash to lend?

Ex-pat Bill is the answer. Oddly, ex-pat Bill is the question too.

Ex-pat Bill stays at the Sailom, or rather, he "lives" there. He says he is an ex-pat American businessman living in Bangkok, and on the pretext of wanting to establish a business in Laos, was granted a one year, multiple entry business visa. He has been here for weeks; long enough to have a daily routine: up at 6:00 running, breakfast at the bakery/café next door. He has cash, but more importantly, he can leave to Nong Khai, get more money and return. No questions asked. He will lend Paul the money.

The bill arrives: 2200 kip. For a warm Pepsi and a plate of greasy pork and rice. 300 more kip than the Chateaubriand dinner at the Santiouk last night. Excuse me? Paul says that I didn't ask, that I shouldn't assume too much, that I can't be too careful. The Mekong is his favourite restaurant. His local. He is running out of money fast enough to be talking about hawking his clothes.

If you have to ask the price . . . I didn't think there was a need for anything but assumptions.

At the Sailom, more rumours. The writer from *Lonely Planet* has already been here. I assumed that meant the author of the Thai guide and I searched the registry in unsuccessful stolen glances for his name. Nowhere. I hope it is only a rumour, that he hasn't already been here. Laos doesn't need a *Lonely Planet*. The book's name versus its reality is too oxymoronic.

It is the Bible of the backpacker in Asia, worshipped with too often the same blindness and carried with the same unquestioning acquiescence. People who don't know where to go use *Lonely Planet* and almost no one knows where to go.

The most popular destinations are the ones listed as "unspoiled". Defloweringly we race, guide bible in hand, until some "unspoiled" village at the outer reaches of "the real China" has fifteen guesthouses, each with the requisite cassette player and collection of Rolling Marley or Bob Stones tapes or whatever zeitgeist pop music is offering. Osteoporotic grandmothers left in charge of the guesthouse run the recorders on half-juiced batteries leaving Mick sounding undulating and diseased, and in his whine, oddly Cantonese. Not knowing that Mick should sound Mandarin, and not understanding the complaints from the unspoiling guests, nothing ever changes. In that regard, the villages are safe. Depressingly, menus in English offer the promise of banana pancakes and muesli and pizza and fruit milk shakes and magic marijuana curd shakes. Worse, they fulfil the promise. Worse yet, nothing tastes like it should. What's the point of selling out to tourism if you do it badly? You gotta make up your mind: either sacrifice the local culture to attract tourists, or keep it and drive the tourists away. Or vice-versa. You can't try to do both. Local wannabe entrepreneurs seize the moment, selling bags of hashish and marijuana and opium for those that don't find the fifteen time zones, alien culture, lack of toiletries and complete inability to communicate enough. That a place is "unspoiled" because tourists don't go there seems somehow lost in the equation.

There is no book yet for Laos. You talk to others, you listen, you explore. You think, and in the thinking you find the Vientiane and the Laos that is yours and not someone else's. I suspect that was the goal of *Lonely Planet*. Certainly the original book came out of self-initiated discovery, out of joy. It just isn't the reality now. Monk Thong Liam Inthvong would never make it past the second rewrite. Or he would be the cover.

11

South

T he third floor of the guesthouse is completely dark, the hallway narrow and straight enough to grope quietly along without losing sensibility. The second floor landing comes easier, a soft yellow glow seeping into the blackness. There is a light at the bottom of the staircase—a single, frosted bare-bulb nightlight. 4:00 A.M. Three people are crowded together in the foyer at the foot of the stairs: one David, two women and three large backpacks. That is two women and two backpacks more than I expected, two travellers more than comfortably fit into this little wood-panelled space, and I don't remember the Sailom having a foyer. Four is not a crowd. It is out of the question: I retreat back up the staircase, teetering my pack on one of the stairs. The foyer is makeshift. A dining table has been pulled up against the hand railing, blocking off the rest of the lobby. The thick, yellow glow from the light the old woman manageress left on for us is near useless. In this cramped little entrance too many shadows fall across our shoulders and heads for me to see either my feet or where I am standing. At least I assume the old lady manageress left the light on for us.

I met these two women yesterday in the guesthouse and forgot their names as quickly as they were told to me. David re-tells me. Jackie and Pamela. Yeah. Great. The air is suffocating and humid. Stagnant. There is no breeze; only the heavy, moist odour of stale cooking oil. Claustrophobic. I am sweating already, and when I breathe, I can feel the grease coating my lungs. There is no space to move in or to except in unison and together. The two women are Mekong River View Guesthouse alumni too. Yeah. Great. It is 4:05 A.M. and I am hot, sticky, sleepy and I can't breathe.

Open the door and a clear lemon spotlight lights the gravel path in the front of the guesthouse. Fresh air. A duller, more pervasive yellow comes from the streetlights on the avenue. The dry gravel scrapes under our feet and then there is nothing but silence. Bangkok would never be like this. Neither, for that matter, would Nong Khai. From somewhere, regardless of the hour we snuck out of our guesthouse, something would have broken the silence: a shout of *hello taxi*; the hollow, punching, Briggs & Stratton-esque echo of a tuk-tuk; the click-click-clicking of a sāam láw tricycle rickshaw. Something. Someone. Thailand doesn't sleep.

The women say they heard David and me yesterday discussing our bus reservation plans, had no better plans of their own, like us had limited options, and decided to go south too. They say "go south too," but they mean "join us": the "We have no plans. We'll use yours," method of travel. I say "Hmm," but I mean, "I don't want you guys here." It's not like there will be two buses. They made their reservation late last night. Yeah. Great. They both just arrived in Southeast Asia. They aren't travelling together. They only met in Nong Khai. This is their first time to the Third World. What I want to know is why are they here? With David and me now, and in Laos in general? What are they looking for? Are they even looking for something? Do I even like these people? Do I care? What are their names again?

The street narrows to a lane, the sidewalk to gravel shoulders and then deep ditches. We approach a small wat complex and I try to steer our path towards the middle of the pavement, away from the dogs I assume own the courtyard at night. There is no response to our intrusion. Nothing comes but more silence. The humidity and blackness hang, absorbing our echoes, smothering them like footsteps caught in a snowfall, filling the contours of my body as though pressed against Cassie. The sound of cicadas follows our footsteps, waves building and collapsing as we approach and pass each tree, asking and answering, crescendo and diminuendo. The sound of humidity and sensuality. The sleeping dogs lie.

Fewer people than I expected mill about the bus station. In the darkness the office doorway glows like a Japanese wood-fire raku kiln, silhouettes bobbing and shimmering across the light as if moths drawn to a flame. I wave to the woman behind the desk who sold us our tickets. She waves back. This is the right place.

A small pushcart coffee kiosk does a brisk business on the street, a basket of persimmon-orange coals creating impenetrable black shadows against the ground through the iron frame. The menu is two pots of coffee and six wrapped baguettes. David and I buy a coffee and baguette each. Instinctively I cup my hands around the glass and huddle my shoulders together, pressing my arms to my sides, my half-awakened unconscious understanding that 4:30 A.M. and black equals cold. It doesn't.

Our "bus" is a lot doi san; a five-ton truck body with a wood frame carriage built onto the back bed. The bus is painted tangerine and sky-blue. The wooden carriage is orange with yellow and green detailing. We are meant to be seen. Maybe not now, but in a few hours anyway, and from far away. There are no panes in the windows, only empty spaces between the supports. I feel like I'm riding in someone's hobby.

The conductor shouts and passengers crowd the bus to load. There is no hurry. We don't have tickets: we have seats, and seats are better than tickets. Seats are guaranteed. The conductor directs us from a chart on his clipboard: David and I are in the third row back, left side, at the window. Jackie and Pamela are in the same row, right side, at the window. There is room for one more person on each bench, plus a fold down seat that fills the centre aisle for a seventh passenger. We're a sandwich: Laotian on white. With a calm and order, the bus quickly fills. There is no pushing, no shoving, no scrambling for a seat for yourself or your bag or your goat. This is not India. This is not China. The bags are on the roof, everyone has a seat and there is no obvious livestock. Competent. Organized. Dignified.

We are the only foreigners on the bus.

The orderliness does not seem to owe itself to the simple consequence of having a conductor. Existence in Laos seems to come with dignity. No compromise of behaviour is offered and none is required; the boarding procedure is a simple acceptance that the characteristics of this bus journey—the lack of space, the early hour and journey length—do not demand a reciprocal loss of integrity or dignity. If there is a cause and effect relationship happening here, it has nothing to do with internal combustion and greed.

As quickly as we are gone, the stillness turns first to a breeze and then a biting chill, and I regret no longer having my coffee. Coatless, I button my shirt to the collar and roll down my sleeves. At least David's shoulder is warm.

Is it dangerous here? Are we going to be attacked? When will we be attacked? Like that, the safety net of Vientiane is gone, replaced by the fear of the unknown and its requisite questions. My fear is honest if not ignorantly romantic, manifested from and nurtured on stories of events that passively could be and events that allegedly have been; events that happened somewhere else to someone else's imagination; times and places and thoughts that are too easily transposed to here. My questions make only as much sense as my accompanying ignorance allows, but there's the rub: how do you disprove possibility in the face of ignorance? Every trip I take, every adventure I begin, starts with fear and unknowing. It isn't the presence of these two qualities that sets Laos apart, just the present awareness of them. Laos is not unique in that respect, just new, just different. And yet, unlike the Nepalese bus or the Bangladeshi ferry, there is an immediacy to this perception of danger, a perception of probable reality instead of a possible future. I am more likely to be killed here and now than I was then and there because I've learned to accept bad driving and worse roads. I haven't learned to accept gunplay, even if the game is run by rumour. Everyone knows most accidents happen in the home. Statistical analysis proves it. Can statistical analysis prove a rumour?

In the summer of 1985, I hitchhiked across Canada from Vancouver to Toronto to find my relatives. Four time zones and

I didn't even have to exchange money. It was camping in my own backyard, except the backyard was 2700 miles long and camping in my backyard had always scared me. Dwarfed by all the things I knew, though, were the possibilities of chance and fantasy I didn't—the questions of destiny and reality that couldn't or wouldn't be answered, and in their unanswering, left large gaps in my strength of decision.

What if there are no rides? What if I'm stranded in the middle of nowhere? What if my ride is an axe-murderer? What if I run out of "What ifs"? Finding excuses to delay was as easy as finding things that had to be done first and items that had to be bought second, until in the first week of June a woman I knew agreed to take me to breakfast and then to the Trans Canada Highway entrance east of Vancouver and I could no longer refuse. Even at breakfast, which fell into brunch, I tried one last time to stall as I watched my watch tick to 11:30 and knew it was too late to start then. But go I did, and, saying good-bye to me at the highway, she kissed the palm of my hitch-hiking hand with fresh crimson lips for good luck and then sat watching from her car as I walked down the highway approach in the drizzle that had begun as we said our good-byes. With each step I felt more alive and less afraid, as in my heart I had known I would, until I smiled and laughed at each car that passed by without consideration before one stopped and I was gone.

On the lot doi san, there is nothing around us now except foliage and darkness, and in our haste it is impossible to tell the difference. Occasional vehicles come upon us from both ahead and behind and not until the lights fall into the distance and then disappear am I sure they aren't about to turn around after us.

I want to sleep, to fall away into the drowsiness the combination of the pre-dawn, the rocking of the bus and the indecipherable scenery has brought on, but it is impossible in the cold. The only place my ego will allow me to rest my head is the back of the seat in front, but to do that means freeing up my arms to use as a head rest, those same arms pressed tight against my sides in rigid resistance to the freezing wind. Unable to fight my drowsiness, I fall into a sleep against David, and when I awake later into the first mauve of dawn I let it carry me off again, until into the emerging pastels of sherbet orange, powder blue and vanilla comes a warmth and awareness of humidity.

As morning turns towards midday, the breeze blowing through the bus window frames thaws from freezing to comfortable, and, as we slow for the uneven surface and increasingly tiresome potholes, to warm. At eleven, when we stop for lunch in a dust-choked roadside village, the breeze dies, and the temperature turns to stifling and suddenly humid.

The land is parched, the soil a quarter inch of desiccated earth the consistency of sifted flour that rains down on my feet from the cloud that forms with each step—puff, puff, puff. Walking slower only slows the puffs; they catch in mid-cloud and hang, billowy, and then settle, smothering. Sweat trickles and then races from my groin down my thighs and calves to my feet. It pools into my Birkenstocks, mixing with the dust, and surrounded by drought, I am walking in mud, sliding back and forth within the sandal. "$85. Ruined," I think. In my pack is a pair of cheap canvas sneakers I bought in Nong Khai. Four dollars. They're new, and unless I wear socks, blister my feet. The socks would get dirty, and so I rejected them this morning. I didn't want to have to do laundry in Pakxé. Such is the logic of 4:00 A.M.

Our meal is tepid orange Miranda soda in a gritty glass bottle and a noodle soup in a less gritty porcelain bowl. The essence of highway food is universal: Husky Gas on the Trans Canada east to Toronto, Denny's on the I-5 south to L.A., Mama Lao's on this dirt highway south to Pakxé. Not food to be savoured as much as consumed, not food as much by taste as by presentation. At least in Southeast Asia, you get coriander. And yet, after hours on the road, sought after, relished. Utensils are mismatched wood chopsticks from a communal bamboo cylinder. The trick with communal chopsticks, I learned in southern China, is to sterilize them with hot tea; you fill your cup, swirl your chopsticks, throw the greasy tea into the street and rinse your cup. Everything is clean, everything a little less communal, and in the dry season, it keeps the dust down. In a country of 1.1 billion, even a little goes a long way. All this for the cost of a few mouthfuls of tea and the time it took to learn to not walk close to outdoor restaurant tables. In Laos, tea is not the lunchtime beverage of choice, and warm soft drinks disinfect considerably less well. At least the soup water is boiled, and what boiling hasn't killed, the chillies will. The chopsticks wash off in my soup.

Pamela, the older of the two women, has what Jane Russell euphemized for Playtex as a "full figure" and Monty Python chose to call "huge . . . tracts of land." She has enormous breasts. God's generosity notwithstanding, she is short too. Maybe 5' 4". Maybe less. Proportion is a cruel joke. Short *and* squat. At 4:30 A.M. she had thrown on a black nylon anorak. Removing it in this heat, she is bouncingly braless under a loose-fitting black muscle shirt. Surrounded by Laotians—men and women—buttoned to the neck, she is unmissable. Certainly none of the other men have missed her. Neither, for the most part, have the women. Worse than unmissable, she is unaware. Either that or fully aware and uncaring. There is a time and a place for everything. This is neither. People cover up here. People dress and live conservatively here. The incongruity of Thailand's sex trade notwithstanding, Thailand is a modest, conservative society. Laos is even more so. Monk Inthvong covered his cleavage.

Whether Pamela's fashion statement is acceptable or even desirable by my standards or Western standards or her standards (people wear the strangest things away from home) is not the issue, although many in Britain or Canada could make the argument that her standards are not universal even within the confines of our alleged cultural homogeneity. Certainly my Southern Baptist grandfather could have made that argument. But that, to a large extent, is the counterpoint. "Decent" is difficult to define, determined culturally by the era and individual. What is proper "here" may not be proper "there", and what is proper today, perhaps improper tomorrow. So we define "decent" by the values we were taught, the values, rightly or wrongly, that we internalized. Whether our individual values define decency through agreement to or in rebellion against is another question. Regardless of what I "think" now, what I grew up learning came from my father, and he from his father and he from his father. I shift and I grow and

I learn, just as my father did, and his father before him, but my family culture is turn-of-the-century Southern Baptist, and what I learn today is a product of where I came from. The contradiction of life: I am my own man. I am a derivative.

So the problem is this. Acceptable, arguable, comparable. They are all irrelevant. Her clothes are out of place here.

Everywhere I go, I take myself with me. No wonder I'm confused. And so we bring our culture when we travel, consciously and unconsciously, an ethnocentric tendency that bestows the norms and rights of our society with some universal quality, and through that universality we, in our self-wisdom, *justifiably* transfer—we are *obliged* to transfer—those rights and actions into other societies. "You can't do that to me. I'm an American." Hollywood's version of a new world pecking order, a version that thousands take with them every year (IF THEY CAN'T UNDERSTAND, I'LL JUST SPEAK LOUDER). Inundated with American influences, Canadians take it with them too. "You can't do that to me. I watch American movies."

What does "I'm an American" mean to a police officer in third world Asia? A police officer whose education is perhaps a few years of schooling, whose English is perhaps rudimentary at best and non-existent at worst. Whose stereotypical image of Westerners, if arrived at from those same Hollywood productions, is easy women, Rambo men and fabulous teeth. The policeman lives in his world with his rules and his values. Asian rules. Asian values. In the West, people would expect him to act upon his rules and to hold on to his values. But as with my views, his views are not wholly of his own creating: however individualized, they are a reflection of his country's culture and values as a whole. Whether in agreement or disagreement with those values, it is not my place to challenge them with my own sense of identity. This is not my country.

A friend told Cassie before we left for Nepal not to worry about bathing etiquette. "It doesn't matter," she said. "Strip off, wash and get dressed again. Just be quick about it. It doesn't matter. You don't live there. You aren't going to see these people again. If they stare, it's not your problem. Its theirs." She's right. It is their problem. If they don't like nudity, they should have thought of that before they allowed themselves to become dirt poor while living in a Himalayan paradise. Is it *my* fault they developed an indigenous system of religious morals and standards? I mean, didn't they know travellers and tourists were coming? Who do they think they are, telling *me* what to do?

She is wrong. It is us that impose the problem on them. Her logic puts the responsibility on their response and away from my action, but this is not a debate over affirmative action or gay rights. This is their country. It is not up to them to learn to accept us. This is not "We're here. We're queer. Deal with it". At least it's not supposed to be.

We are too caught up in being tourists to remember to be people. We look, we photograph, we smile, we purchase. We observe and we walk away and our camera has captured an image and our diary has been written in and we then see something else and then something else and then something else until we are at the airport and the trip is over. The people we gazed at are still there, today gazed at by yet another tourist with yet another camera pointed and clicked. We are too busy on vacation to remember the people we are seeing aren't.

Listen: November 18. Marpha village, Nepal. The apple pie western (both capital and small W) half of the Annapurna circuit, part of either the ancient salt route between Lhasa and Bombay or where all travellers in Nepal go in October, depending on your sense of history and cynicism. Mani Rimdu: the four-day Tibetan Buddhist festival that celebrates the bringing of Buddhism to Tibet by Padma Sambhava in the eighth century and its ascendancy over the indigenous animist B'on religion. The height of the trekking season. A village that is normally crowded was bursting. I was looking for photographs the afternoon before the festival began, and wandered into a private yard I thought was public. A Nepalese man saw me and pointed out my error. Covering up my embarrassment and stupidity I said, "At least I'm rich." It was a joke. Stupid, but a joke. I felt rich. I had just come from Japan. I was talking about myself relative to myself, not myself relative to him or Nepalese. I was talking about myself, relative to my feeling of stupidity: I might not have brains, but at least I had cash. He walked away muttering "I hate tourists." I heard him and said, "So do I." I was talking in general. He was talking about me.

Where is the respect for other cultures, the cultures we have spent a fortune and travelled halfway around the globe to get to? We have some, but it all seems so set in the obvious. We take our shoes off in a Japanese home, leather off for Hindu temples in Nepal; we learn *please* and *thank-you* in Thai or Mandarin or Nepalese, and how to order beer in all states of inebriation. It is the subtle we cannot see, and it is in the subtlety we show our ignorance and our Selfs because the subtle is not subtle. It just requires observation. True, honest, unprejudiced observation. Westerners swim topless in Thailand and fail to see that topless beaches are our predilection and not the Thai's, and so our transient indulgence offends what our money already monopolizes. We are blinded because the thought processes and actions are based in our society. Topless is *our* selective normalcy, and we never think about it because normal is only that, or if we do think about it, we bite our tongue because "We're here. We're bare-breasted. Deal with it." And it is only *our* because I am white. Topless is European normalcy. This may be their country, but this is my vacation. Thailand is sexland. *It ain't famous for its temples, you know—nudge, nudge, wink, wink. I mean, Bang. Kok. Bang. Cock. Get it?* And so we compare our actions to hookers and dancers and justify our public behaviour accordingly. Or Westerners in Japan demanding with self-indignation that Japanese women rebel against their socio-economic-sexual status and take charge of their lives. We miss the societal changes taking place in Japan because we see only a snapshot, a misunderstood moment confused by our comparisons to our knowns; we miss that the questions we ask stem from the zeitgeist of our philosophies. We miss that too many men in Japan need to rebel against their own socio-economic status, that the power brokers that control most of society are few. We miss that Japan is not our country. These are our definitions and demands. This is their situation. Even Perry Mason knows this is incomplete and misleading: the truth, the whole truth, and nothing but the truth.

Arguably it is our duty to introduce truths to others. But since when did telling ever equal understanding? And what *is* our "truth"? That the female nipple deserves—no demands—the same disrespect that the male nipple enjoys? That women should be afforded the same opportunity to be culturally exploitative, insensitive and ethnocentric as males? Unarguably it is our duty to understand that others too have truths. I am fortunate to be here and to be here now, before Laos has been co-opted by tourism into what I think I want it to be, or worse, by what Laotians think I want it to be.

I want to say something to Pamela. I want to stand up for what I know to be true, for what I believe needs to be said. I want to.

As the day progresses, it becomes clear that the fear that held me earlier was unfounded. There are no guerrillas. It is all too mundane. More fearful is the road condition, which in the early afternoon deteriorates into a barrage of potholes and washboard rivulets. With each jolt the wooden frame of the bus threatens to explode into splinters, creaking and splitting against itself like the timbers of a tall ship. Long stretches are reduced to a deadening repetition of sharp jolting shots that throw us forward and side-long into each other and the straining, whining re-emergences that bounce us against the seat back snapping our necks as though we were caught sitting on a trampoline.

I run my fingers through my hair. It stands on end, the dust and sweat congealing into a mousse. The trade-off for sitting next to the window and keeping cool. A slap against the leg of my shorts leaves a dust print. I begin to crave a bath at the end of the day, a hot supper, a tepid beer, a soft bed and cleanliness. I begin to crave craving. I make the same mistake over and over. Where is the here and now of craving? Where is the satisfaction?

12
South

The 4000 kip cost of the bus trip includes overnight accommodation. Where our accommodation was had gone unstated, but logic tells me it must be past the half-way distance and in a town large enough to support a guesthouse. Savannakhét seems the answer, and I imagine a guesthouse like the Ekalath, only plainer, more Communist. I can see it in my mind, and for some reason, walls the colour of peach appear, with a cramped bathroom tiled in small, odd-coloured ceramic squares with a creeping blackness in the grout. There is shag carpet in the hallway, and the corridors smell like old apartment buildings and cooking. A Savannakhét guesthouse. It becomes my sustaining attachment as the sun slides behind the trees: not out of sight, not setting, just low enough that sunlight floods the road in patches. As the light scatters, the warmth of the breeze changes and I grope to roll down my sleeves and re-button my collar.

Long after twilight, in the fading moments of dusk, the bus lurches to a halt in front of two small bamboo dwellings. There is a large covered bamboo porch. In front is a small red candle-lit *phra phum* spirit house: a Barbie-doll sized wooden "good-fortune" house perched like a birdhouse atop a wooden pole. Adjacent is a second porch with picnic tables set up in front. We will stay here for the night. Such is the price of craving.

There is a well in the back to wash from, David tells me. I nod, the information only partially setting in.

A confusion of bodies continues to move around me as others

find food and make their way to the toilet and well. I stand alone at the back of the bus waiting for my bag until, exasperated, I climb onto the roof myself and see our luggage secured under a net tarp. Inside my pack is my towel, soap and toothbrush, as well as my long pants, socks, mosquito lotion and mosquito coils. Where has my vision gone? A room, a bed, a shower. To get me through the night I have my camera, passport, wallet and flashlight? What good will these things do when it becomes cold, when the mosquitoes appear?

By the time I get to the well, the hint of dusk there had been is gone. Only the glow from the streetlamp at the road offers any light, throwing deceptive shadows across the cold stepping-stone path to the barrel.

In the rush to wash much water has already been spilled, the mud indistinguishable to my eye in the darkness even after my foot finds it. There are three others at the barrel washing and scrubbing with a ferocity I thought impossible in this dark. I try to rinse the road off my arms and face, but with the water once poured splashing into the mud below, the effect is to trade clean arms for muddy legs.

Dinner is rice and chicken. The rice is pasty white, tasteless and dry. The chicken is honey brown, tasteless and dry. Last to wash is last to eat. Perhaps the food was better half an hour ago. Perhaps not. We are still, technically, on the road. David and Pamela and Jackie are together under the metal awning to the left, the bus driver, conductor and about ten other men to the right. The centre is an uncomfortable no-man's-land

"Hello you!"

The ten men laugh. I know this game. At the other three's table, there is no acknowledgement of the moment. I had hoped there might be more support coming.

"Hello! Hello!" and this time there is a wave. When I look confused, arms reach out, waving and pulling me forward through the space while on the bench the others shuffle to create room, followed by more laughter and smiles.

"Hello. How are you?" the young man asks, at last in command of the moment. "He is the bus driver," he says pointing, and from across the table a glass is raised. "He is his friend," the young man says. Then there is a pause. "No," the young man shakes his head. "He is my friend." Everybody laughs and the young linguist mugs for his friends.

The only women I can see are the two older cooks and two teenage serving girls. He has seen the women too. My newest best Laotian friend's posturing is physically mine, but psychologically the other males' and the women's. There are smiles everywhere and I don't feel the need to burst any bubble being a smart aleck back. It is easier to let him have the stage and just enjoy the moment. Sometimes, even dancing bears like to dance.

"Yes, you want drink?" and he holds up a large white plastic glass of alcohol. It looks like laokao, the apparent poison of choice in Laos. A few others hold their full glasses high in camaraderie and then drink them back empty and laugh. The women join in. The faces are a little redder. The laughter a little louder.

"Here you drink. Good! Good!" and the showman says it twice for emphasis, to help convince me.

A gesture of friendship or hazing? A happy drunk or a conniving Laotian? Both are acceptable tonight, but friendship demands sincerity and acceptance. Hazing demands caution and assertiveness in the guise of sincerity and acceptance. Both are outstretched hands, but one has a joy buzzer in it and the light here isn't that good. Regardless, neither of us has that much invested in this interaction, but while disillusioned friendship turns to indifference, disillusioned hazing holds too much chance in anger. Accepting their conversation gambits over my friends—my *kind*—at the next table was a deep first step: I am already involved. Step two is to take the drink. Step three, to sit down. What do they expect for four? Is this a twelve step programme? Does my intellectualist hesitation appear to them as reluctance and fear? Another rite of passage, of the transcendence from touristic curiosity to person.

"Hello please you drink," and they offer me an already poured glass as two men push over to create me a space. The women stop to watch, and the table of men sit and stare and smile and poke each other with their hands and their elbows. I glance at David, Jackie and Pamela; they are lost in conversation, either oblivious to or hiding from this moment. I force a smile and take the glass, feeling awkward and displayed; the guest treated with deference and warmth, expected to entertain and cajole at his own expense in receipt of the hospitality. The hesitation has changed the direction of the moment and the background in which it is played.

"Hello you. Drink please," he pleads. Two gulps and the laokao repeats into the back of my throat burning, the sour look on my face making them laugh and smile. Now they know: it must have been fear. The woman behind the cooker has been impressed. Does she impress easily, or is the ante raised with every bus that pulls into the village? What hoops will the next victim jump through?

"More? Hello you, more?" he asks, and all the men's glasses are filled before I can answer. I am their trophy. "Drink!"

"Hello. You want girl? Here," and he pulls over one of the teenager servers. Again? No. Thank you. I don't want a girl. And again the question is asked and again I refuse and in my refusal, there is a change in the atmosphere, a change in the joking and in the good-naturedness.

"Why don't you want a woman?"

I am uncomfortable with the question, but more uncomfortable at the tone. Trophy wives don't say no. Why should trophy foreigners be different? That there is, or may be, offence is only a small part of the issue. It is their country, there is a language difference and I don't know what they consider offensive behaviour. Are they upset because I said no? Because of how I said no? Because they suspect I want a girl, but not that one? Because they suspect I want that girl and I'm just being polite? Because he isn't really offering the girl, but the tone of my "no" suggested that I thought he really was, and now he's offended? Because *there goes ten dollars* or whatever fee they were going to charge, ten dollars that maybe they'd already spent on laokao? Because now the cook is unimpressed, and so *both* of us aren't getting any tonight? What is their relation to the girl? How do I refuse without being offensive? That is the true question here. A refusal, I am sure, is what they expect. The girl is not the issue for them. This is a two-part test.

The art of refusal is as an intricate a skill as the art of acceptance, and it all starts at the start: is it a real offer, or a polite offer, or a joke offer? Perhaps it is all no more than a joke. After all, the vulgarities seem to be what we choose first. Perhaps too, it is genuine. She is available. That too is a dilemma, for then my botched refusal is not social but instead commercial, a comment on the girl being offered and by association, the man making the offer, the men at the table and even the village. *Come to where the flavour is. Come to hooker country.* I have sat with these men at their table and drunk their whisky and now I call them and their judgment and their women into question through social ineptness? I smile and shake my head and smile and again it comes: "You want girl? She good, yes? She beautiful?" If I say yes where do I leave myself? If I say no? And for a moment I stop thinking of the answer and let my eyes move over her. She is beautiful, a round face and long black hair. Slim, her sarong tight against the contours of her hips and buttocks and thighs. I feel the warmth of the laokao and the desiré it acknowledges and I think about holding someone and not being alone, and I look again and she is just a teenager, and I remember Bangkok and recall the seedy reality of Pat Pong in contrast to the image I clung to booking the ticket and I remember I don't want that in Laos. And I look again, and she is so very pretty. So I smile and laugh and make odd sounds and raise my eyebrows and give no answer and no explanations.

"Drink!" someone shouts, and everyone raises their glasses and takes a mouthful. The hazing is over, the trick finished, the girl gone off to finish her chores, the women back to their cooking stalls. Just like sport fishing: catch and release. My friend, now exhausted of his English, talks to his friends and leaves me ignored, a new toy at Christmas fussed over until its novelty has gone and it's back to the road hockey game with your friends, Alastair Sim on the TV and *When'll the turkey be ready?* I finish my drink and slip away to the other three.

Time for bed and it seems the straw mat on the front porch behind the *phra phum* is our accommodation. Just the four of us. There is no blanket. There is no pillow. There is no wall. There is nowhere else. We choose up our places: Jackie and Pamela, then

David, then me: sardines on bamboo. It is not yet cold, but it is still four hours until 2 A.M. I expect no miracles.

David rumbles next to me and half-awake I hear murmuring and shuffling. 4:30 A.M. The spirit house is still alight, two light bulbs dangling naked from the rafters over the mat floor. We are leaving. A man holds up his watch and points to the five. I nod my head and realize I didn't wake up in the night scratching from mosquito bites. I check my legs anyway, but there are no bumps. I stumble for a tree to relieve myself. David is still putting on his shoes. Jackie and Pamela have gone off somewhere together.

On the bus, the others are sitting as though they slept here in their seats, as if only we four slept away from the bus and in honesty, I don't know that I'm not right. The order and patience is tangible. It surrounds me and I feel unhurried and secure, as though I were young again and wearing my father's suede jacket. Our places are open, and the interior is warm and welcoming. It smells of sweat and clothes and food, almost sweet. I undo my collar button in the warm stillness. At 5 o'clock the bus erupts and we are gone.

13
South

At 2:00 P.M. the lot doi san pulls into a large, dusty open court ringed by squat wooden buildings. The impression is more American Western than Laotian, but more spaghetti than John Wayne. This is Pakxé? Instead of a scramble to get off the bus or rush to be first, there is a collective sigh of exhaustion. Everyone is too tired to hurry and too stiff to jump. In tentative, measured progress, the bus empties. It's like learning to walk again.

My body is covered in ochre powder. I slap my shorts and the dust lifts off like a mist, the ghost-print even better in the extra accumulation. I slap them again, then the other leg, then all over again. Fun comes from the strangest things. I touch my hair and it is hard and matted. Immovable. It pulls and knots in my hand like mange on a dog. The fun stops here I guess. Shouting taxi drivers are upon us like burial plot brokers at a retirement home, but there is a twist: in Pakxé taxis are motorcycles and sidecars. Someone asks about a hotel and our bags are gang-loaded into one of the already revving sidecars, the assumption both that the four of us are together and that whatever our long-term plans, staying in this dusty square isn't one of them. All at once all of us ask everyone English questions, but the motorcyclists speak Laotian. Not wasting time not speaking English, they are nothing if not efficient.

The Hotel #4 is a cluttered, deserted, half-finished cement and ceramic tile shoebox. A floor to ceiling galvanized steel accordion gate is rusted immovable in its runners, unwelcomingly stranded at three-quarters shut. The aesthetic is third world institutional, designed for practicality and function unburdened by any sense of comfort requirement. Only in colour is the Hotel #4 not grey.

Three employees sit behind a reception desk that looks like a 1970s era rec-room bar. The front moulding strip is coming unglued from the plywood top, trying to droop and instead jutting and bouncing like an unleashed erection. Yes, they have rooms. There are two, both on the third floor. David and I follow a man to the back of the hotel and up the staircase.

The air smells of mouldy cement dust. The staircase is littered with piles of broken concrete and wall plaster chips. On the second floor, all the room doors are boarded closed. The central, communal sinks at each landing are dry and stained, the hallway piled with broken construction supplies and scaffolding. The ceiling fans are dead. Everything is covered in a dust. The image is white gossamer, Stevie Nicks dancing Rhiannon. Not death, but euthanasia.

The room is a large square cement box. Fractals. Surprise. Inside are two four-poster beds, each with only three posts, mosquito netting over each bed, an en-suite bathroom, a portable standing Thai fan and electricity. Square and concrete must be a stipulation of foreign aid. The amputee four-poster's are "local colour". There is no water in the toilet and the shower taps spin and spin and spin. The fan works. So do the room lights. The switch for the fan is on the base of its stand. The switch for the room lights is in the hallway. Short 2x4 and 2x6 planks lean against the boarded-over doorway across from our room. There are no fresh nail holes in our doorframe.

"The toilet and shower," the manager explains, "are downstairs."

The room is languid and smells stale. The walls are dishwater white and dishwater green. David and I look at each other. The other room is down the hall.

The hall-walking manoeuvre to negotiate the second floor eco-system is a series of pirouettes around scattered piles of plaster and concrete chips, through half assembled scaffolding, and a duck under a fallen 2x6. The extremes people go to when they can't afford a real Twister game. Our down-the-hall alternative is smaller, with more must and no fan. This must be where the poor travellers go. For our $6, we will take the other room. The way back is easier: we just follow the footprints. The door doesn't close when we get back: the lock won't catch. Where are the other three hotels?

By the time I get to the shower, I am already number two in a line behind an Indian man. Jackie appears number three, a fuchsia and vermilion pattern sarong pulled and tied behind her neck, the material tight across her breasts and thighs, her strawberry-blond hair spilling across her shoulders in far too dangerous a sensuality for this steamy yellow light and the grey cinder blocks, her nipples lost in the design. My sarong is less tight, less pulled. Not yet anyway. This is not Japan. Our eyes fleet together and then abstain. For a long moment I consider inviting her in. *You want girl?*

The water is backed up to the top of the threshold three inches deep. The cappuccino surface crust breaks and recongeals in my steps, the film banking along the edges, the pinwheel of residue a pathetic swirl stagnating above the clogged drain. I have neither rubber thongs nor choice. A single 25-watt bulb hangs sweating from the concrete ceiling. Safe too. Above the water line, the brick is green with algae.

At the rear of the Hotel #4 a second unwelcoming steel gate is rusted immobile somewhere between open and closed. In fairness though, the rear doorway is smaller than the one at the front and, three quarters shut, would restrict its useable clientele to anorexic supermodels, most of whom, I suspect, stay at Hotel #1 when in Pakxé. For the effort of sucking my rib cage into my gut, the reward is a step-down into a shaded, narrow alley of rusted machinery and chunks of broken buildings. The two children playing in the door-well of their home directly across from the hotel's rear exit look me straight in the eyes. I turn away and then look back. They are still watching. I feel very rich, and very uncomfortable.

At the end of the alleyway is a dying French colonial manor, the white stucco walls streaked and stained by rainwater in the pattern of Bridal Veil Falls. The effect here is not becoming. It looks like runny seagull shit. The door lintels sag and there are clear gaps in the roof tiles. The gutters empty into rusted oil drums below, the downpipe ending far short of the cistern, the back-splashed water staining the white stucco yellow and thick like a bed-wetter's mattress. Opposite the manor in a canary yellow building is a barbershop. Four chairs, two barbers, two walls of mirrors, and no customers. No waiting.

I love straight-razor shaves. I indulge myself whenever I can and covet them when I can't. The cost is minimal and I tell people the room gained in my pack without the razor and blades is worth the indulgence. A closer truth is self-indulgence: straight-razor shaves feel wonderful and I am too embarrassed in my pleasure to not have to justify it. An even closer truth is their sensuality, the touch of human-to-human, male-to-male, inherent sensuality without explicit sexuality. That is what I've convinced myself.

The barbershop is a bastion of male authenticity, a sanctuary uncommercialised through tourism and uncompromised by enforced gender equality. There is nothing unisex about a third-world barbershop. It is the pocket of truth and reality that I have come searching for. I tell others and they react as though I've suggested shooting up in the main street. The image of a strange brown man with a straight razor at your throat unsettles them, and my explanation of sensuality and touch only confirms their suspicions. Shaving is mundane, but in the mundane is truth and honesty, and truth and honesty, I am convinced, are beauty.

Some insist they regret only the things left undone and never the things done. It is inaction then, that at the root causes regret. Action, it seems, by the very nature of the word, is unregrettable. To an extent it is true. Actions once taken rarely prove as bad as their imaginings made them, and most after-the-fact judgements from non-participatory outsiders have little validity because, firstly, regardless of their opinion, they are commenting on a situation from a perspective of observation and not experience, and secondly, having not participated, it becomes their obligation to their Self to defend their non-action. But regret out of non-action is a false God. Non-action is action. The answer is not about a choice of one option over another. The answer is why. The answer is fear. Always.

I regret too much. I strive to regret less. On the conscious level, regrets come small, regrets come large. That they stay around suggests they are all large subconsciously. Perhaps it is not the inaction itself, but its motivation that looms large.

1984. December. Days away from becoming sick with hepatitis. I was alone in Luxor, Egypt, and afraid to step out of that aloneness. An act of cowardice. Cowardice suggests large actions from large moments of physical danger, of confrontation and challenge. When I say fear I see income tax officials. The cowardice that kills is not large but small, the tiny, daily fears strung together that make a life. Each one demands a step outside. The character trait that defines my life. In adventure. In love. In happiness. To deny in the face of want is fear. It is so easy to write.

It was late in December in Luxor, the afternoon's light and warmth giving way to a grey and biting cold. Three times I walked past the Arab barbershop, the men and mirrors half hidden behind the cloths that draped the entrance. Three times I started to enter, three times I hesitated. One time I walked back to the hotel.

A Pakxé shave is 100 kip after asking, and climbing into the chair, I explain I am not Soviet: Canada. The difference between a new sharp blade and an old dull one is enormous.

The first time was in Thailand. It often is. It was a weathered coconut-wood barbershop on Koh Samui in Mae Nam village. The man was slim in his 50s with a white-speckled stubble beard and his hair oiled and parted. He wore a white sleeveless undershirt and sandals. I wore blue shorts and a nut-brown tan. There was an old scarlet leather barber chair, a white propeller ceiling fan that skimmed the air without disturbing it; the only light came in through the open door and two shutters. He reclined the chair and stood over me, taking in my face with his eyes and hands.

Dipping a small cotton wad into a shallow metal dish of soapy water, in short, quick strokes he pulled it over my beard, stretching my cheeks tight with his left hand, drawing the razor across my skin, wiping the whiskers from the blade across the fleshy crescent between his thumb and forefinger. And then again pulling with his thumb, tugging and cleaning and smoothing and checking until satisfied. He spilled talc deep into the upturned bristles of a white brush and smothered it into my face, covering my temples and forehead and throat and ears. And again pulling, scraping the blade across my face, taking the short, golden hairs from my forehead and temple and the space unsure between my eyebrows, gripping my ear lobes and shaving them, leaving me naked and powdered and limp. Uprighting the chair from behind he wrapped his hands around my head, searching with his fingertips, finding my temples and caressing into their tightness, swirling fingers sliding away into my jaws and ears, finding the cartilage of ears and folding it flat, pulling backwards, pushing the pressure through the ear, circling the flaps and folds until tugging down through the ear lobe and easing out of my body. Clean. Finished. Surrender. His hands on my neck, his thumbs caressing my nape: his hands on my crown, spreading his fingers wide, massaging and tapping deeper and deeper into my scalp: gripping my forehead with split fingers and pulling, sliding his hands to the back. Exhausted. Tranquil. Spent.

Thailand. Laos. *You want girl? You want shave?*

Nothing disappoints here. 100 kip is well worth it. David is unconvinced. Tonight, the barber will just have me.

Regret is never about action, but fear. Joy is never about action, but life.

I feel joy.

On the dirt block behind the Hotel #4 is a second mystery-numbered hotel. It looks much quainter, less institutional, less grey. It looks yellow. Next to it, a small bar displays its menu selections on a long church-hall table, covered in a pink and orange and white chequered vinyl cloth: cabbage, pork, noodles. At the end is a small glass display case of cigarettes: Benson & Hedges 555, Special Gold, Gauloises, Capstan, Samet from Thailand, and Dunhill. Next to the cigarettes, bottles and cans of Pepsi, Fanta, Sprite and Heineken, huge bottles of Beer Lao and tins of Hall's Mentho-Lyptus.

Most inviting to David and me though, from the top of a white

Kelvinator refrigerator, is the suggestion of *cold* beer. We accept. It is only polite.

We are into our second acceptance when a lone Western woman appears. She is well dressed in her late 50s or early 60s: confident, a woman at home within her surroundings. I look at her expectantly, the way I have grown accustomed to looking at Westerners— friendly, acknowledging our alien co-existence so far from home. In Nagoya, I said "hello" to every *gaijin* I saw. I thought our similarities there outweighed our differences at home. Whatever we were to ourselves, what we were to them was "not-Japanese," and in Japan the group is everything. Some groups were Toyota-employees, some groups were golf-friends. Some groups were not-groups. I was a "not-Japanese" group. So it goes.

Too many Westerners in Asia are open only to the foreign and themselves, conscious only of their trip and their objectives. People are here for days, for weeks, for months. I am what they have left behind. I am not their experience.

Their experience, of course, is Asia. Surrounded by the target culture, alone in a sea of Oriental voices, washed over and freed by the sounds and smells of the East. To be alone: unintruded upon. "Hi" forces recognition of your outsidedness and commonality. "Hi" breaks the spell.

"I can meet Canadians at home." I've said it before myself, the justification to exclusivity. I am wrong. It is not the traveller from Vancouver, or Canada or even North America that intrudes upon my Asian experience. It is me. In my desire to fulfil the images I have created, of both Asia and who I am and who I want to be. The desire becomes a demand and demands do not allow freedom, only results: an exercise of searching to find rather than seeing what is.

It is the removal of the thought, the "I" from the action, the removal of the expectation that eliminates the preconceptions and allows true experience.

She is here with her husband, on a group tour of Laos. Their tour is genuine; they are the group. They don't like tours, but in Boston Lao Tourism told them it was the only access. She is more than a little surprised to see us here unchaperoned.

They are here in Pakxé for the same reason as we are. Wat Phu. They are going tomorrow with a guide, flying back to Vientiane the next day. She is Margaret. He is George. A conversation of smiles. She is nice.

George is older, perhaps late 60s. They are off for dinner with the guide—some restaurant on the Mekong. He couldn't remember the name.

Unlike George and Margaret's, our transportation questions are not going to be answered cleanly or effortlessly. There is supposed to be a local bus, but when it leaves, where it leaves from, how close it gets to the wat or when it returns, we have no idea. And whom do you ask here anyway? The *joy, joy, joy* of unescorted tourism is that there is no unescorted-tourist information. *Yes, we have no pamphlets, we have no pamphlets, today.*

Lots of questions and very few answers. Disturbingly similar to life. None of them ultimately matter though. In both instances. At 9:30 P.M. as we are walking back to our hotel, stopping in the street to buy some steamed Chinese *bao zhe* dumplings, George and Margaret reappear, excited to see us, so eager in anticipation it takes them a moment to catch their breath. They mentioned us over dinner. The guide volunteered they were welcome to invite us to join them—free—if we would like to go tomorrow. There is room for two more, but only two: the women will not be able to join us. Are we interested?

14

South

Long tail boat is the English translation for the Laotian *rua hang yao*. A rua hang yao is a long river boat built of wood, narrow enough for only two side by side, with a Ford V-8 engine mounted like an outboard motor on the stern. The propeller trails about fifteen feet behind, at the end of a long steel drive shaft. The prop throws a huge rooster tail when the Ford opens up. It's noisy as hell, and it goes like stink. The only thing better than riding in a rua hang yao is riding in a tuk-tuk, and tuk-tuks have two large strikes against them here: they don't float, and there aren't any in Laos. As part of their "official" tour, Lao Tourism had arranged a long tail boat with a canvas roof for George and Margaret, their "official" guide, his Chicago educated supervisor, a driver, and by default, David and myself. The trip to Wat Phu would take about an hour and a half, going with the current. It was not a problem. George loved to talk.

The year earlier they had been in Vietnam. Years earlier, they had been to Angkor in Cambodia.

Nepal as well, arriving in Kathmandu in 1966. Everywhere I had been they had been as well, years, sometimes decades earlier.

Nepal was only opened to the West in 1959. Seven years then would have been almost nothing. In 1988, tracing Hillary's 1959 Everest approach route, I had been deprived of neither Coke, Cadbury's nor English for the twenty-eight day trek through the Khumbu. Transportation neither. For me, the Everest trailhead village, Jiri, was at the end of a twelve-hour bus ride. For Hillary, the trailhead village was Kathmandu and Jiri was still six days' walk away. For cash I had brought rupee notes and $100 US bills. The black-market coveted large denominations. It was easier to smuggle one one-hundred dollar bill than a hundred ones. Hillary had ported his cash reserves in thirty-five sacks of coins.

Now Kathmandu has the 31 flavours of Nirula's Ice Cream and Nirula's has a uniformed Ghurkha doorman. It was still the Kathmandu of consciousness, but what it was conscious of was business and entrepreneurial possibilities. I treated myself to Nirula's Ice Cream a couple of times and bought the *International Herald Tribune* to follow my hockey team's sad progress, but I would not have missed either if they hadn't been there. Ironically, part of the responsibility is Hillary's. Now I get to share in it. There is enough to go around.

The Serengeti too. George had been there in 1958.

1958.

I was born in 1958. Hell, I was conceived in 1958. At home I am a "world traveller". But away from home I look about me and see many travellers and I know the difference between the reality of perception and the reality of reality. What I have done, comparatively, is all about more or less; to some I have more time, more money, more energy, more ignorance, more courage; to others I have less time, less money, less ignorance, less fear. Perhaps it is as simple as a stronger stomach: a traveller, after all, marches on his or her stomach. Perhaps I just have more emotional baggage to rid myself of, and baggage acquired, accumulated and grown attached to can't be hurried. Maybe I don't want to know how much baggage some of my travelling compatriots are carrying. I exist, it seems, on a continuum.

And so: George Meegan lives in Nagoya. He was a friend of a friend, but he was a *gaijin*, a foreigner, and in Japan that made us friends. I met him coming out of the subway one day, on the way to a friend's wedding. Both of us in ties and jackets exiting a rather out-of-the-way subway station, I put two and two together, introduced myself, and asked him if he wanted to share a taxi to the reception. He said no, he'd rather walk. I didn't realise how funny that was till much later.

George's hero growing up was Sebastian Snow, a British adventurer who had tried to walk the Americas from Ushuaia in Tierra del Fuego, Chile to Alaska. Snow raced through South America to Panama, but broken financially, physically and spiritually, his walk ended there. Meegan read Snow's account of the walk, *The Rucksack Man*, and was hooked. Snow's unrealized dream became his to complete. In January 1977, with Snow's blessings, Meegan and Yoshiko, his girlfriend of only six months, started from the same spot in Ushuaia. Where Snow had exhausted himself carrying his rucksack on his back, Meegan pulled his behind him in a modified shopping cart he christened the "yoshikart". Meegan's logic was simple. In macho South America, how could a skinny, hunched-over gringo pulling a grocery cart be a threat? The bag-lady theory of safety. In September 1983, in the exhaustive desperation of watching a life's dream come to fruition, he finished alone at the Beaufort Sea, Alaska. During the walk Yoshiko became his wife and two children named in Japanese Don't Stop and Keep Walking, were born. Using an elaborate ritual to ensure the unbroken integrity of his line, he traversed the length of western South America, Central America, eastern Mexico, the eastern seaboard of the United States into Canada, west across Canada to Vancouver, and from Vancouver north to Prudhoe Bay, Alaska. 19,091 continuous miles. Almost seven years. He wrote a book: *The Longest Walk: An Odyssey of the Human Spirit* and dreamed of wealth and celebrity. His publisher went bankrupt. Another publisher bought the book, saw the title and filed him under religion. Inexplicably, sales fell off. Walking, he only had to rely on himself. It's a strange old world.

The driver pulls the long tail boat up to a ferry dock on the Mekong's west bank and a second guide joins us. The tide is low. Our itinerary has been changed. We are still going to Wat Phu, but it seems that along the way, there is another, much older wat. Wat Upumong. Our guide knows *of* Upumong, but not *where*. Not the Chicago guide, but the Laotian guide. The Chicago guide knows that he wants to *see* Upumong; that in spite of apparently knowing little about either Pakxé, the local villages, the river or Phu he is the supervisor; and that the Cubs will never win the pennant. The new guide knows where Upumong is, but not precisely where. What he knows is which village it is near. He has no idea what a Cub is.

The village of proximity is on the east bank of the Mekong. The low-tide-exposed silt is burning hot, bleached white and cracked in the heat. Although the boat will wait for us, the boatman will stay with the boat, and there is no one else around, Chicago supervisor advises not to leave anything behind.

At the top of the bank, hidden by a thick line of palms, are four thatch huts on stilts. There is a family: a man, a woman, six children from toddler to pre-pubescent, and a dog, age unknown. Words are spoken, and I am handed a piece of fruit pulled from the tree we are standing under, the skin sliced open exposing the flesh. The family is standing in front of us and words are still being spoken. The skin of the fruit is soft and discoloured like a bad bruise, the flesh a rich creamy white surrounding soft lines of seeds. A *noi-na*, a custard apple.

George, Margaret and the tour supervisor slurp at the crumbling fruit. I feel embarrassed, a group of white people appearing out of nowhere, mumbling indecipherably, devouring this family's fruit as they huddle together watching.

The buckled rinds are tossed into the dirt and another fruit sliced open, a confusion of purple and white mashed and dirty in the dust.

"Eat! Eat! They're delicious," George says. The supervisor insists. The intrusion and domination is not just for the Laotians.

This is not a tourist spot. These villagers are not a part of the "industry". They are people who live along the Mekong, who farm and fish and procreate. Perhaps they have never seen a Westerner before. Perhaps the point is they have. Perhaps what they know best is government officials. And still we eat and litter, my objections waved off by the director.

"The pigs," that I neither see nor hear "will get them," he says.

There is an exchange of money between the American-Lao

and the villager-Lao, producing one smile on our man's face. Money replaces food and we buy our arrogance away. Money has value because we give it value, we accept it as having equivalence in value to other goods. We believe in its worth, and as we do, so it becomes. It costs therefore it is. Cartesian economics. For value to be transferable, doesn't everyone have to agree?

It is hard to bargain over a piece of fruit already eaten.

Click, click, click.

George and Margaret are snapping pictures of the now husbandless, fruitless family crouching huddled behind a fallen log, the mother clutching her baby, the other children crowding around her clutching each other. This is a zoo, and not even a petting one at that. A display of natives that even the supervisor could not help but indulge in. More serendipity. We have had no genuine interaction with these people, no organic process leading us into this moment unless bullying and usurping can be considered genuine and organic. Perhaps they are organic in Chicago. We are here. They are here. Nothing more. We are foreigners, we are the government, we are important. They are villagers. They are fisherman. They are not.

And still, the study of body language is inconclusive, a "soft science": if the *object* of the sentence is results and the *verb* interpret, then the degree of our assuredness depends on how sure we want to be, right? Easy. Is the family huddled together behind a fallen log because it is easier to take a family portrait when they aren't spread out, or are they scared. Can we *really* be sure?

"Smile," says Margaret. Click, click. "Look at the little one. Isn't she darling." Click, click.

What is it about the rules of human behaviour and dignity that make them suspendable for tourists? Because we have paid money to come here, we can just do whatever we want? The pictures are taken because the villagers are different from our norm, and in that difference challenging, and in that challenge, rewarding, and in the reward is justification?

Would we accept the game if the roles were reversed, if it were they that were rich, they that appeared out of a Greyhound bus onto our front lawn, stripping the apples from our trees, crowding around our children taking pictures, condescending to each other over how we live, how we dress, mumbling indecipherably to and at us, the difference indistinguishable; laughing and joking and us having to choose between friendly and mocking because we can't tell the difference? A busload of Japanese?

"*Kawai de ne!*" Click, click. "*Hayaku. Shashin o torimasho. Sugoi de ne.*" Click, click. "*Chi-zu onegai shimasu.*"

Click, click, click.

Huh?

We are rich. They are not. That is the justification. I tried once to explain it to an Egyptian temple guide harassing me for *baksheesh* that in Canada I wasn't rich, that I didn't have money to give away. "Yes," he nodded, "but you are rich enough to be here, and I will never be rich enough to go there." It is hard to argue against truth. Is it mere coincidence that so few travellers talk of plans for Japan that don't include work?

I do want pictures of these people. Too many people in Southeast Asia have lost themselves in the name of tourism and money. So I take these people's picture to capture their uncoopted quality and in the taking, they lose that quality, and the only difference is that I am first. I feel sixteen all over again, and I wonder if I have to say *I love you* too? I wanted the photos. As the world speeds towards homogeneity, they are endangered too. It's all right. I'll pull out before I cum.

It is justifiable. It is justifiable not. She loves me. She loves me not.

One more time: In 1986 in Thailand, through serendipity and ignorant lust, I ended up in Mae Hong Song, a northwest frontier town on the Burmese border. Across the border, the countryside was controlled by the insurgent KNU, the Karen National Union. The KNU are one of the ethnic factions fighting the Rangoon government. They had been fighting for autonomy since Burma's independence from Britain in 1949. The Karen are the "long neck" people that live in the legend of Ripley's. Those families that can afford the expense extend the necks of their female offspring, beginning in the girl's infancy, with a succession of brass rings that stretch and separate the neck vertebrae until by adulthood, the neck is about twice its normal length. The ring-necked Karen. It sounds more Audubon than Ripley. There is no mention of the brass ring technique being used penilely.

Flowing west out of Mae Hong Song is the Ping River. The Karen lived along the Ping in two small settlements. It was possible, by offering bribes to both Thai and KNU border guards, to flaunt international legality and follow the river downstream into Burma to see the Karen. To accommodate the external demands by Western travellers and tourists for unaffected hill tribe experiences and the internal demands by Thai entrepreneurs for wealth accumulation, two local operators had set up trips. The bribe was hefty: 500 baht at the Thai crossing, 50 more to the Karen. Inside Burma, to guarantee our safety, an armed Karen guard would accompany us. After considerable deliberation, I went with a German couple, led by a Thai who called himself Paul.

Thai Paul was everyone's friend; honest, legitimate, concerned, ethical. Over the three days I was in Mae Hong Song, it became apparent that for money, he was whatever you wanted him to be.

At the Thai border I made a pathetic attempt at adulterating my name by changing the o in Boyter to an a. It wasn't so much inspired deception as nerve-wracked apprehension. At the last minute, I couldn't decide which offered the greater dilemma: being illegal in Burma with my right name, or trying to get back into Thailand with my fake name. The way my family name looks when written, an a for an o was common: Bayter instead of Boyter. It was only a big deal when my Southern Baptist grandmother wrote letters. She insisted on honorifics: Mr., Mrs., Miss, and for me as an under eighteen year old man, Master. Birthday greetings were always fun. Back in the boat, having left Thailand behind, I seriously questioned the wisdom of this "experience" need. Our Karen guard sat armed at the bow of our rua hang yao. Thai Paul sat beside him, took the guard's cap off, and wore it the rest of the trip.

At the village there were three women wearing the brass rings, two teenage girls and an older woman. The younger women understood both the game and Thai Paul, allowing but not creating photos. The older woman alone in the shade of her veranda quietly sewing understood the game too, but in a much more subservient way. Seeing the two girls leave and take with them our photo-op, at Thai Paul's impatient beckoning the old woman put down her sewing and moved into the sunshine, walking the length of the village to us, standing in front of us as though at auction in a Bangkok bath house, her arms dangling at her sides, her face acquiescent and obeying. Twirl and spin, twirl and spin.

I had paid a lot of money and taken a great risk to see these people. A satisfied customer is a repeat customer, or at least tells a friend. Here was my money's worth. I tried to engage her, to acknowledge her humanity, to dignify the intrusion. Bowing, I raised my camera, questioning with my eyes for a picture. My discomfort and bow confused her, and Thai Paul, quickly mis-judging the situation, intervened, tugging at the woman to stand straighter, to not be so difficult.

A few years later, the Karen moved up the Ping onto the Thai side of the border. Paul, I suppose, never forgave them. Maybe he went to Chicago.

George and Margaret are still shooting. I raise my camera and begin to shoot. A competition. I do not want them to have some-thing I would not. A family pack of karma. *My joining in will make no difference—I owe it to myself to take these pictures—I will hate myself if I get home and have no pictures and recall this moment and that I lost it.*

Click. Click.

In a moment it is over. Time to move on. It is getting late. Time to remember why we are here.

The guide our guide knows has done his job. We are in the right village. We are not there, but we are close. The boy children will lead us to Upumong.

The forest floor is covered in a thick layer of hard, brittle amber leaves. It surprises me to see a North American autumn forest floor in Laos in February. A huge Banyan tree the colour of weak marmalade pulls out of the ground like forced, extruded concrete, twisting and climbing into a canopy. Through the leaves, points of broken pillars and curved edges of staircases show through; mountain summits through low clouds. The leaves look unrustled, as though for a long time they have lain unwalked upon.

This will be over too soon. The time I desire for understanding will not happen. Every second counts. This moment won't come back. This wat won't come back. Am I really wasting this truth on archaeology?

Upumong is dead. The viharn is intact, but light streams through the laterite stone blocks that were built light tight. The stone building blocks themselves are perfect. A James Bond temple: the walls are shaken, not toppled. Elaborate balusters lie fallen in the dirt, covered in leaves. Inside the sanctuary a carved pumice-coloured door lintel sits in the grass leaning against the wall. The image is a Khmer king, with long pendant ear lobes that fall to his collarbone, a long sword raised high above his head. In the courtyard near the viharn is a broken nāga. In Buddhist iconography, the nāga is a cobra, the serpent king Muchalinda. It is a frequent image in Khmer art. The nāga image represents a story occurring in the third week of the Buddha's enlightenment. The Buddha was deep in meditation on the shores of Lake Muchalinda when a violent storm arose, raising the level of the lake, threatening to engulf the Buddha. Muchalinda, the Serpent King, came from out of the water to protect the Buddha, coiling himself around the Buddha, fanning his hood up over the Buddha as an umbrella. In nāga images, Muchalinda is depicted as a seven-headed cobra, his body wrapped around the base of the Buddha as he sits in dhyānamudrā meditation, right leg over the left, his hands cupped right above left, Muchalinda's seven heads fanning out over top the Buddha's head. The fanning cobra ribs look like a Shell petroleum sign. Only six snake heads remain. Amber everywhere. It seems an appropriate colour. The definition is lost in the darkness. A bulk, an outline. And then we are gone.

15

South

It is still another hour upstream. A Land Rover will be waiting. Lunch is bananas, bottled water, sticky rice and sweet Laotian sausages.

"The children were wonderful," Margaret says.

Huh? Were we looking at the same children? Does she mean the little girl huddled behind her mother, the little boy who stared us down defiant and protective, or the baby that clutched at its mother's bloused tit and cried.

"I wish we would have thought to bring some balloons. Something to give. If only we'd known. We usually bring balloons when we travel. Just a little gift, and it makes the children so happy. We heard about the idea years ago. Now we do it everywhere we go. We tell our friends to do it too."

"Yes," George says. "We always bring something, but we didn't know today. We never thought that we would be meeting any children. We were just expecting Wat Phu."

Balloons. Absolute generosity corrupts absolutely.

"They're better than candy. Better than money. They don't rot your teeth. They don't turn the children into thieves. They're just fun. A complete extravagance."

Yeah. And the check is in the mail, I love you and . . . It's an old argument. I've heard it before. I've even read it in guidebooks. Hell, once I thought it was a good idea too, but I thought twice and what sounds like altruistic giving is really ethnocentric condescension and self-gratifying satisfaction. Who asked these people to bring gifts? Do they take gifts to the rich kids too, or the poor white ones, or just the poor brown ones?

For all their innocence, balloons might as well be gold bullion. In fact, if I were a kid, it wouldn't even be a contest. Balloons intrude into the village, its socio-economic system and both its short and long term investment portfolios. Money is valuable because we give it value; why not balloons? Balloons in fact, are more obviously and immediately valuable than money, for money requires a second object to realize its value. Balloons just are. You can blow 'em up, fill 'em with water, wear 'em like a hat. Again, how altruistically would we see things if the roles were reversed, if it were a bus load of Japanese tourists disembarking in front of our homes, running up to our children in an indecipherable condescension of language, handing out origami paper and miniature lanterns to the children. Would it still be "a complete extravagance" or racism and nationalism and economic superiorism and *Who the fuck do these people think they are?* Would we stand for it, or would we just demand more? How long before you figured out that they gave you folded paper, but they carried digital cameras and wore Rolexes? The gratuitous, near anonymous donation of balloons or money or chocolate is neither free nor faceless. The cost is minimal, the inconvenience minimal, and the immediacy of response fills the giver's heart with joy to have "made the children happy". Is it my responsibility to make these children happy? What even makes us think they're unhappy? Have we confused dirty clothes and no bicycles with unhappiness? Are we simply making ourselves happy? What if what made the children happy was for tourists to stay the fuck away from their village?

What is my obligation to a favour? Is my obligation to myself or the owed party? Are there degrees of indebtedness? Do I owe more because of Upumong? Which will let me sleep best?

I don't want to be argumentative with George and Margaret, and I am only at the best of times more constructive than argumentative, especially when through deliberation I have said nothing—not because I believe the introspective silence calming, but because at those non-best of times, I am more sure of my rightness than my ability to present my position calmly and without judgment, and then the debate becomes the delivery and not the issue. I wanted to say something but I didn't. (First Pamela. Now balloons. There's an unfortunate parallel.) We still have three hours left together and they are nice people. They really are. It is a question that I still have no answer for.

A banana peel floats by. Then a plastic bag, then an empty water bottle. Thank God we haven't eaten enough yet to evacuate our bowels. The culprits are the Laotian crew in the front. The floating-garbage effect is as un-obvious as Margaret's balloons-in-the-mist effect. It is here, it is gone. What garbage? Only the motor breaks the silence, the engine chugging against the current, more to keep than make our progress. The sun is stifling, the water dancing and sparkling up against the hull.

I am as much at fault here as is the guide at the front throwing the garbage because I have witnessed and done nothing. But he is only here because of me. I come here, this boat takes me into the river, and the cycle begins. I tell others, they tell others, and quietly, burgeoning tourism overwhelms the resource. In the hedonistic rush to capitalize on the boom, to achieve the promise of the Talàat Sao, the environment is lost. "Unspoiled" is all perspective. The futility is the irony, and so the circle goes.

Another plastic bag goes by.

"Don't do that!" George hears me.

"Yes," he joins in. "Don't throw this over the side," and he holds up a water bottle.

A surreptitious banana peel floats by, dropped unseen and unheard, like the self deceiving smoker hiding the illicit cigarette cupped inside the palm of the hand, the smoke curling up the wrist and arm, the smoke everywhere but without a visible "cause," not real. The "If I close my eyes, you can't see me" school of logic. There is a difference between the bottle and the peel. One is organic, one inorganic. Maybe history has shown that waste can be discarded, that it either decomposes or is eaten. Regardless, it goes away. Now there is plastic, but where is the understanding that this waste will not go away as well? And of course, it still does. The current carries it down to the sea and out of sight. But it doesn't go away. The behaviour hasn't changed. Only the items discarded. Don't go away mad, just go away? I want to see the fish that eats plastic drink containers. Everybody sing. *Cruising down the Mekong, on a Sunday afternoon . . .*

The conversation turns sharply towards tropical diseases and malaria.

I look at George and Margaret. For their generation, hell for my generation, they are part of the enlightened and adventurous few. That giving balloons may be detrimental notwithstanding, their actions are taken with a kindness of spirit and giving mind. The simple act of choosing balloons takes enormous experience and consideration. To sift the options of giving on a personal level, beyond the necessary realm of foodstuffs and clothing, beyond the most obvious detriments and corruptions of candy or cash. Balloons. A toy. Valueless but for enjoyment. George and Margaret are part of the enlightened few that travel ahead of their time and outside of their safety. And still the result is food taken for curiosity instead of bought for food, pictures snapped of natives instead of photos made of people, rivers polluted by objects nature never intended.

Why am I here? What has driven me to Laos, rather than Japan or Indonesia or Malaysia, or even back to Canada? I am not an anthropologist. I am not a pink-skinned head-shaved Westerner wannabe monk begging from wat to wat for a forest monastery to call home. I cannot claim to have any defined purpose, any reason to be here, apart from the fulfilment of some vague indetermination. Am I in Laos because of Paul and some absurd machismo to equal him, or because it is another notch on the bedpost of my passport? Is it because I don't know what to go home to? Did Mallory just say it all? Am I here because it's there?

The earliest mention of Wat Phu is in the *History of the Sui*, written in 589 AD and chronicling the rise of the Funan empire: "Near the capital is a mountain called Ling-kia-po-p'o, at the summit of which is a temple always guarded by a thousand soldiers and consecrated to the spirit P'i-to-li, to which they sacrifice men. Every year, the King himself goes into the temple to make a human sacrifice." In the second half of the 5th century, a vassal from the Chinese empire of Funan, Shresthavaraman, was victorious over the Chams at Champassak, the city now at the base of Phu and the name of the province that Phu is in, and founded a city at the base of Wat Phu, Shresthapura. A princess from the maternal line of Shresthavaraman, Kambuja-Rajalakshimi (Raja meaning sovereign; Lashimi, the Goddess of prosperity and beauty) transmitted the heritage of Shresthavaraman to her spouse, Bhavavtman, who became one of the original leaders of the state of Kambuja-desa, what became Cambodia and then Kampuchea.

In the 9th century, the Khmer Empire began with its centre at Angkor, lasting to the 15th century. Over 900 temples were built in Cambodia, southeastern Thailand and southern Laos in symbolic representations of the Hindu cosmology: Siva, the Destroyer and Transcender; Vishnu, the Preserver; and Brahma, the Creator. One feature in Khmer architecture was the mountain pyramid shrine. Phu is built halfway up the side of a natural stone pyramid mountain, the only known Khmer temple constructed on the flank of a mountain. Reminiscent of other megalithic structures in Southeast Asia, archaeologists believe that long before the Khmers, or even Shresthavaraman's victory four centuries earlier, the site was already holy. What the four of us are looking at now was built in the 12th century. Astonishing. Simply astonishing.

The Khmers, as they became more Indianized, came to see certain mountaintops as being the natural lingas of Siva, Svayambhuvalingas; lingas of the Self-existent. Lingas are stone phalluses. The literal translation from Sanskrit is "gender" or "sign". A more generous translation is penises, and rock hard at that. Size is less important than shape: cylindrical, with a rounded head and etched bands around the head. Svayambhuvalingas, Self-existent penises, were the most prestigious of all the rock genitalia. Phu, in its sanctity, proves the truth we men cling to in the face of our partner's reassurances and in spite of what the adult industry and Long Dong Silver would have us believe. Laos is full of similarly sized mountains, but only this one is venerated. Phu was re-named in Sanskrit Lingaparvata—the linga of the mountain—and became a temple of Siva in the incarnation of Bhadresvara, the national deity of the Khmers. When you can snatch the linga out of my hand, Grasshopper, then it is time. Until then, touch me . . . here. And Grasshopper . . .watch the circumcision scars.

The footpath-approach to Phu is a long avenue of waist high square pillars through a grassy plain: a promenade of miniature phalluses that cuts through the middle of the temple complex and establishes the symmetry of the wat with the mountain peak. The grass is dry and brittle, a crisp hay that breaks under each step.

The temperature is oppressive. An overpowering, still heat. George and I share an entire bottle of water at the base of the great stone genital.

What are left are the crumbling square remains of the women's and men's palaces; long, deep laterite stone passageways and fallen, shaken archways. Chunks of blocks lie in piles around doorways, tumbled together into a jumble of geometry like swept-up building blocks. Outside the courtyard, more piles form; a giant, building block puzzle half completed, the joined pieces to one side, the unfitted pieces left unclaimed next to it. On a passageway lintel, the image of the Hindu god Bhairava, the angry, terrifying manifestation of Siva. From his mouth come snakes, curling upwards into his hair, his teeth huge and fanged. Inside his snake beard on either side, two female images hold erect penises while sitting on the coiled rings of a serpent.

The heat is penetrating. I wonder if there are snakes. The grass is dead, the burnt amber hay radiating colour and heat into the walls. It is brittle in my footsteps. The base of a standing Buddha image rests in the middle of a squared courtyard, two planted feet, thick toes facing forward, the right ankle adorned in a wide, elaborate anklet. In the hay-coloured grass the sleek decapitated torso, limbless, lies supine next to it. The Buddha image wears only an antaravāsaka, the bottom half of a monk's robes, the folds pulled between the legs, pleating and tugging against the thighs, a muscled stomach showing above the belt, the chest full and round. A heat so hot even the Buddha strips off. A Khmer Winged Victory without the wings. Beside the fallen "god," a broken nāga sits propped upright, scattered chunks of disassociated veneration littering the burnt, brittle field, casting long coffee shadows into the dead vegetation.

The staircase up the mountain is sprinkled in magnolia petals, the approach billowing and fragrant in Parisian canopies of white blossoms. In the ascent, the staircase opens up into a series of stone viewing platforms and benches, each elevation a progression of coolness, each space accented with more remnants and shards of Buddhas. To the humid southeast are the hills of northern Kampuchea, northern Kambuja-desa.

"This is quite a climb," Margaret says. "I hope George does okay." There are ninety-five steps. "He has to go slowly, that's all. But this heat is dreadful. It's really quite a climb. How old do you think he is?"

I hate guessing ages. There is never a right answer. Only degrees of wrongness.

"Late 60s, early 70s."

"He is 78 years old," she says. "He refuses to give in to 'old age'. Refuses to stop." Full of life and vigour is how people should be at 78. Too many people are old at 65. Too many at 35.

The viharn is crumbling, the bricks lost to erosion and decay, precision lost to essence. Out of decrepitude, Zen. The heaves of the ground dictate to the foundation stones like waves to a rubber raft, the line following and moving with the surging earth instead of fighting and losing. A lintel carving shows an adorned triumphant Khmer Buddha King riding a three-headed elephant, his hand raised high in victory. In a second, a warrior splits with a single sword his adversary length-wise to the waist, the two halves falling away limp. That the wat is penile in nature makes the image even more discomforting. The image may be descriptive, but the Zen is clearly symbolic.

The ferry is a barge deck of thick steel plates and girders riveted together in military olive green, connected to the other side with a heavy steel cable. The river in the sunset has calmed, reflecting in ripples the air still and cool and the glow of the warm earthen banks.

If I return to Vientiane by truck with David and then continue by truck on to Louangphrabang, I will spend the next five days on buses and trucks. Seven of the last eight will have been spent in transit, and if I return overland from Louangphrabang, at least two more. This is nuts. There is a plane for Vientiane every morning at 10:30 A.M.. George and Margaret are flying out tomorrow.

The motor thumps into reverse and the steel plate edges into the dock, fighting the current, scraping steel against steel. Another truck pulls up behind. Almost 5:00 P.M. We are the second last crossing.

The Land Rover climbs to the top of the far bank and stops. At the top of the landing is a small cluster of bamboo stalls selling the usual suspects of tobacco and soda. Through the tinted plastic windows everything is a monochrome of amber. I'm caught inside. I can see it: I can feel it: it moves, it is soft, warm, protective.

Suddenly I am struck, grabbing the vinyl seat padding and the steel seat frame, lifting myself up and out of the vehicle, my mind seeing my hands already at the door, my body already outside. Déjàvu suspends me, a lifetime experienced in a second, a revelation felt and lingering, known and yet unknowable. I have already done this. I have seen this moment before. I am, and I belong. Right here, right now. I am electrified, engulfed in waves and filled. As if I have been descended upon by an angel of the Lord and filled, its presence moving through my flesh and soul and, in spite of my difficulty with the analogy I can find no others. Language does me a disservice, and yet it is true, despite my struggle to deny the image. Even in this moment of realization and recognition, in this moment of transcendence, there is still a me to see myself, a me to try to define the moment. The recognition stops me from leaping outside. *I* know it would be impossible to explain. Revelation always is.

Pamela and Jacqueline have been to Muang Pakxong, a cowboy town thirty-five long, dusty, cramped miles into the hills east of Pakxé. They want to say it's been a good day, a worthwhile excursion made in intelligence, worthy of the adventure getting this far had been. With no guidebook to offer suggestions, with no other Western travellers to query, it was made in as much intelligence as could be mustered. That it was good . . . Tomorrow they will go to Wat Phu. Local transportation. On Monday they are flying back to Vientiane. Air Lao.

They bought their ticket today. $85 US. Buying the ticket had required official permission from the local immigration official, permission that allowed them to be in Pakxé without an internal passport, the internal passport in theory required to purchase the air ticket. It was no problem. The officer was very kind. They are invited to his home this evening.

One more thing. They met an American who claimed he had driven his car across the border at Ubon Ratchathani, paid $15 US, and had received a two-week tourist visa. He was not part of the embassy. He was not in the military. He didn't work for the government. Just a tourist, he said.

16

South

At 7:00 A.M., there is an incessant pounding on our hotel room door. It is yesterday's driver and guide.

"$50 please."

"Huh?" The Andersons said free. "No."

"Money for gas?

"$10?

"A tip?

"Money for cigarettes?"

And then they are gone. Empty handed. A shakedown attempt in our hotel was the last thing either of us expected.

And so I've decided: I'll try for the Vientiane plane today, the plane George and Margaret are taking. From there, one night in Vientiane, then the next morning's bus north to Vangviang. I have three hours. A quick coffee with David, then to the airport to see if there is space on the plane, back into town to get official permission to buy the ticket, then back to the airport. At least the Pakxé airport is not far out of town. Thank God for small miracles. The air is already hot at 7:30. It is getting hard to breathe.

In a small café near the hotel, there are maybe twenty cramped inside. The lone empty table is at the front of the café, almost in the street. A small chipped porcelain plate of croissants and rolls appears without a prompt, followed by the last two glasses of coffee from a wet beer-parlour serving tray.

The glasses are old, the shine and squeak long since dish-washed away. The sun catches the ribs cut into the glass and it sparkles newer than it really is. Through the glass, the beige coffee-milk floats in sedimentary layers swirling, rising, falling silt-like. The movement inside highlights the film of water legs and droplets spotting the outside. My instinct says "dirty".

My travel logic makes no sense.

These glasses are no dirtier than anything else, and to be concerned in the face of water spots is to resign myself to expensive restaurants, expensive imports, long bouts of expensive starvation, an unhealthy dependence on Coca Cola, and water spots.

After having worked so hard to get here, to allow bureaucracy to dictate my itinerary is lunacy.

The coffee is chocolaty and pungent across my palate, a sliding sweet thickness over my tongue and into my throat. Be the water spot, Grasshopper.

That I periodically allow external impediments to dictate and control my behaviour, forgetting why I have come to a place, forgetting it is not the souvenirs that make the trip but the people selling them, is not the point. *To know and to not act is to not yet know*, and I am just starting to know.

I haven't even seen Pakxé. David remains non-committal. He is leaving tomorrow by bus to Savannakhét; a meandering return to Vientiane. In six days he is leaving for Vietnam, a time frame that reduces alternatives to one. His ticket to Vietnam is a return to Vientiane, and upon re-entry he will get another visa. In the leisure of a new two weeks, he will attempt Louangphrabang on a more realistic schedule. That is his logic anyway.

The coffee is gone. Too sweet to enjoy. The heat is growing. Now I know. David is right. The hard dirt street is throwing heat into the coffee shop. It is getting very, very hot. Already.

17

South

A broken line of birds sit in meditation on the telephone wires in front of the café, back-lit by the sun, vibrating in a ring of neon energy. How is it that they so effortlessly achieve their stillness? With whom do they study? Beams of light and shadows scatter in the dirt street, cutting the soil into shapes and lines of black and gold. The waitress with the tray of coffee makes another pass, quicker now with fewer customers, the earlier demand for bustle still in her stride. It is almost 8:00. The café is half full.

Funny, I crave a cigarette. I feel so close, on the edge between the veiled proximity of the one-way mirror and being a part of the entity, engulfed in the moment without excuse, the consciousness all through the day of "I, me, mine" lost in the reality of "we, us, ours". What a joke. A cigarette. Another artificial boundary to bonding, to self-realized peer acceptance. I'm willing to make myself sick long-term for acceptance short-term? I keep me from myself over drugs and desires? The birds are just birds. Am I just Mark?

I feel relaxed—for the first time in what feels like days, and my shoulders droop into my stomach, smothering effort instead of demanding it. Travelling is more than following itineraries. The airport is too much effort on an off chance, too much denying a given in anticipation of a maybe. I swirl the sediment in my glass. Tomorrow.

Pakxé immigration is behind thick plastered canary-yellow walls in a large quadrangle compound. Regardless today or tomorrow, if I hope to buy an air ticket, I'm going to need the same official OK Jackie and Pamela got yesterday. David is still non-committal; he will wait for me in the café. The wrought iron entrance is manned, but with apparently little concern over who or what enters. I am not waved through as much as neglected through. Inside, the grass is burnt dry and brittle. A solitary water buffalo the colour of worn asphalt grazes, pulling and grinding in snorts and huffs, its hoofs scraping across the exposed, dry soil. The plaster walls deaden the street noise and the quadrangle produces a tranquility and an astonishing coolness.

Immigration is easy to find. There is one English sign. The ceramic floor tiles are worn and yellowed, the propeller-blade ceiling fan redundant and languid in the freshness. The man I want is short with a small round face and short black hair, parted on the left. He is in short sleeves.

His clipped, educated pronunciation belies his friendliness and smile. Funny how right accents out of the wrong mouths disassociate instead of confirm. Can you learn a foreign language *too* well?

"Yes. I know the two girls," he says. "Jackie and Pamela. They were at my house last night. We had an English lesson. They wanted to buy an airplane ticket, but they did not have an internal passport." He asks for my passport and I lean over the counter to point out the Laotian visa. He nods and leafs. He is enjoying where I have already been, not searching for what he can't find.

"Yes, you do not have an internal passport either. You are not supposed to be here. Did no one tell you in Vientiane?

"I will sign something so that you will be able to buy a ticket here, but when you get back to Vientiane, you must go to the immigration office and get an internal passport. They will give you one, no trouble at all. How do you like Laos? How do you like Pakxé?"

I explain the visa situation.

"Yes. Two weeks is very short for a visit. Why don't you have a longer visa?"

And the Thai travel agent.

"Yes. Travel agents are difficult. Yes. You must go to the Laotian embassy in Bangkok yourself. There they will give you a visa for, I think, perhaps 300 baht, for as long as you like. One or two years. Long enough to really see our country. By the way, what do you think of my English? I learned it twenty years ago at least, but I have not used it for a long time. I have only started to speak English again in the past few years. What do you think? Is it good?"

It is Margaret's gift in a different wrapper. The question is never yes or no, but how much, and the expectation is not low.

"Thank-you. Thank-you," he says through a big smile. And of course, he already knows. He just wants to hear it, as he must have last night, from a Westerner, and an English Westerner at that. "Miss Pamela said my English was very good too, but I don't know. It has been so long." He hands me my passport. "It is all signed now. You will have no trouble getting a ticket.

"It is a shame," he adds, "that I don't have a name card to give you with my address on it. I usually have some, but today I can't find any," and he shuffles through his papers to prove it. "If I had one, we could correspond with each other by letter after you go home."

Indeed.

I like this place.

18

South

At 9:00 A.M., Pakxé's talàat is sweltering. Despite the length of the shadows, the sun feels high overhead.

The sellers, regardless of stock, seem to fit into two categories: poor and not-so-poor. The not-so-poor are protected from the sun and heat under large umbrellas and covered stalls. The poor, mostly old women selling produce, squat in the unprotected spaces between the stalls and umbrellas, towels wrapped around their heads, conserving in immobility what the others find in the shade. To their favour, squatting forces the buyer to squat too, and in the exchange, the power shifts from buyer to seller. If not rich, at least they are smart. As the sun shifts across their neighbours, they gain and lose the little shade that fleets from proximity. Most don't even enjoy that, themselves and their rubberizing vegetables abandoned to the heat unprotected. Tied to their produce as they are, they seem more responsible for their goods than the others do. Even here it is impression that sells. It is the difference between buying ears of sweet corn from out the back of a pick-up truck on the roadside and from a bin in the Safeway.

Under a sheet metal roof on a small wooden slat table stands a row of reclaimed spirit bottles—Johnny Walker, Schenley O.F.C. and Bacardi Rum—plus five large white plastic containers, "Texaco" still visible on one. Two are laokao, the other three something brown. At the bottom of the brown bottles are respectively a leech, a scorpion, and something that looks suspiciously like brains. There are some things I will never know the taste of.

An old man wearing a tan fedora with a tri-coloured hatband beckons David and me, his thin arm lost in the sleeve of his red polo shirt. Behind the display, at the back of the stall, are a second man, a woman, two adolescent girls and more of the large white containers.

The large second man on the stool in the shade says something and the two men laugh.

I feel unhurried. My visa has been handled and the incentive to worry is gone. There is nothing to do but live the moment without the obligations. Free to be just me.

I waste too much time living up to my own expectations of who or what I should be. The expectation becomes competitive, and out of necessity, derivative. I am never enough, but I never know what exactly enough means, only that it is more than what is. Moreover, I allow myself to get caught up with the perceptions and expectations of those around me, their perceptions irrelevant to my own true nature, but assumed regardless. Rarely taking the freedom to just be, in rarity do I become just who I am. My actions end up representing myself rather than embodying it.

David and I have nowhere to go, nothing to do, no one to be.

"Laokao?"

The man in the tan fedora nods. Again he turns and smiles to the second man.

The laokao burns, rising out of my stomach into my oesophagus and back into my mouth. It is a good burn. It is a good breakfast.

And then there is a powder blue wooden stall selling fabrics—*sihns*, cloth, shawls. The front of the stall is bright and soft, but unlit, the rear falls to shadows. Inside against the wall, an explosion of colours: madder red, honey gold, black, silver, white.

Sabadee, she says. She is beautiful: high, round cheek bones, her hair pulled up and back into a ponytail, a pink and white chiffon top, buttoned to the neck. A gold Buddhist amulet hangs to her breasts, bouncing as she walks to the light to greet me.

Sabadee.

"How much?" She turns to pick up her calculator, punching in numbers I can't see. 1800 she shows me and smiles into the wall, turning away from my face, hiding her blush. 1500 I show her back and smile into her face and then into the floor and away, joining her in the game. Am I that obvious? Does the laokao free emotions or create them? I'm supposed to bargain, right? Yes, she nods. 1500, and she folds the material. *Will you marry me?* And I'm not even sure. Did I say that out loud? Sometimes I forget. She smiles. It is not her first proposal. Not even today. *Will you?* And I see. There is a ring. She already has.

An old wrinkled woman squats beside a large rattan mat covered by eight perfect piles of fluorescent, shimmering aquamarine. The shimmer moves, like light playing on the threads of a silk dress: the pile seems to float, the light shifting back and forth across the surface. Beetles, upon closer inspection, swarming like a rugby scrum, burrowing to the ground, pushing others back up to the surface like cold cream in hot coffee. Then cabbages, bananas, vegetables, tobacco, fruit. More tobacco. A dry goods stall of sponges, plastic pails, dishes and mesh shopping bags. Extruded-petroleum sandals splash candy-apple red and grass green and dodger blue next to hideous lime-green and electric tangerine pink. Pencils and cheap lined notebooks and pencil sharpeners. Then more bananas, more fruit, more toothpaste and soap and towels and hideous plastic footwear. And in the stalls, the light cuts through the ragged rips in the tarpaulins and the imperfect joins in the roof, the colours changing from cool blue to a warm gold to hot white as though a Peter Greenaway movie set. The stalls smell of wax and unfinished pine.

A colonnaded concrete pad at the end of the street is the new market; twenty-foot steel girders still in red primer, a corrugated metal roof. A Pakxé Parthenon. There are noodles and spring rolls and baguettes and coffee, sweet coconut desserts, but no beetles. They keep running away I guess. We are the only Westerners at the table, the only Westerners that I can see, that I have seen. Walking through a market gives the illusion of exclusivity, but in the movement there is always doubt, always the play of chance. To sit immobile is to acknowledge certainty.

A physically and mentally handicapped beggar approaches us, her hand searching. Halfway to us a second woman intercepts her, turning her by her arms away towards another table.

"They know her," David says. "She's accepted. She didn't choose us because we were foreigners. We were just another table.

"The woman pulled her away because we were foreigners, but she didn't pull her away for us. Why would she? We're foreigners."

From that table to another and another she moves, never a gesture out of place, never a misplaced step. We have both grown accustomed to assuming gullibility, to being seen as targets. We are white. We are rich. We are dupable.

And he's right. No one is being rude. No one is brushing her off. Like any good intervention, it had been articulated at the centre, not the periphery. The acknowledgement the interceder offered us was not compassion but distance. We were not the ends. The line is not beggar and tourist or even beggar and shopper. The line is Laotian and foreigner. It is us that will frighten her.

And so: Khao San Road is Bangkok's main street for budget backpackers. In 1986 Khao San Road was a quiet little street of guesthouses and restaurants that specialized in fruit salads and Indonesian satay and breakfasts of sausage and toast and coffee and big smiles and clean rooms. I stayed in the Hello Guesthouse. One morning I was up even before the kitchen staff, standing alone in the middle of Koh San Road feeling the morning break against my skin. The road, that part of Bangkok that I'd laid claim to as mine, was peaceful and calm and delicate and the air smelled fresh. In the Cleopatra Guesthouse on Khao San Road, where I stayed later, a hand-printed cardboard sign on the wall just inside the door that was locked quiet at 11:00 P.M. read:

> *This is not a brothel*
> *Thai girl (prostitute)*
> *cannot stay here*

By 1989, the Hello Guesthouse restaurant had become an all-night bar of Mekong Whisky and Jimi Hendrix to patrons half of whom hadn't been born in the 60s, half of whom had never left.

You could still get breakfast, but without the smiles. It was hard to be up before a kitchen staff that didn't sleep. The rooms weren't as clean, and while Cleopatra Guesthouse still promised integrity, more and more promised locals in blue-jean micro cut-offs with red toe nails in gaudy plastic flip-flops and enticing coffee-brown cleavage in tie-dyed, barely-tied halter tops.

They sat in the laps of the new adventurers at the cafés and pubs that complemented the five Sikh clothiers and two silk merchants and two leather outlets and the overbearing confusion of sellers tables that *excuse me* dominated the sidewalks, forcing *excuse me* pedestrians to veer into a road increasingly *excuse me* congested by food stalls and pineapple sellers *beep-beep* and tuk-tuks and *beep-beep* taxis and patrol cars. The tables offered a full line of fake designer clothing, rip-off pirate cassettes, near-genuine hill tribe artefacts and for our dining and dancing pleasure, two Sikh mystics carrying laminated name/rate cards, insisting them into the paths of the shopping *excuse me* impaired pedestrians and the genuinely apathetic excuse me asking for "a moment of your time friend and to guarantee an excellent reading." Medium-friendship was available for three different budgets and "*What is your good name friend?*" and "*Where are you from?*" which seemed strange questions for mystics to be asking. Only 900 baht. About $40 US. A good meal and wine at home. Or forty-five bootleg cassettes here. Or fifteen nights in the "this is not-a-brothel" guesthouse.

Apart from change, the other constant in those three years was three small children who worked the street selling packets of tissue for five baht. Expressionless and mute, they started at one end of the road, entering each successive restaurant, shoving their way into the centre of each conversation or newspaper with a ragged piece of cardboard covered with saran wrap and scotch tape; they were from Pakistan; they had no parents; would you please buy their tissues for five baht. The encounter completed, they rushed on to the next table and the next and the next and in a kinetic hyper activity, an entire restaurant swarmed in moments. Rarely did they make a sale. New arrivals to the road accepted the demanding card and read it before rejecting it, the old Asia hands from yesterday's

Thai Air flight acknowledged the already annoying cards intrusive to their beer and conversations in a dismissing wave.

I saw the children, one night, sleeping in the entranceway of an office building under the mango yellow security lights, lying on pieces of cardboard beside an older man. It was a few hundred feet off Khao San Road, but it was in a direction no one took and no one needed and it might as well have been a million miles. The children appeared, the children disappeared. No one knew. No one cared. The entranceway was on the corner of six-lane Ratchadamnoen Klang Avenue. Even at 11:30 P.M. the traffic was intimidating. The good news was, you never noticed the noise because the exhaust pollution was so bad. Home. It's where I want to be. Indeed.

19

South

The ticket officer that afternoon at the airport is much less cooperative. He points out that I don't have an internal passport and states that he can't sell me a ticket because of it. I point out the hand-written approval to be in Pakxé from Pakxé immigration, dated this morning. The whole purpose of getting immigration approval was to be able to buy an outgoing ticket. He sees it. He doesn't care. I don't have an internal passport. He won't sell me a ticket. I point out that he sold Jackie and Pamela tickets yesterday, and that they didn't have an internal passport either. They had hand-written approval from the immigration officer in Pakxé. The same hand-written approval. The same immigration officer. The same ticket request. He doesn't remember them. I ask him how many white foreign women have come into the airport to buy tickets that he can't remember two English women yesterday. It doesn't matter he says. He remembers them. Yes. That was different. He doesn't have authority to sell me a ticket anyway. He has to check with his superiors. I should come back.

"But you're the ticket official, right? You're the only person here, the only person in the office, and the only person in charge of selling tickets, right?"

It doesn't matter. I don't have an internal passport, and he has to check before he can sell me a ticket. I should come back tomorrow morning, when the flight is leaving. Then, maybe, he can get me a ticket. But by then, the flight might be sold out I say. By then, it might be too late. Indeed, it might. There is nothing he can do. He has to talk to his superior. I tack into the wind.

"I understand," I say. "A long time ago, I was in East Berlin. The East Germans there, even though it was their own country, they had to ask the Soviets what they could and couldn't do. It's a shame when you don't have control in your own country. I understand."

He wants to know what I am talking about. He wants to know why I am saying such a thing.

"It's okay," I say. "I understand. Laos is a poor country. It's a Communist country. It gets money from the Soviet Union. The airplanes Lao Aviation uses are Soviet. Laos depends on the Soviet Union. I understand." I tell him I'll come back after he's asked his Soviet superior if he will allow him to sell me a ticket. I tell him it's just a shame when you have to ask foreigners if you can do something in your own country. But I understand.

He doesn't have to ask anyone for permission to sell me a ticket he says. This is his country, and no one is in control of Laos except Laotian people. He does not do what Soviets tell him to do. He does what he wants to do. He demands my passport.

My flight to Vientiane leaves tomorrow at 8:35 A.M. Sunday, February 25. It is $85 US. Cash. Don't be late.

Two half-naked teenage monks are playing ping-pong in Wat Sim Luang's courtyard. Three more are standing next to the table watching the game. The afternoon has turned overcast, the sky losing its brightness but none of its heat. The five boy-monks are wearing only the under clothes halves of their robes. In the soft, even light, their antaravāsaka skirts radiate pumpkin-orange into the shifting perspiration on their teakwood skin. Their arms and torsos are flawless, the monks' ribbed muscles pumping and hardening with each reaching step, with each reacting swing. They are perfect, and I envy them their perfection. It is a beauty I will never see again without effort. A sixth monk stands nearby, close to the game, but not a part of it. Watching.

"Hello. My name is Tommy. How are you?" It was not the moment I expected.

He is seventeen. He lives here. He has for many years, he says, since he was a boy. He studies English he says. His uttarāsanga is pulled high, covering his shoulder and his chest in an unnecessary, unshared conservatism. First Monk Inthvong and now Monk Tommy, except that Monk Inthvong was happy and smiling in his modesty, a modesty that suddenly occurs to me might have been out of his huskiness and not his beliefs. Monk Tommy seems much more determined in his dress; there is no smile, there is no joy. The feeling of his cover-up, given the five to one split, is less shyness and more disdain and distance. My personal history is covered rapid-fire and rather less modestly. Where am I from? What is my name? How old am I? What is my job? Do I like Pakxé? More question forms. Is there only one English textbook in Laos? He is eager to speak and eager to learn, in a stiff, alienating, language-vulture kind of way. He stares at my camera, gesturing towards it with his head, his arms folded across his chest. "Why do you make a picture of my classroom?" He has been watching me a long time.

He pulls me aside away from the others. "Hello. Please can you give me $100 American money?"

I shake my head no in reflex, but the abruptness and magnitude of the request leaves me confused and intimidated. A second Pakxé shakedown, and I still don't know what the rules are or how far the game's parameters get pushed. My "no" feels tainted in a questioning.

"Please, you give me $100 American money. Please. You are a rich man. I am a monk. I have no money. I am a poor man. Please, you give me $100 American money." The words sound more desperate and pleading than his eyes explain. The fix to be had is neither drugs nor money but probability. The question seems more based in experience than need. My fears of the unwitting foreigner alone in Laos evaporate in Tommy's move from demanding to begging.

"Okay. Please you give me 100 Thailand baht," the pleading provoking more anger and disdain in me than anxiety. Funny how we mirror what we see.

"Okay. Please you give me 100 kips," and I realize there is no emotion in Tommy's request, no abruptness or anxiety. Maybe 100 is the only number he knows.

I shift away, back towards the others, trying to remove myself from the perception of intimacy.

I feel betrayed in the request. By Tommy of course, but Tommy is the symptom, not the cause. The betrayal is in the desire. I keep trying to transcend the opportunism that characterizes friendships and interactions. It is not my desire to befriend someone in the expectation of acquisition. And of course, reciprocity is the nature of friendship, of mutual benefits arising through the interaction of humanity, the sharing of one person to another.

We talk, and in that talking acknowledge our humanity and co-existence. I always expect to find it in churches and temples and wats. I expect it because of the purity and altruism that rests at the foot of spirituality and religion. I want to take refuge from the ills of humanity and Self in God and Selflessness so I can emerge clean to re-enter that same humanity and Self and see them as glorious. I want the monks and priests and novices and masters to instil in me, for that moment of inter-relation, for those moments of deliverance inside their temple or church, the essence of their spirit so I can carry it with me in mine; to relieve my need to escape, to alleviate my fears in desperation and stolidness. To allow me, in these Buddhist sanctuaries or Christian churches or Hindu temples, a re-baptism into the calming and inner joy of knowledge that for fleeting moments I have held in my hands and that now I hold securely only in the distance of memory.

100 kip is nothing: 23¢. It is the attack to the spirit that dampens and disillusions. Even here, in Wat Sim Luang, there is no purity of spirit; even here I am cast down as a tourist instead of uplifted as a human. I want to soar in the embracing spirituality of God and humanity and love without contention. Offered and accepted because I live, because I am a creature of God. Instead, the moral suasion of alms through a triad of guilt: spiritual, economic, cultural.

He wants to show me inside the viharn. Words are spoken and one of the ping-pong playing novices runs off to get the key. The remaining players leave their game to join Tommy and myself. The group of us cluster in front of the viharn door. The novice returns with the key and a second, older bhikkhu, their forearms locked into each other's. "My English teacher! This is my English teacher!" Tommy shouts and I look in reflex, but I am not the subject of this sentence. "My English teacher. This is the Canadian." Embarrassed, the teacher-monk's yin-reluctance is prodded along by the tugging novice, his own yang-ecstasy outpacing the boy's steps, dragging them both up the steps towards the door; a Pushmi-Pullyu bhikkhu. In the conflict he is just awkward. At least he knows enough not to sing any Chuck Berry.

I extend my hand in a gesture of English and speak "hello". The teacher-monk answers, but his answer is lost through indecipherable pronunciation, subject-verb disagreement and exterminated vocabulary. In doubting benefit I continue, ascribing his illiteracy to exuberance in the unexpected confrontation with his subject and inabilities. Soon it is clear. It is not exuberance and I am not George Harrison. He is hopeless. I feel sorry, the monk out of respect and love stripped naked by his own adoring pupils before an acknowledged expert. Eager to bask in him, eager to have the integrity of their education verified—the novices encircle him shouting as he drowns, embarrassed, pressured, aware of what he doesn't know and afraid to use what he does.

His students translate what I say for him and what he replies for me. I smile at him and shake his hand again, holding it tight and long. I ask him simple questions, repeating each thought syllabically even before he can stutter "pardon?" and his students can translate, letting him wallow in the question without being obvious that he is wallowing or that I know. I listen to his answers and nod in appreciation and comprehension without understanding even half. I hope he can tell I am supporting him.

The tour is over. He has had my undivided attention. Again I shake his hand, and offer as reverent a good-bye as I can forge in the barrier of our language. He smiles and walks alone back to his room. It is late in the afternoon. Time to walk away, indeed.

20
South

The restaurant specializes in lychee-ice shakes and steamed *bao zhe* dumplings. This is where David and I had arranged to meet the women. The last night in Pakxé for the four of us, my last night with David. In the corners above the front door two small wooden perches support cups filled with burning joss sticks, the ragged ends of dead burnt sticks dangling limp. The poster on the wall is a nameless, interchangeable Japanese pop idol, the impression pathetic and needy removed from her native context of Japanese pubescent sexuality. Next to the false foreign idol are Thai Pepsi ads with the ubiquitous and increasingly tiresome Miss Universe 1988—Miss Thailand, Porntip—and a Thai rock band clearly influenced by, if not the music of the Doobie Brothers, at least their album art; the pose is *Takin' It to the Streets* all over again.

The small round wooden tables are covered in vinyl tablecloths. Their odour reminds me of my grandmother's log cottage on Lake Erie: the maple tree in the back yard; the lush, cool grass filled in the evenings with mosquitoes; cracking window ledge paint the colour of a Guinness head; the smell of the varnish over the brown-stained timber; coal-oil heating fuel; a wall of fishing poles, one for each son-in-law and grandpa; row-boat oars stacked in the corner. I can hear her voice. I can see the family, the dinner table. In the kitchen there were always tins of cookies and pies lined against the wall, five or six: oatmeal, chocolate-chip, date squares, cherry, blueberry, rhubarb. There was always food, always people. I never felt at ease there.

At the back of the Chinese-Lao restaurant beneath a small red illuminated Buddhist shrine there is a Japanese cassette deck.

It is Saturday night and by 7:00 the restaurant has filled, boys on the left, girls on the right. One of the boys is in sunglasses, brown chequered shirt buttoned to the collar, and leather jacket. The others are just neat in a style that says innocent-next-door. The girls are all in sihns, plastic flip-flops and blouses. Cool must be a guy thing. Someone turns on the stereo and music blasts into the concrete cavern, distorting far too loud to be heard or spoken through. The boys shuffle their feet and sway in pre-amble, crooning with the songs to the girls who seem more interested in each other than the boys. You have to play at least a little hard to get. Pakxé posturing.

Jackie and Pamela arrive. Across the street is another larger, more luxurious Chinese restaurant. A long carved Chinese screen room divider zig-zags across the front, separating the streetside tables from the oppressive, hospital-starched whiteness of the dining room. The other restaurant is empty. And quiet.

A schizophrenic rain has spotted the afternoon and early evening, coming in downpours, tumbling out of the sky and then as quickly stopping, the pattern repeating itself as if the weather were a whim to be played with. The potholes are brimming, bigger than I had remembered them being dry, and now that they stand out, more than I remember as well. More teenagers arrive. We tiptoe into the mud and around the pothole field.

Jackie is twenty-three, a schoolteacher from London. Pamela is thirty-five. She trained as a social worker, and after leaving college entered the job where she has been ever since. Jackie didn't have much money and wasn't sure about either this trip or herself: who she was, who she wanted to be, or even where she wanted to be. She misses her boyfriend a lot. Though she has been gone only a couple of months, touring her way through Greece, Turkey and India, she has already been back home once, and is in fact planning another return after Laos.

Homesickness. When she got too lonely, she bought a ticket to England, spent a week or two with her friends, did some supply teaching if any was available, and then left again. She doesn't want to go back she says. She wants to travel, but as soon as she gets away, she forgets the reasons she left England, misses her boyfriend, becomes insecure, questions why she's here, and returns home.

I try to tell her about my experiences with homesickness: the presumed disillusionment with travel that was more about too much unfamiliarity than too long away, that within days of returning home, after seeing my friends and family and going to some favourite hang-outs, the boredom that had driven me away returned, stronger and more determined in the light of the new comparison of fact to dreamed belief. In the tide of returning, the reasons I had originally left for re-swept over me, engulfing all I had accomplished in a wash of doubt. The reasons that had brought me home, so pleading in their moment, seemed illogical and whimsical in retrospect, the adventure of travel lost to the craving for a drink with a friend at the pub. No one at home seemed to understand my experiences, and the more I tried to explain, the more I doubted my own understanding, until despair set in as I watched all I thought I had learned crumble around me under the weight of familiarity and numbers. Moreover, the effervescence of reunion gone, within days few even pretended to care about the misunderstood moments of experience and knowledge and life that travel had given me. Life at home was life at home: my absence had not changed that. On the contrary, it had reinforced it. For my friends, life had not changed, nor had it needed to. For me the perception was 180 degrees divergent, and life at home was only more ensconced in its commonality and repetitiveness.

An American friend in Japan had had a theory about homesickness. After watching himself twist in the emotional wind for two years, he concluded it was cyclical, coming in six-week oscillations. The key to homesickness was in its refusal. Denied reactive emotion, the desire dissipated. The problem was in the reacting, in the grasping and clinging, refusing to understand the passing nature of the longing. If you didn't let it go, if you responded with phone calls and letters and video rentals of home the way you wanted to remember it and not the way it was, the dislocation would last and last and last. The indulgence wouldn't cure the pain, and neither would it upset the six-week cycle. The trick was to see the sickness for what it was and not what you wanted it to be: to *see the moment, as it is.* You reap what you sow.

I try to tell her about my experiences with homesickness, but since when has telling ever worked? She isn't listening: she doesn't care. She feels homesick just talking about it, clinging to it like a longed-for wayward lover returning from the arms of another with fresh kisses and new promises. She wants to be homesick. The homesickness proves her love for boyfriend, friends and country: the widow cast forever in black, remembering a love that when alive was never as true and never as devoted. Like a rejected lover, the wounds of separation still fresh, the heart a mass of struggle between love and pain that doesn't want to be told that this too shall pass, a heart that instead wallows in the joy of pain and self-pity, in a final grand proclamation of the lost love. She wants to be homesick. It is a right she will not be denied. I know it far too well.

She is attractive, with strawberry blonde hair and freckles more provocative than childish, tall, with the legs and bust of a runner. Her self-piteous musing and lack of strength, depth, undercut it all away. The shell of a beauty, filled with indecisiveness and emotional insecurity. I'm not sure the trip isn't just a way of seducing her boyfriend into a commitment.

Pamela wants to be here.

Not specifically here Laos, but specifically here travelling. Living a life moment to moment instead of working an existence day to day, conforming to expectations and dreaming of living a life.

After twelve years, her job no longer provided the fulfilment popular mythology had promised. All her money was going into her house, her car, her clothes and food: was that why she was working? To survive? One day she realized there was no real point to her existence. She was living someone else's dream under some-one else's rules. It and they meant nothing to her.

She was thirty-five years old, already old among her neigh-bours. Prematurely middle-aged, as if thirty-five was past her prime instead of it being the start.

So she quit. Her job. Her lifestyle. Everything. No leave of absence. No tethering umbilicus to assuage the fears. She quit, said good-bye and came here. She never mentioned a man. She never mentioned a woman.

Except for a short holiday in Morocco, she has never been out of England. She has never travelled like this, with a backpack, without an itinerary, with the goal indefinable, yet absolutely clear.

She wants a challenge. Some excitement in her life. I admire her decision. In my dislocation, I had never had so much to lose.

I had been disillusioned with my education from the day I graduated, and with my career almost before I began, and still the divestiture had been un-easy, the freedom of responsibility for my life, taken into my hands seven years ago at twenty-five, still looked at by co-workers and family with a mixture of suspicion and envy. At thirty-five her life had been set. A house, a car, a career. Freedom at thirty-five was not popular, and from those intimidated and threatened by her strength, she had taken her share of criticism and comment. But she was here, and she was alive. In every bone she felt it. With every breath.

Uwais the Sufi was asked one morning how he felt. Like a man, he said, who having awoken in the morning, did not know whether he would be alive in the evening. But surely, the questioner replied, that was the case of all men, wasn't it? Yes, replied Uwais. But how many *felt* it?

She hadn't been too late.

The years pass. Quicker every year. It is the truth I was always told as a child, never understanding the sentiment because since when has telling worked, and truth as we know it colloquially is never really truth but experienced perspective. Children grasp the concept of age, but not the concept of aging. Next Christmas seems forever away. The leap from age five to twenty-five is a five-fold increase. To the child's mind, it is an impossible jump, and to the twenty-five-year-old, the mere fragmentation of memory: an album of class photos, faces clear in recognition, names lost in aging, stories related by parents and relatives of events they remember to your nodding, vacuous agreement. Twenty-five to thirty-five is not even a halving, and while to the twenty-five-year-old it seems a leap of almost the same magnitude as from five, to the thirty-five-year-old it is your youth that was in your hands, believing it would never fade, that there was always time, but now the time has passed, and the past dangles before you alive and vibrant and just out of a reach that pulls with each day further away instead of closer. The mistake, the Buddha said, is believing there is time.

In the final weeks of my first job as purchasing agent at Dare Cookies one of my regular phone contacts confided his envy at my decision.

"I got this job," he told me "in my twenties. It paid well, it wasn't too difficult, and it held the promise of some challenge as well as stability and advancement." He sold edible animal oils, the boiled down remains of pigs and cows. "So I stayed, learned my craft and became content. One morning I was driving to work and it hit me, like a slap in the face. I'd been doing the same job for twenty years. I'd been driving to the same office, along the same road, sitting behind the same desk, for twenty years. And I didn't know where they had gone. Twenty years. I was forty-four. The numbers had never meant anything to me before and it hit me. I was forty-four and I realized I wasn't going to travel the world, I wasn't going to do all those things I had accepted as unassailable in my youth."

How long would she be gone for?

She didn't know. Maybe she could find work overseas. Maybe after a while she'd become bored and want to go back home. None of that mattered, none of that was important. What mattered was the break, the leaving. Being here now.

I asked her if her friends understood, if her parents understood?

Her friends, she said, were divided into two camps. Some supported her completely, envying her courage and freedom to quit and travel, the courage to be herself, or at least to search for that self.

The other half couldn't understand. In their eyes she had it all, and she was abandoning it in the ravings of a pre-mature middle-aged panic for an irresponsible fling that, once completed, would see her back in England, broke, regretting, humbled, unemployed, and at thirty-five or thirty-six or thirty-seven, unemployable.

It had been most difficult to walk away from her job, at a time when thirty-five-year-olds were looked at as entrenched rather than developable. But it was that kind of suffocating, demanding, arbitrary philosophy she was fighting against, that kind of philosophy she wanted to leave behind. To take a leave of absence, to ask for an extended holiday, was to taint the experience in caution even before it began, and besides, the trip was not the end but only the means. The end was to break free of the bonds which and who kept her from what she really was and who, to fulfil longings of the soul instead of obligations of the mind. It was all or nothing.

I liked her. I liked her a lot. I felt bad about what I had thought about her. You learn as you go: in time, her about clothing: in time, me about myself, about others. I kept deluding myself I had come to understand people, that somehow after all this time and energy, I had found the intangible of wisdom. I had in the past, but in fleeting glimpses, never long enough to not see it slip away in often its first test of conviction. I fell back into knowledge and the perception of wisdom instead of being. I liked her. Whomever she left behind, they lost something special.

And so: I found my relatives in that summer of 1985. Twenty years since I had seen some of them. Forever for others. They weren't lost, they weren't hidden. They were just … a long way away, behind too much day to day living to be done here, not away. The rationale wasn't one sided. "The planes fly both ways," my mother always said. She was right. Is right. I spent a week alone with my by-now widowed grandmother at that Lake Erie cottage. Just the two of us. We walked the old paths and cut the lawn and collected bits of broken glass from the beach and put the bits in jars just like we had those twenty years earlier when I was just seven. At the end of the week, there was a family reunion. Everyone was there except my parents and an uncle-in-law who had died. 2700 miles away was a good excuse, but there were always good excuses. Thirty-six people. Just like olden times when I was 5 and life was not as innocent as I lovingly remember it to be. And then we all left, all at once, all of us; back to our new homes, our new lives, our own beds. We just left her. All alone. A week later, the cottage was up for sale. A couple of months and it was gone. Two years later, she was gone. For that, my parents went back.

The mistake, the Buddha said, is believing there is time.

Tomorrow I will be back in Vientiane and alone. Again. My time here is racing.

21

North

T he Monday morning bus out of Vientiane to Vangviang leaves at 7:30 A.M. from the old, out-grown bus station next to the Talàat Sao. My information was 6:00, so I have had one and a half hours to eat breakfast and drink too many glasses of coffee to feel comfortable with the idea of a five-hour bus trip. I could have stayed and eaten at the bakery next to the Sailom. Life.

I am going to Louangphrabang, overland, from Vientiane. It is supposed to be a three-day journey. Time, discomfort and illegality notwithstanding, travelling overland to Louangphrabang is not logistically problematic. Then again, it's not like I have another choice: I still have no internal passport. I still can't fly. And now that I have a hand-written entry in my passport from Pakxé immigration, I can't play stupid either. The note from Pakxé immigration might get me an internal passport, but then again, it might just get me deported; I guess it depends whether Vientiane immigration chooses to see the O.K. from Pakxé immigration or the fact that I had to be illegally in Pakxé to get it. Moreover, since everything is closed on Sunday, it would have meant staying in Vientiane at least one more day, and the internal passport just lets me do legally what I'm going to do illegally anyway. What it won't get me is more time: today is the 26th. My visa expires in six days.

The route to Louangphrabang follows the only road north out of Vientiane, through the villages of Vangviang and Kasi, before

132   Crescent Moon Over Laos

the final leg to Louangphrabang. From Vientiane there is daily bus service to Vangviang by one of a fleet of brand new Mitsubishi buses. That's what I am on now: a brand new Mitsubishi bus. I taught at Mitsubishi Motors in Japan. The factory in Nagoya Port is for automobiles, not buses, but the possibility that I know some of the workers that built this bus, tenuous though it is, makes me feel less alone and less vulnerable. The sign over the driver's head reads that the buses have been provided through a "Japan-Laos joint economic cooperation and friendship agreement". Mitsubishi in Nagoya built Zeros for the Imperial Japanese Air Force in World War Two. Cooperation comes in many faces. The new bus station the older buses didn't necessitate is being built next door to the old bus station these newer buses have outgrown. A large billboard near the old bus station says that the construction of the new bus station is being handled by a joint "Japan-Laos construction consortium". Elephants wearing walkmans pulling big-screen TVs, I guess. Why a billboard in Laos erected by Japan is printed in English is an excellent question. Laos is still full of excellent questions.

There is also, allegedly, daily bus service between Vangviang and Kasi. Kasi is the end of the public transportation route. Buses arriving in Kasi stay over the night, then make the return trip to Vientiane the next day. From Kasi, transportation, if there is any, is via transport truck, if there are any. It is just a matter of waiting until one comes. Simple. Allegedly. But some of the same folks that told me this also told me about the internal passports, and like I said before, I haven't met anyone holding one. And I'm not going to.

I am the only Westerner on the bus. I was the only Westerner in the entire bus station parking lot. I kept looking for another Western traveller to arrive, someone to confirm that this was the right bus, that this was the right station, that this in fact *was* a station. In the end, the only person I have to confirm anything for me is me. In the most unexpected places, Zen. Or Camus. Sometimes it's hard to tell the difference.

The bus is crowded without being oppressive, my expectation still one of impassable aisles full with produce and livestock, and plastic vomit bags used prophylactically in the parking lot. Once again I am wrong. The seat I guarded through two rushed trips to the washroom and one to confirm I was on the right bus was in no jeopardy. Even without a conductor there is civility, an acknowledgment of space and dignity. This is still not India.

Nor is it Japan. People talk here: out loud, in public, and quite possibly, to strangers. The seats hum with conversation, food passed across aisles, and the tobacco trinity of offer, acceptance and smoke. We are a community, one secure enough to leave it unobliged to notice me as anything but another human being. Whatever I am, what I am not is gaijin. It all seems so normal. But still, I am heading north. North is where the fighting is. North is where the guerrilla attacks happen. The south was safe. Vientiane was safe. The danger is in the north: everybody says so. It must be in the north. And so come the questions that in spite of this apparent normalcy I can't escape.

Who would want to shoot us?

Who would want to shoot me?

Just before we make our lunch break, we pass a work crew cutting a new road into the Prince Edward Island-red soil, followed quickly on its heels by a small works yard with a chain link fence around a storage compound housing a bulldozer, a grader, an excavator and a roller. The driver, the conductor and myself are the only ones to leave the bus. It has been almost three hours since we left Vientiane. The rain that's threatened has come and gone, leaving the morning cool and damp and the soil thick and chunky; footprints aren't left in the earth so much as picked up and carried along on the soles of my shoes. The others' reluctance to stretch their legs worries me that they know something I don't, that consumed in false security, I will wander off to photograph the village only to see the bus pull away without me.

Two large, heavily loaded military transport carriers are parked in the middle of the road. The back bed of each is crowded with forty-five gallon drums, draped over in camouflage netting. I watch six soldiers get off the nearer of the two trucks. Only two seem past their teens. A bazooka and Khalashnikov lean against the drums. Do they know I am not supposed to be here? Do they care?

The village, or at least the stretch of village earth our bus calls home, belongs to the children. Playing photographic hide-and-seek, me with the camera, them with the smiles, each cajoles the other to go first, to go closer, leap-frogging into my proximity and then too close, retreating in an adrenaline explosion of shrieks, scattering screaming behind doors and each other before the game begins again. I am new, a toy that walks, talks, is unpredictable, and will not be here in an hour.

Each approach is closer, each approach braver, each retreat louder. They want their curiosity. They want their play. There is neither reluctance at my intrusion nor resignation to their fate.

It was not the village reception I expected. The usual routine is much more financial in nature.

Postcard racks in Bangkok flood with photos of hill tribe people, offering photographic fortune to the shooter and, from those of us who bother to turn over the postcard, fame. Whether these images in their creation bestowed the Karen, Lisu, Akha and H'mong with fortune as well I don't know, but I am left doubting. There is no question about the fame: more and more trekkers with more and more cameras stumbling through more and more of their villages, searching in vain to reproduce that manipulated postcard image or capture the mystique of adventure in the image. Sought out because of their uniqueness and exoticness, for the H'mong, Akha, Lisu and Karen to not share in the profits was to watch their marketplace asset decline in value, with no offsetting income generating source. It's the "pay me the money now, because who wants to see a sixty year-old stripper" theory of income accrual. The problem is, the dowager dancer theory is valid. The hill tribes' assets are both depleting and finite: exoticism, authenticity, unsophistication. And so, with each photo we take and with each resulting demand for money, especially demands that translate into hard coin, the uniqueness and exoticism we attach to these Hill Tribe folk and the primitiveness we demand from them disappears and with it, the devaluation doesn't just accelerate, it races. No traveller wants a photo of a H'mong or a Lisu in a Yankees' ball cap and Laker's jersey, and no adolescent Lisu wants to be the only kid without them, nickels for photos be damned.

In Mae Sai, Thailand, on the Burmese border, tourist posturing is big business for Burmese hill tribe women. Taking advantage of Thailand's border generosity, Mao and Lisu in full tribal dress cross the Sai River from Thakhilek in Burma to pose for tourist dollars not thirty feet from the no-man's-land of the bridge, a no-man's-land filled with hawkers selling elephant and cock opium weights, World War Two Japanese occupation currency, and packets of more recent fiscally reneged currency, notes which were legal tender mere weeks earlier until Burma's Military central bank's sleight-of-integrity monetary policy eliminated overnight three denominations from circulation. Imagine if tomorrow you woke up and 5s, 10s and 100s were no longer legal. Imagine if you kept all your money at home because you didn't trust the banks. Imagine if your recourse to the de-nomination (if shutting up and smiling didn't work for you) was prison or death or renting your daughter to foreign backpackers. Imagine if your recourse was gluing the worthless notes to pieces of cardboard to sell to tourists on the Friendship Bridge at Niagara Falls, or from the asphalt under the "Welcome to Tijuana" sign.

I am burdened by the history of travellers unknown to me, of situations and circumstances that are a part of someone else's travel diary. Often the burden of travel history is my own. Here, there is no photographic travel history to be burdened by. There are no out-stretched hands for money. Unencumbered by their inhibitions, I lose mine too. They laugh and I laugh and they pose and I shoot, all from our safe distances, all the time in the moment. The burden here is just beginning. Now I am a part of it.

Looking back home at the photos of the hide-and-seeking children, there is no self-consciousness to break through, no dissatisfying loss of the moment. Able to think "not-Mark," there was no consciousness of "Mark trying to take a good photo" to cloud the moment. Unfettered, the process was simply "taking a photo" and the photo is simply "children playing," or even simpler, "a moment". Perhaps that is the problem with travel history. It suggests and repeats the moment with too much ease and too often, and in acted-out orchestrations of moments, there is no joy, no spontaneity, no life. The joy of travelling is the moment, the serendipity of life unfolding before you in situations that, in their essence are but normal occurrences. Laughter, smiles, waves, conversation. Out of their familiar context, they become less the mundane and instead the unique. It is the difference between saying and feeling.

In the end, the other passengers knew nothing I didn't.

At the northern frontier of the village is our first police checkpoint since Vientiane. On our approach, tens of adolescent boys swarm half naked into the roadway facing the sentry box, surrounding the bus in a bravado of strength through numbers, their authority established more through self-administered accountability and the group dynamics of shouting *Lord of the Flies*-adolescents than through any government agency. Who is in charge? What is in charge? Do they know I'm not supposed to be here? What are the possibilities, given the apparent ascendancy of randomness and adolescent authority to the status of order of the day? I lie better when I'm telling the truth, and I don't tell authority even the truth well, especially when the authority comes from armed children. Then again, maybe it doesn't matter. If randomness determines fate, then what difference does truth or untruth matter?

I need not have worried. The young warriors' only interest is in extracting the transit fee of the day. The toll collected, the stone-weight barrier is lifted and we are on our way.

22

North

1:30 P.M. The bus is almost empty. The rear doors accordion open, and the conductor points. "Gueshause."

"Gueshause," he repeats. "Vangviang." The three remaining passengers understand both the situation and the Lao-lish, and in an effort to get their stalled trip moving, join in.

"Gueshause. Vangviang. Gueshause. Vangviang."

This must be the guesthouse.

A small man approaches me from the stairs of a white wood frame building, smiling Laotian, speaking English. His name is Chantravong.

"The bus makes a circle of the town, then comes back here for the night," he says. "I am the only guesthouse in town. The driver and conductor were trying to help you. They will stay here tonight too. Tomorrow they will go back to Vientiane."

I am the only traveller at the guesthouse tonight, which makes me the only Western traveller in Vangviang. I was the only Westerner on the bus, and to the best of my knowledge caught the only bus to Vangviang, but I never put it together that I would be here alone. I have never been alone anywhere in Asia. Quite the contrary. I have gone places expecting to be alone and instead found guesthouses full of other equally displaced, beer-in-hand Westerners, comparing travel experiences and must-see destinations, complaining that "this chocolate cake" in this "unspoiled" backwater village on the Chinese footsteps of the Tibetan plateau "doesn't taste like the chocolate cake back home." I just assumed another Westerner would be here.

There are six large rooms. Number three is reserved for the bus drivers but Chantravong offers that I can take number six across from it if I want. Both rooms are near the back door, where the toilet key hangs. Chantravong tells me this twice. Why the toilet needs to be locked I'm not quite sure, but once locked, being near the key is clearly the place to be. The wooden floors feel like my grandmother's cottage on Lake Erie.

A large shuttered window opens onto the limestone karsts across the river. The dominant geological feature of this area, karsts are formed by the dissolving action of CO_2 against the bedrock, in this case, limestone. It's called the "the carbon dioxide cascade". Rain picks up the CO_2 which dissolves in the droplets. This "acid rain" percolates through the soil and picks up more CO_2 to form a solution of carbonic acid. The limestone simply dissolves. If you've seen a Chinese scroll landscape, or *Goldfinger*, you've seen a karst.

The room sleeps however many travellers can be squeezed into four big, musty, four-poster beds. Mosquito netting hangs over each bed, tied into a bun above the covers. Tonight, the answer is one. 500 kip.

"Would you like to see caves?" he asks, and he unfolds a hand-written sales pitch.

> Would you like to see caves? Please enjoy our beautiful scenery from a caves nearby. There is also a cave with many Buddha statues, and a pond for swimming if the day is good. It is nearby for walking. Ask Mr. Chantravong. He will be your good guide. Cost is 1000 kips for each person.

Then, in pathetically-proud sincerity, he produces a hand-written testimonial. To my surprise and his credit, it is from my "tour" mates Andy and Laura, who, only days ago, enjoyed the trip "thoroughly". How had he sold the trip to them? Even in acknowledging Andy and Laura, the farce is more naïve caricature than sincere entrepreneurship. Nothing clouds caricature like knowing the perpetrator by name.

Testimonials are almost as big a scam in Asia as teaching English for free for your hotelier/monk/bar pick-up. Every rickshaw pedaler, tout, and handicraft peddler in Asia has a testimonial. First comes the patter: "Hello friend. I show you Agra marble factory/old Thai pottery/antique Chinese vase. I will be guiding you all day for only 49 rupees/baht/yuan. My great-great-great-great father/brother/dear uncle worked on the Taj Mahal/Sukhothai temples/Great Wall. Please I will show you a shop/market/village. You do not having to buy, but if you look only, I will get two rupees/baht/yuan." Still, perhaps Chantravong's sincerity is genuine: what is caricature after all, if not a good idea overdone? The problem is, sincerity is often the only thing that is genuine in the exchange, and at that the sincerity is in their desire for you to hire them as opposed, strictly speaking, to the testimonials. Then comes the finish: Autograph books full of European and North American names and addresses and recommendations that this "is the best tour ever" or that "I had my doubts, but Mr. Flim-Flam is as good as he promises" and that they "highly recommend him to all tourists". It is easy. You get a name. You get an address. You get a dictionary and phrase book and a pen. The rest really is easy. As my acting teacher always said, the key is honesty, and if you can fake that, you can fake anything.

In the small food stall on the corner where the bus left me off hang two signs. Photographs of military personnel or equipment are not allowed. I will be sent back to Vientiane if I'm caught taking any. And, the cook does a cave trip. In Vangviang it seems, there is not much to do.

Listen: I have a set of Austrian-made nail and cuticle clippers. They come in a small black leather case along with some other tools for cleaning and manicuring nails. It had been my Southern Baptist grandfather's set, from a trip to Europe he took late in his life. He died when I was thirteen. I hardly knew him. Somehow the set became mine. I don't remember when. I don't remember why. It was always just there, tucked away in the bookcase in my bedroom, beside my cub-scout manual, hockey annuals, deer antler handle folding knife (with spoon and fork), and red leatherette breast-pocket edition Gideon bible that would save me from an enemy bullet to the heart in the event of war.

I never used the tools. I took them out and looked at them sometimes, wondering what everything was for, but I never used them. To be honest, this describes my feelings towards the Gideon as well. My manicure was never that important to me. My religion either. Both seemed too constraining and not nearly fun enough for a child. I was used to the little pincher action clippers that my parents had. My grandfather's pliers-like clippers and their accompanying pointed and bevelled tools and buffing brush intimidated me. There were too many instruments I had no idea how to use. Their passing resemblance to dental equipment did not help. The Gideon remained a mystery.

By the time I was eighteen, I had sufficiently mastered the clippers to take them with me to a job I had lied my way into working in the Rocky Mountains near Revelstoke, BC. For a few months I had the best cuticle in my life (as well as the best cuticle in camp), but one day we moved our base camp and they were left forgotten in the cutlery drawer. I never got around to buying a replacement set. Instead I lived with either the cheap, inefficient pincher version that my parents had lived with, or with the much less acceptable, although equally as inefficient and substantially more participatory method of biting and pulling that left my cuticles ragged and bleeding, always accompanied after the fact with the vow that this time, I would buy replacement clippers for my grandfather's set.

In Japan, growing richer and richer with each paycheck, my old desires of acquisition and possession fuelled by the consuming affluence around me, I decided to buy some. I knew what I wanted: an exact copy of my grandfather's now long-lost clippers, based on the unquestionable exactness of the image seared into my brain. Of course, Japan being neither Canada nor Austria, I could never find quite the clippers I wanted. Oddly enough, they were all too Japanese.

Driven to purchaselessness by indecision and exacting demands, I ended up with a comically over-sized pair of pinchers bought in a twenty-four hour Lawson's convenience store on the way to a Time T.I. staff party. My Japanese boss, Suzuki-san, was in the same store, on the way to the same party. He was buying bananas. He always brought bananas. I never understood that. I suppose he never understood the clippers. They had a large, plastic penguin glued onto the thumb lever. The clippers, not the bananas. In the humidity of the summer that followed the clippers rusted tight. Party favourite that they were, the bananas never had a chance to rust.

Arriving back in Canada with what to me was outlandish wealth and a banana addiction, overwhelmed by choice and quantity, and believing I would within the year return to Japan, I bought the clippers, the deciding factor their price: they were on sale half-off. They were not the mirror image of those in my memory, but purchasing the matching cuticle trimmer as well, I took solace in at least having a matching set. My concession to adulthood.

Waiting for Chantravong to return after my lunch, I take out my Baptist grandfather's manicure set. On the bus for five hours, crowded and noisy, the windows steamed shut through excessive breathing, there hadn't been much to do but think and examine myself. My teeth need a good cleaning too, and in spite of my gorging in Vientiane and Nong Khai, I'm not too fat. I wonder if I really do think too much.

In the midst of this grooming, a girl wanders into my room out of room three across the darkened hall. She sits down on the bed, picks up the leather case and begins turning it over and around, taking each instrument out and examining it before returning it to its proper slot. I put down the nail clippers to pick up the cuticle trimmers and she picks them up, squeezing them together in the air, testing their manageability in her hand. I show her how they work. For technology to help, you need to understand it first.

Chantravong arrives. The girl hesitates a glance at me and, apologizing, offers me back the clippers. "No," I shake my head. "You take them now, and give them back to me later, okay?" Chantravong reminds me to lock the door, to be careful. Of whom? There are no others here but for the bus drivers. He must mean the toilet trespassers. I lock the door and follow after him.

To get to the caves, we walk back along the main road for about one kilometre and then zigzag our way through rice paddies before coming to the edge of the wide, shallow Sang River. Three small streams separate us from the base of the karst. It is dry season.

"They are not too deep," he says. "We can walk across." Chantravong neglected this detail in his sales pitch. I notice, however, that he is wearing short pants. The cook's tour had promised a boat ride, with a suggested tip of 500 kip. I wonder what's in the water? Leeches? Snakes? Snails? Meningococci bacteria? Chantravong forges headlong into the water while I am still removing my sneakers and pants. It is a bit late to think about disease. It is also a bit late to think about short pants. At least I'm wearing underwear. This morning's choice was an excellent one: clean, no holes, no bunnies. I don't see a boat around anyway. The water is freezing.

The climb up the karst is easy, if not altogether romantic. A gentle rain has begun, drops slapping on the leaves, wetting the rocks and my footing. The ascent looked much steeper standing in my jockeys in the middle of the river. The entrance, hidden in the dense undergrowth and forest that clings to the karst, is halfway up the side. Call me Indiana.

The cave is a cavern of stalagmites and stalactites that bores through the karst to a second entrance on the opposite side, a common geological characteristic of limestone karsts. The second entrance is much larger than the opening we entered through, with a small natural balcony, guarded by large boulders around the edge. Fifteen minutes away on foot, Vangviang is invisible.

To the depth that daylight seeps into the cave the walls are covered with graffiti. Some of the scribbling looks Chinese, but most seems either Laotian or Thai. The odd inscription looks to be French, but sounding it out using English phonetics makes no sense. Chantravong insists it is all Laotian. It could be. My phonics were never that strong.

The caves are popular in the summer time because they are cool he says. Also with the young people in Vangviang, the students. This is "make-out" cavern? In the distance, three echoing booms carry across the plain in front of us. I look at Chantravong. "Road construction," he volunteers. "There is no fighting here. Nothing for you to worry about."

Re-fording the river, I decide to not remove my shoes. In the deepest sections, the current is strong, and there are too many sharp objects on the stream bed for me to feel stable and confident in my bare feet. A hundred feet downstream on the opposite bank, three girls watch us, giggling. Then again, perhaps not us, but simply me, a skinny white tourist standing in his underwear and sneakers holding his pants over his head surrendering in the middle of a stream in the rain. I'd laugh. There is more dignity to pants than I have been aware.

We turn back towards Vangviang in the falling late afternoon, Chantravong bounding ahead through rice paddies and fields, me sloshing behind thinking none of it looks familiar. It is too late for wet-shoe regrets. From a grassy school playground comes a cascade of shrill sabadees. Fifteen children, the oldest perhaps seven, the youngest still a toddler riding its elder sister's jutting hip wave and shout and jump. This must be how Ronald McDonald feels. I return their invitation and approach. They shriek and run away laughing. The game is on. Photographic hide-and-seek, part two.

Was I their first Westerner? Probably not, but not as "probably not" as was my foolishness arriving in Nagoya in 1986. Waiting for my then new boss Gordon in the railway station of a city of five and a half million, I absolutely positively believed that I must be the first Westerner the Japanese walking by had ever seen. The fact that in the fifteen minutes I waited I saw no other white folks confirmed my posturing. My then new now ex-boss Gordon arrived. He was from England, dressed in black biker leathers, a Fu-Manchu/Village People-esque moustache, and too much stubble to have been only one day's growth. His then-girlfriend was olive-skinned Mera from Michigan. On our way out, we passed the McDonald's. The most popular baseball player in Japan was Randy Bass, a decidedly white slugger who owned the triple crown and had a candy bar named after him. Interestingly, there are the same number of *i*'s in naïve as there are in stupid.

Attracted by the disturbance, a father bounces across the field on his bicycle carrying his infant son in the front wicker basket, coming to a stop in front of me. Smiling, he holds up his son, although whether for me, himself or his son I am not sure of. Maybe none of us are, or at least, none of the adults. The boy knows. He is terrified, screaming and windmilling his fists in defence. Both the father and I are embarrassed. Scaring little children is not why either of us has come here. He smiles again, says something and peddles away.

The rest of the children stand still. Game called on account of tears.

I sit on the grass and take my shoes off. My feet are wet and cold, the grass warm and soft with a hint of the moisture that had fallen as we ascended the karst. I take out my camera and wave the children to come closer. They line up straight and true, all smiles and grins and taunts for each other. I take the picture, and the girl with the infant riding her hip chides the boy next to her with her elbow for his fear.

I wave good-bye, but with the word half out of my mouth I realize I don't know the Laotian word for good-bye. I feel awkward in the silence, and fight hard to not blurt out good-bye just to ease my tension. The children wave back and call out.

"Sabadee!"

Sigh. Thank-you. "Sabadee." Indeed. I wanted to say sabadee, but I thought about instead of doing: a critical mistake in language acquisition. Sabadee. I won't forget again.

At the guesthouse I set out my wet shoes to dry, put on a sweater, set out my candles and find my flashlight. I thought my return would also signal the return of my clippers. I expected them slid under my door or on the floor in front of the threshold. I check twice, but there is nothing. There are no sounds from the bus driver's room. Sleeping, I figure. I don't knock. Later.

In their reference for Chantravong, Andy and Laura wrote about a second restaurant in Vangviang. At first Chantravong is unable to even recall the reference, and when he does he is unable to explain the directions. Vangviang seems too a small town for its only guesthouse operator to not know about a restaurant that by definition has to be close. I suspect he owns the food stall as well. Business ethics, it seems are universal. I don't believe his stumbling ignorance, and all my doubts over Andy and Laura's letter rush back. Did they offer the testimonial, or did he ask for it? Maybe he wrote it himself? Maybe next time, an ancient relative will have written the graffiti. Maybe next time, Chantravong will have a shop with little bits of the karst for sale.

The food stall in front has an English menu. Already. That is to say, it has a Laotian menu in English as opposed to an English menu in Lao-lish. It is no help. The lady working behind the wok speaks no English, reads no English, cooks no English. In the end I point, she points, and vegetables and sticky rice is what I get.

In the evening, the stall fills with local men: sort of a combination Chinese tea house and Left Bank café. The purpose is simple and universal. The three C's of Asian male socializing: coffee, cigarettes and conversation. It is the camaraderie of the group, the familiarity of the ritual, the daily bonding. Camaraderie. I guess there are four.

It will not be long before this café is taken over by tourists. Vangviang is small, beautiful and close to Vientiane. Even more lethal, it will be described as *unspoiled*. There is good public transportation, and as word of Laos filters through the backpackers' hostels of Bangkok, as it becomes the new "hot" place to go, it will be discovered. Guidebooks will recommend it, Western travellers will Westernize it, our money will monopolize it. The next time I am here, these men will not be. They will not know what hit them. Chantravong will welcome the change. It will mean full rooms, full cave trips, full pockets. 500 kip a night will be as much a memory as this place. The men will find other places to go until we find them too.

The inn is lit with candles and a kerosene lamp. Chantravong and the lady who works with him sit in the front parlour looking out into the street. Chantravong is working on his English with an American-English book that has already been studied to dog-eared death, the same book that Monk Thong Liam Inthvong used. He has learned all about the Statue of Liberty and the Golden Gate Bridge and picnics in the park. There are even pictures. Useful conversations about laundry and shopping and television programs.

In spite of the book, he has learned well. He asks if it is any good. What can I say? It is out-dated unapologetic American propaganda, but a British book would consist of pub dialogues, references to the Queen and picnics on the Common, interspersed with out-dated unapologetic British propaganda. There are no Canadian books. Too cold for picnics I suppose, and we apologise at the drop of a hat; all the sentences would start with "Sorry." Regardless, the answer he wants is "yes". Reassurance. Confident. "Yes" is an easy nod. Smiles all around.

The bus for Kasi, he says, arrives about 11:30. It goes right past the guesthouse. I can catch it here or at the marketplace. It doesn't matter.

In the back of the house, on the steps leading to the locked toilets, a man and woman sit together. I ask Chantravong if that is my clipper girl. "Yes," he says. "She's the daughter of the people who operate the tea stall." I still have not received the clippers, but no problem. I'll see her in the morning. At 8:30, in flickering candlelight and pitch black, it is bedtime.

23
North

My thoughts have been consumed by Cassie, my Self choosing to pull pain and hurt out of longing and desire. I wallow alone. It is all illusion. For all my anguish, I am still alone, and I wonder for whom is this pain? Would there still be this response if in return for the letters I have mailed there were answers instead of silences? I create my reality, regardless of responses mailed or unmailed, regardless of desires spoken or left silent. It is the act of asking the questions that allows one to recognize the answers when they appear. This I understand. What I wonder is whether I really want the answers?

Outside it is cold and damp and grey. I know it even with the window closed. Grey is a feeling: light black is a colour.

The karsts outside my window stand languid in the mist. It feels like autumn. Neither Chantravong nor the woman is around. The bathing water in the washroom cistern is cold, the surface covered in mosquitoes, each plunge of the dipper stirring them into frenzy. After a night sitting out, my shoes are still wet.

At 10:00 Chantravong appears and I ask about the tea stall girl; later is now and I need my clippers to finish packing. She is at the tea stall he says, but she doesn't have my clippers. The clipper girl isn't the tea stall girl. The clipper girl is the sister of the bus driver, and it has gone. That much I already knew. The bus was parked under my window. I heard it and felt anxious at the sound. Instead of acting, I chose to gloat; it was 7:00 A.M. and I didn't have to get up. Funny what the subconscious knows.

Didn't I ask him about the girl last night? Didn't he tell me it was the tea stall girl? "Nothing like this has ever happened before," he says, but I don't care and in that not caring don't believe him. I try to think, but I am furious, and fury has no logic. Fury just is. That is the danger of fury. It thinks it has logic.

The bus makes the trip back here every two days Chantravong says, struggling against the current to find a positive spin. Today Vientiane, tomorrow back here. I need to leave Louangphrabang Sunday. I calculate the days. Monday might work. Chantravong says he could just ask the bus drivers to leave them with him the next time they are here. Then meeting them wouldn't matter. "Nothing," he says again, "like this has ever happened before."

Chantravong's woman helper arrives. There is excitement, there are shouts. There is Good News. The clipper-girl from room three has not left for Vientiane. She is in the marketplace. The assistant pedals off to bring her back. Chantravong is happy again, smiling, relieved. So am I.

There is Bad News.

The clipper girl gave the clippers to the driver. He was supposed to return them. Life. The Lord giveth and the Lord taketh. There is nothing I can do. There is no one left to vent at.

Chantravong assures me the Kasi bus will pass the guesthouse at 11:30. Exactly. He will watch with me. Over and over, "Nothing like this has ever happened before" and "This is the first time any trouble here" trembles through the guesthouse. He chastises me for not having taken enough care, reminding me of his warning to lock my doors, right. He told me, didn't he? "The driver is honest. He will bring them back," he says. The assistant and the clipper girl stand by. If honesty is so prevalent, what was the need to lock the doors? What was the need for the warnings? Why is there a lock on the toilet? "They are from bus number seven. Every time, they are the same bus. Bus number seven." Craps.

The four of us wait for the bus in the street. Each passer-by in turn hears the story. Now it is embarrassing and annoying.

At 11:30 the bus arrives. Chantravong is right. This is a good sign. I expected another Japan-Laos friendship bus, but instead, it is a bursting lot doi san, the roof piled full with belongings and riders. The conductor and two others hang out the back door, arms waving, pointing. There is space on the ladder at the back, and in my hesitation and confusion, he points up. On the roof, my pack still on my back, I teeter on other bundles and bales looking for a foothold among the warren of bags and splayed bodies, searching for a place to throw my bag and myself. The conductor slaps the cab. We lurch off. The choice is made for me. I will sit. Through the dust cloud, Chantravong, his helper and the clipper girl from room three wave me good-bye.

Ya all come back now, ya hear?

We drive straight one hundred meters, turn left another fifty, and in front of the market stop. Lunch time. One hour.

Only a foreigner would do this and I am tired of being the foreigner. I am tired of being an outsider. I already stand out here. I don't need to make myself any more conspicuous by looking the fool. Worse, Chantravong has proven himself right in a most ineffective, un-understanding way. "The bus comes at 11:30," was correct, but "and then stops at the market for an hour, " would have been a nice addendum. I could have walked. *The driver is honest. He will bring them back* is not nearly as confidence inspiring as I'm sure Chantravong meant it to be—and it was—five minutes ago.

24
North

A line of bicycles is parked along the front of the market next to some food stalls. Inside, the selection is clothing and household products. Hanging from a frayed blue nylon clothesline is a black cotton *sihns* with a repeating pattern of embroidered gold, red, purple, forest green and white triangles. Neither elegant nor over-wrought, it is just simple and honest. It is exactly the nature of Vangviang. I point to it, and the lady in the stall gives me the price. *Hâa phan* kip. *Hâa phan* kip. She repeats it twice.

I haven't a clue, and I count on my fingers to confirm it. Five something? I shake my head. Where are the calculators when we need them? She searches for paper and finds a torn scrap and a fat kindergarten pencil, and suddenly we have success: 5000 kip. No wonder. I don't know the word for thousand. This I tell myself out loud, covering my embarrassment with intellectualism. Covering up more, I bargain hard. Language non-proficiency does not equal stupid. I write down my counter. 3000

She points to the 5000.

I write 3200.

She shakes her head and picks up the sihns, placing it back on the frayed blue nylon clothesline.

Still, it is a game. That much I understand. I walk away, trying to lose myself in the sparse crowd of short brown Laotian women. Returning from my ploy, I lift down the sihns and write 3500. I've done this before, and I know what I'm doing now. She points to her 5000.

I write 4000. Then I write 4500. Then I write 5000.

She nods. *Hâa phan* kip. She folds the sihns into a white cellophane bag. 5000 kip. A good price. Worth a walk around the market. Worth the wait.

25
North

Pummelo trees line both sides of the road north out of the market, their branches twining together into a cool leafy cathedral canopy. The branches are heavy with the green thick-rinded fruit and hang low, whipping above our heads and slapping into our forearms as we try to deflect the branches away. New riders litter the roadside north of the market like evacuating refugees, their belongings wrapped in cloth sacks stacked beside them in the dirt. Our momentum out of the parking lot fades to a crawl. New bags come on and old bags come off, tossed into the dirt below while waving hands shout instructions back and forth from the conductor and passengers on the roadside to the roof riders rooting out the correct luggage. As the road opens up outside the village pushing the trees back, the pummeloes are less dangerously picked in a "stab and duck" attack. The previous attack method, "stab and get whacked," involved more actual foolishness than fruit. Besides fresh air, unobstructed views and the chance to jump off if the truck overturns, plundered fruit is the single biggest advantage to roof travel.

A tangential advantage, although no less important and certainly as appealing, is the chance for these young riders of the roof to throw these thick, heavy rinds at the teenage girls we pass. Each new target precipitates a locker-room laughter and jostling, each toss building more and more excitement, each near miss raising the stakes on the succeeding pitchers, each targette more helpless, the anticipated if unattainable "success". I try to suggest that using the girls as targets is wrong. Dressed in standard white cotton dresses, they already contend with the choking clouds of dust that swirl after us. My roof compatriots' interpretation is disapproval at their poor throwing rather than their intention. Steadfast in their confusion, they rectify the problem by simply trying harder. And yet, no one is ever hit, no throw ever successful. The game is not to hit. The game is to shine.

It is, I suppose, their way of cultivating a male bond while preening for the female of the species, a courtship ritual struck in the awkward years of pre-adulthood. I remember having to run faster, to skate better, to wear the "right" clothes and adopt the right hairstyle. Often even that wasn't enough. I remember as a grade five boy sprinting in exhibitionism the fifty steps it took to my neighbour's house because a classmate, a girl, and her father had happened along the street at that same instant. Coupling my embarrassed attraction with the fear of exposure, I ran past her in a blinding "hi" to escape what I knew would be *my* father's taunts and their red faced consequences in the front yard. When even younger, I recall showing affection with punches and pushing. Younger still, I kissed the girls behind the closed doors of the cloakroom.

It seems, in retrospect, a regressive progression towards adulthood. To have been so bold as a child, so confident of my emotions and so demonstrative in their admission at a time when my peer group sought refuge in the opposite. By adolescence it was my peers that turned outwards while I grew shy and unsure, embarrassed at exposing my emotions and desires. Where did the change come from?

What makes someone cool here? In Thailand, Vuarnet sunglasses is clearly the answer. In Japan, magazines are published monthly to leave no doubt. It can't possibly have anything to do with ice skating.

Through the afternoon we pass a number of villages, some no more than a scattering of elevated huts along the roadside, others large and sprawling. Some are just deserted, abandoned without even a hint of life or of the direction it escaped.

Ghost villages. Villages I always assume must be populated, ghosts that I always assume must be in the fields working, but that same wave of assumption makes me think there should be at least one grandparent too old to be in the field, one child too young. There never is, and I never spot the field.

Ghost Villages. The truck doesn't even slow down.

In the larger, living villages, villagers and children line the roadside awaiting our arrival, their expressions flush with expectation and wonder. In these quiet hills, they must have seen our dust cloud miles before our arrival. We are the Wells Fargo Wagon and this is Meredith Wilson's *Music Man*, larger than life and living in a northern Laos as innocent as any Mid-western—"next stop, River City, Ioway"—town. Like the more American version, we are an aberration of spontaneity; a planned, yet inherently unknown event. If we are the Wells Fargo Wagon, then that makes me Professor Harold Hill, and the question is, what can I sell you, friend? Like the arrival of the Wells Fargo Wagon, we are an aberration of spontaneity and excitement in an otherwise predictable existence, the embodiment of possibility.

> *hi ho the lot doi sa-an is a, coming down the road,*
> *please don't let it pass my hut*
> *hi ho the lot doi sa-an is a, coming up the hill,*
> *I bet that there's a Soviet on the truck*

As the song says, there could be something special in that wagon, just for me. Or you. That the Wells Fargo Wagon was usually for someone else didn't matter. It was knowing you were a part of something bigger at a time when what lay 100 miles away was as foreign as what lay 10,000. If the wagon was here for you, great. If it was for someone else, that was great too, because that quality of random selection that had chosen him or her guaranteed that the next time, or the next after that, it could be you.

> *I got some sticky rice from Kasi last December,*
> *and I've ordered some Thai underwear*

So the children, the travellers and the simply curious swarm onto the village banks rolling above the road to watch. Today their vigilance has been rewarded: there is a foreigner on board, a white—a Soviet. That I'm not a Soviet isn't the point. The carnival is not about truth, it is about fantasy. Every child that witnesses my coming vocalizes it; *sabadee Soviet*'s thrown at me in overlapping cascades that build upon frantic waves and more frantic screams. Who knows when they will see a Soviet again? Who knows what the last one produced? Running to the road today, they didn't know I was on board. I am a bonus. It is the truck that captures their imagination. Their Wells Fargo Wagon.

a book on fruit-rind throwing is on order,
the book store in Vi-en-ti-ane said they'd deliver here!

The dilemma is in the response. Today I am the clown in the travelling circus. Tomorrow a new circus will bring a new clown and I will be forgotten. Today I am the star and tomorrow is a long way off. There is nothing Zen about tomorrow.

Hi ho the lot doi sa-an is a, coming into town,
I haven't seen one passing through in days
hi ho the lot doi sa-an is a, coming into town,
I want, I wish a Soviet there to gaze

Being white in Asia guarantees the conspicuous attention and documentation that is the preserve of the celebrity. In China, in Thailand, in Japan; I am never one of them. I am never Asian. I am always looking in, always being looked at.

I got some laokao from my uncle down in Pakxé,
we drank it with the roast suckling pig

The elevation to celebrity without the justifying accomplishment, the ascendancy to stardom for my latest role. The role is now. The role is here. In just being, I fulfil it and in fulfilling make it valid. The proof is in the being: to pose for pictures, to give autographs, to entertain in sincerity conversations broken by lost verbs and interchangeable gender identifiers, sentences that amount to little more than homework and little less than the opportunity to grab the moment and claim a part of the serendipity for themselves.

My aunt in Lou-ang-phra-bang still expects me,
she's sprucing up her roof with metal from a Russian MiG

But the novelty of "star" wears thin and abrasive when the substance is genetic composition, and an awkward one at that. An accident of birth realized. Success and fame conferred in the consequence of the unavoidable; something that is entirely you, yet in its entirety is not you. The juxtaposition of emotions: the sex symbol and celebrity opposed to the face staring back in the mirror and wondering why. Substanceless substance. A birthright denied and undeniable.

In that last evening at the Ekalath with the Englishman, it was a struggle that after his two weeks in Laos had left him with many questions and few answers, that even those, at that late moment, felt uncertain and incomplete.

Hi ho the lot, doi sa-an is a, rumbling through the hills,
I think I spot a Soviet!
hi ho the lot doi sa-an is a, making noise and fumes
I wonder how many Soviets we'll get?

The reality is that I am among the first Western travellers here, that stepping outside of Vientiane, just stepping into Vientiane for that matter, is stepping into a world still preserved from the raging tourism that characterizes Thailand. It is a preservation compromised with each tourist, eaten away particle by particle, unnoticeable day to day, but over a month, a year, a decade, undeniable.

he could be waving!
or smiling
or he could be hiding,
or he could be,
taking photos,
just of me!

The Englishman's Wells Fargo Wagon ride had been with three other "Soviets". The distance had given him the chance to observe both the Laotians and his compatriot travellers. For his solo return to Vientiane, his conclusion was to be as much the observer and as little the participant as possible: to see Laos by exposing himself to its realities, not by imposing his upon it. For example, he would not ask the bus driver about time. Time of arrival was his corruption. He wasn't sure it was theirs. The reality was time did not matter to the Englishman either, since he had no control over it. In trying to, he would succumb to the very influence he strove to defeat. The truck would get to Vientiane when it got here.

Hi ho the lot doi sa-an is a coming

Hello is the other problem. *Hello* is English, and people here speak Laotian. *Sabadee* is Laotian. Too easily *hello* rolls off the tongue and into the vocabulary of others, supplanting the native language equivalent of greeting for foreigners. We are different. We are foreigners. Us and them. As if all our other differences are not enough, we must add greetings to the list.

Don't you dare be late . . .

Back in Vientiane on the other side of the coin, Paul told me how sick he had become of *sabadee*. A week earlier he too had taken a Wells Fargo Wagon to Louangphrabang. The children that today race to see me once raced for the Englishman and Paul.

You don't know when
it will come

Big finish:

baaaaaaaaaaaaaaaaaack

"It was okay at first," Paul said, "but it just comes and comes and comes at you until you just want to scream NO MORE

SABADEE!" They are two sides of the same problem. The obvious side, of course, is language. The other is recognition, the denying of one's ability to just be. It wasn't *Konnichi wa* that had driven me mad in Japan. It was the recognition. Paul's reaction wasn't about sabadee. It was about space. To be offered sabadee is to be welcomed. To be offered a hundred sabadees is to be abused, denied the chance to fade into the fabric and exist in the whole instead being a touristic curiosity. It is an impossible sentiment, an impossible demand.

How to respond? To wave back is to acknowledge their friendliness, but also their perspective of me as a curiosity. And of course I am a curiosity, but that same curiosity that sees children run out shouting "hello" and "sabadee" will eventually lead to an attachment to my language, my food, my culture and my possessions. Finally to my money, and when a dollar-based economic class system replaces the present agricultural and trading economy, the result is the subordination of the hill tribe and village Laotians to Westerners since we have all the money, and them that has, gets. Just ask a low income earner about taxation if you don't believe me. Traders in the cities will find their own way to survive. They always do. Besides, they have already chosen to play the economic game.

To respond is also to become the centre of attention on a roof where everyone is, or should be, equal. It is a distinction I do not want to cultivate. And once I acknowledge the inequality, once I agree that I'm different, that the attention I'm being thrown is justified, how do I convince the others on the roof that my status embarrasses me? I have been held up as special, and in responding give it validity.

Major stops produce a clamour of women selling arrowheads of barbecued chicken on bamboo sticks, watermelon, sticky rice and fresh fish. That is always the sign for me that our destination is near: fresh fish. No one buys a fresh fish with six hours left on a bus. For the roof of the bus at least, the watermelon is a no-brainer.

With each stop producing more roof riders and more luggage, as the afternoon progresses our centre of gravity shifts upwards. With the added weight, the bus can no longer negotiate even the smallest dry hill without long roaring run-ups, and too many hills are neither small nor dry. Of our tendency to upwards mobility, I am terrified we will topple over. The probability seems not *if*, but *when*, and so the question becomes which way to jump? Into the fall or away? Where is a flight attendant when you really need one? Of negotiating the hills, run ups, much like wearing the right clothes, sometimes isn't enough.

While we never do topple, twice the driver runs out of gears to shift down into halfway up a hill.

And so we all climb down to watch the truck jerk its way up the hill in bursts, each foot gained secured by the conductor running alongside shoving scavenged tree limbs and large rocks behind the rear tire. Our position secure, with the clutch disengaged, the driver revs the engine into a whine, pops the clutch, and lurches the truck forward another few feet, the new gain saved again by the conductor running along side the truck, the sequence repeating over and over until the bus crests at the top. What we would do if there were no tree limbs or large rocks I have no idea, but I suspect the answer has something to do with hitch-hikers, and at a glance I am meatier than the others.

Climbing back up after the second hill, a young man offers me a cigarette. Everyone on the roof smokes. It is obligatory. Cigarettes are offered and everyone accepts. It just is. I am allergic to tobacco. The allergy allows me to be moralistic and self-righteous, but a closer walk with reality is that I discovered my allergy by being a smoker, and after all these years, I still crave, not for the drug, but for the inclusiveness. Once in Europe, another traveller misheard my name and began calling me Michael. It didn't seem important enough to correct him for the one day we would be together, and when he offered me a cigarette, I decided that Mark might be allergic, but Michael wasn't. Michael was. Life. I want to share the moments on the roof, that moment at the base of the hill. As always, my refusal catches the instigator unaware. Like the village children's "sabadee Soviet" which defines me as different, so does this de facto rejection of the moment. I am out of the loop, neither being able to accept their generosity nor reciprocate it. Worse than being different, I have rejected their chance to be equal.

Another hand quickly accepts the refused cigarette, and the tobacco pusher, happy with his generosity, motions for my canteen. He takes a drink and then holds out his left hand, a filthy bandanna knotted loose around his fist like tape around a boxer's knuckles. He slides the bandanna back, exposing a large deep gash, white and puffy, angling across the fleshy inside part of his two middle fingers.

He motions for a bandage. I start to say no, but remember the unused gauze and bandages Cassie had me buy. "Kasi?" I point and ask. If he's going, I'll give him some there, rather than try to root around now in this bouncing and dust. A dubious nod and a vague hand signal is the reply. Again I motion. "Kasi? Are you going to Kasi?"

"Yes," he nods.

Long before Kasi however, the truck stops, he climbs down, and without looking back, walks away in the late afternoon sun down a long, dusty side road.

26

North

Independent travellers live Maslow's hierarchy each day. It is one of the reasons the travel experience of individuals differs from that of groups. Groups have decisions made for them, their itineraries established, waiting to be implemented instead of dynamic and discovered. The difference between "where will I stay?" and "what is my room number?" is the difference between experiencing and following.

At 3:30 we enter a village larger than anything since Vangviang. "Kasi?" I ask. The others nod. Not even four hours on the top and I am back at the bottom of the pyramid. I try to stand, swaying in the attempt to take in the village, to spot the guesthouse or even to just recognize a "most likely" route. It is futile. Our speed is too great, the road too pot-holed and my floor too mobile: what costs $10 at Disneyland I get for free, but the only free lunch in an amusement park is the one you get to enjoy twice. I hunch to support myself with one arm on the luggage and sacks, but in the movement the weight shifts and I have to juggle arm to arm just to remain upright. I give up and kneel, still propping myself up with my arms. The additional vantage is not a substantial improvement. The more I struggle against the jolts, the faster our illusion of speed becomes as though this close to the end, the anticipation is too much for even relativity to contain. Looking straight ahead doesn't give me the information I need, and scanning from side to side gives me too much. I can't process even the fraction I do see. On top of everything else, I have to contend with the frantic waves of "hello," "Soviet" and "sabadee" that bombard me. I wave back in spite of myself, just to calm the noise so I can think over it. I try to acknowledge the cries with waves synchronized to my side-to-side scanning but finally just give up and wave blindly. I'm not sure the difference is discernible.

In the midst of my dislocation and frustration at my inability to see anything, the truck lurches to a halt. Immediate confusion. Shouts from the street see bags rooted out and dropped into waiting hands and debates over which bag is which and whose bag is whose. The inside passengers spill into the street creating a din and dust that convinces me to search for my bearings from the roof. I still have not seen anything I think important to finding the guesthouse.

To the northwest, the cluster of houses falls away and the road opens up and then disappears around a curve. To the left there is a playing field. It looks as though we are at the northern edge of the village. My best alternative is to head back along the road and hope to spot either something or someone who will show me the way. Hoisting my pack up, I back down the ladder into the crowd below. The crowd pushes me behind the bus, squeezing me between the lot doi san and a cement utility pole. There is a large yellow sign: VANTHONG GUESTHOUSE. I missed it, peering out into the distance instead of seeing what was right before my eyes. The story of my life. From the dining room walks a man, white teeth gleaming, a baby against his shoulder. He extends his hand. Welcome to Kasi. The accent is American. He is Vanthong.

Tonight I am Vanthong's lone guest. Last night he had two. The night before, no one. Again I'm alone.

A large wooden room on the second floor above the kitchen, with a window opening up onto the street, and a mosquito net. 600 kip; 93¢. In the centre of the room under the netting is a single, unsheeted futon. On the wall is a poster of a Vietnamese bazooka schematic.

There is a notice in the kitchen. I must "not to take pictures of military personnel or military installations," and there is a 7:00 P.M. curfew. Violation of these rules will result in my being sent back to Vientiane. Apart from the curfew, it is the same sign as in Vangviang. By my reckoning it will be dark by 6:00. At 7:00 I want to be inside anyway, removed from the street and the dogs I assume will own it. What about trucks to Louangphrabang?

"Most days there are some," he says, "but you don't know until they get here what time they will get here, or even if they are coming. Usually they leave Vientiane and drive to Ban Houay Pamon at the north end of Nam Ngum Reservoir, stay there the night, and leave about 7:00 the next morning. They get here about 10:00 or 11:00 A.M., but today the trucks arrived late and did not leave until 2:30. Usually there is a truck every day, but not always. Two days ago there was no truck. But I'm sure a truck tomorrow. For you no problem." How long to Louangphrabang? It has only been eight hours total to Kasi and I am feeling pretty flushed over two cooperative travel days.

"Ten to twelve hours," he says. "It depends. On the driver, on the road, on the truck. On the weather too. If the truck is okay, maybe ten hours. Maybe less. Maybe more."

In the Mee-Krabe Guesthouse's three-ring binder of comments from previous travellers to Laos before the visa-guesthouse coup d'état, one traveller wrote "Laos is where you go to learn to be patient."

The town market is in front of the field to the north of Vanthong's, down towards the river. In the driveway, two teams of boys are playing hacky-sack volleyball. I watched a similar game in the afternoon sun in Ayutthaya with Cassie next to the remains of a crumbling unnamed stupa. In the heat I fell asleep, my head in her lap, and when I awoke, the boys were still playing, Cassie was still there, and for all the world I felt accepted and protected, a part of something larger than just me. A community. A family. I belonged. Like the old Thai men and women at Mae Nam village asleep on the open-air teakwood *salah* on the edge of the beach in the afternoon. I belonged: to the afternoon, to Thailand, to Cassie. I was not the outsider anymore.

A point is won and both teams turn to look. I expect a sabadee in acknowledgement, and in that expectation, I call out sabadee first, but it falls timid and apologetic. The return is laughter. The game resumes.

The market is boring. Worse, it feels contrived. Even worse, I am the only shopper. A huge concrete slab and naked steel girders, without individual stalls but instead tables laid end-to-end-to-end in escape-proof aisles the length of the slab. Once entered, there is no turning back: a gauntlet of goods. Large, heavy canvas sheets are draped along the south and west sides to deflect the afternoon sun away. In their warmth they smell like old tents, and the odour takes me back to a tent my then-best friend pitched in his backyard under the weeping willow in the summer of grade seven. The experience then was much more welcoming. The faces here say "work" and "boredom", and as the lone customer, I feel more intrusive than desired; an unwelcome guest that requires attention when the clear preference is lethargy.

The merchandise is little more than a boring array of inferior Chinese and Thai goods, an inventory belying their end-of-the-line location in the transportation link. I feel the subject of a disdain and disregard that I am convinced comes from my "Sovietness". Perhaps it is not personal, but only a job obligation that resents my intrusion. Then again, maybe not. When I initiate with a smile, when our eyes meet and I offer a sabadee in explanation, there is silence, a stare, a sabadee quickly offered and then pulled away. Maybe it is me, my own unease mirrored back, a residue of the intimidation I felt outside from the boys, and like the dog that smells fear, they have smelt discomfort and growled. Instead of fluidity, my movements become awkward, openness and friendliness lost in reaction and self-consciousness. Instead of seeing I feel the obligation to look and I don't know where. Cultivated paranoia? Perhaps, except alone here, without the sense of belonging . . . what did Martha and the Vandellas sing? Nowhere to run, nowhere to hide? Definitions notwithstanding, there is comfort in at least knowing my paranoia is not completely irrational. The furtive glances among the sellers and my defensive response confirm my "Sovietness". I feel defensive, and worse, aggressive in that threat.

I step into the sun and relief. Martha was wrong. There is a place to run. I feel alive. Run to the light, Grasshopper.

The Lik River skirts the back of the market, to the north the Chinese-jade-green limestone karsts that define the valley. Exposed rocks and boulders whiten the surface in shallow rapids and eddies. Late in the afternoon it is alive with women in sarongs bathing, naked boys, and a mother and daughter irrigating their fenced garden. To escape the sabadees and sabadee Soviets I expect, I walk up onto a footbridge above the garden. I need to be alone. I want to see Kasi without the burden of celebrity, to fade in anonymity into the background and observe. To be invisible and, being unseen, to see. I was the celebrity too long in Japan to covet it now.

I was never a person there but a thing. Always *eigo no sensei*, always English teacher. Always gaijin, always foreigner. Sometimes I was gaijin-san—They call Me Mister Foreigner!— but the categorization still stood. A place for everything and everything in its place. Only for moments when into the night I escaped inside darkened bars was I me instead of a thing, and in hindsight, I wonder how much "me" I was even then and how much just a more comfortable, more inebriated fake.

The naked boys spot me. "Sabadees" bombard me, except that in the illusion of distance, the words are screamed rather than shouted. I acknowledge the first few, but in the acknowledgment the demands become frenzied. I try to ignore the frenzy and gaze into the karsts, hoping the boys will grow tired without my participation, but the pleas continue. This is too friendly. Beleaguered, I squat behind the bridge railing, hiding.

Shortly I am joined by a boy, perhaps seven or ten. He motions his intentions and a question, but the answer is no: I will not be joining him. He strips down to his shorts and red plastic thongs, mounts the railing, looks to confirm my attention, gives a cry and jumps. A small splash, and while I am still looking for his head to reappear on the surface, he is back on shore, sliding up the muddy bank to the bridge. As he reaches the top of the bank, he hunches forward, folding his arms around his chest conserving body heat. The river is in the sun, but the bank below falls in a shade. Water shining on his skin, he skips onto the bridge. He looks towards me, and I smile and applaud with a small bow. Does Japan never go away? Again he mounts the railing. He looks at me. He looks away. At me. Away. At me. Away. At me. He jumps.

And in that second that he jumps, as his trajectory peaks and for that split second he hangs suspended in the air, he turns towards me and shouts.

"SABADEE. FUCK YOU!"

On the opposite side of the river two men working on a Jeep and their children playing under the tires offer sabadees and a sabadee Soviet, but my responses are half-hearted and distracted. I take a different path back to the guesthouse, away from the hacky-sack boys.

Sabadee. Fuck you.

For a short distance I follow a woman and child on a narrow trail through knee-deep grain. Twice she has turned around to notice me and twice she has quickened her pace. I wonder what image of Westerners she carries: I doubt it is the one of vulnerability and solitude I feel. I try to walk less assuredly, making caricatured gestures to tourism, sweeping my eyes all around looking, literally turning in my steps, taking out my camera for pictures. I wonder if these gestures mean anything to her? Has she ever seen a tourist? Is this what the "Soviets" do?

The path ends in a dirt road. She turns to the right, I to the left, towards the main street. We are both alone again. On the deserted main street, I feel more comfortable and less conspicuous. Surrounded by shops and huts, I feel hidden and protected, belonging here and so unseen even in the emptiness.

Vanthong keeps a guest book at the guesthouse. He asks me to sign it. I ask him about being the only guesthouse in Kasi. He tells me that there used to be two others, but that they stopped taking foreigners. "Too much trouble," he says. I don't know whether he means too much effort for too little return or that the travellers were the problem. I am the only traveller in town tonight. Poor economics for one guesthouse let alone three. He leaves the statement open, and I choose not to close it.

Listed in the ledger already are Swiss, Germans, Norwegians and a Singaporean Chinese. A French woman has succumbed to caricature and refused to fill in the age column. Australians, Canadians, Americans, English. *Sabadee, fuck you.* Where did he learn that? Does he know what it means? Who taught him? Who could have taught him? I don't speak Laotian, but I am certain it is not their "Geronimo!" From a traveller, seems the unfortunate explanation, but who comes to Kasi? Only travellers on their way overland to Louangphrabang. Only those willing to spend what now seems a minimum of three days on buses and trucks, running the risk of being shot at, and only those with time to explore, discontented with seeing only Vientiane or being packaged up with Lao Tourism. But who comes to Laos? Only those with a week to spend in Nong Khai and $180 to spend on a visa and a promise. The country has been reopened to the West since June. Seven months.

Sabadee. Fuck you. My inclination is to blame the English speakers, confident a Norwegian or German would find something in their own language, but that is a dead end. It is also folly. Everyone here speaks English. It is the Esperanto of Southeast Asian travel. We are all responsible. All of us.

We are the cutting edge of tourism in Laos, the cutting edge of tourism in Southeast Asia. If first impressions shape and define the future, then it is us who will in large part shape the expectations and illusions of the Laotians and create the climate for all travel here in the future. If we demand bacon and eggs or muesli often enough, they will appear. It is simple economics. If we demand of the marketplace authentic souvenirs and artefacts, they too will appear, replacing whatever low-profit-margin indigenous items sustain the market and the people now. Who cares if there is nowhere for Laotians to buy soap and underwear? So it is with our personal interactions. If we argue and demand, that is what will come to be expected, and in that expectation, given to us even before we can ask for it: catered tourism because history has told people like Vanthong or the shopkeepers that is what we want.

It is not that Laos has never seen a Westerner before. It is not by coincidence that breakfast is coffee and baguettes or that jewellery stalls sell Piastre de Commerce coins. The French were here from 1893 to 1953, the Soviets since the 1970s. The Americans from . . . well, the Americans were never officially here.

We aren't some travelling elite. It is as much a function of time and place as design that I am here. But finding myself here, I am obliged to act responsibly. I am part of the beginning, the cutting edge. To deny it is to deny reality. Even the shortest visit to Thailand proves that to be here now is special.

Listen: I met a lady in Toronto in the summer of 1990 who had been trekking the previous season in Northern Thailand. The company she had gone with claimed all the areas in the north around the small centre of Chiang Rai had been over-trekked, so they offered treks that went further north towards, and clandestinely into, Laos. In 1986, Chiang Rai had been where people had trekked because it was undeveloped.

This is her memory of that trek, that one encapsulating anecdote that in its telling set her aside as part of the group that travels and has travelled and not touristed. This is the anecdote that proves she has experienced life, that proves she has lived and adventured. This is the anecdote she tells with bursting enthusiasm and joy over dinners among friends and acquaintances and strangers. This is the anecdote: She had been surrounded in her clandestine Laotian village by those unaffected, untouristed hill tribe villagers she had trekked through the jungle to see, in the location she had selected specifically because of its promise of remoteness, because of its promise of unaffectedness and purity of experience. And in this clandestine village, surrounded by clandestine Laotians, there had been a campfire, and all campfires need songs to be sung. And so she had taught these non-English-speaking villagers *The Rodeo Song*. The joke, of course, is that they could only mimic the sounds. They couldn't understand the lyrics. It would be hilarious if it weren't so pathetic. There are

Canadians that don't know what 40 below feels like: what are the odds for a South East Asian hill triber, although I'll give you that allemande *is* French, and they *do* have trucks.

Laos has been reopened to Western travel since last summer. The first recording in Vanthong's guest book is July 18, 1989. Today is Tuesday, February 27, 1990. 209 days. I am number 147.

147.

Sabadee. Fuck you. Indeed. One, two, three, four . . . everybody dance.

27
North

Upstairs a narrow wooden sundeck looks out over the street from the second floor of Vanthong's. In the late afternoon, the heat has gone. There is an over-sized brown leatherette armchair covered in dust. The arms are worn colourless and brittle, the seams splitting with age. There is my diary, my Walkman and a Chinese Tsing Tao beer: one playing out confusion, the other Crosby, Stills, Nash and Young's *Teach Your Children*, the other facilitating both. Downstairs inside the guesthouse, there is a ledge that follows the length of the kitchen wall and into the dining room. The ledge is stacked in repeating pyramids of Vanthong's kitchen stores: Heineken, Pepsi and huge, swirling blue and orange Ovaltine tins. Most are empty. There is also a pyramid of Tsing Tao beer cans. Like a Strauss waltz, triangles of colour repeated over and over and over; green blue swirl, green blue swirl, green blue swirl.

The pyramids remind me of the now-yellowed Ektachromes my father took of his grocery store end-aisle display pyramids in the 1950s. Then he was a young salesman, full of energy and life and the belief that what he was doing mattered. Back then he cared. The Ektachromes haven't aged well. Neither, since his retirement, has his belief. Don't ask "why?" indeed.

February 27

What is this concept of waiting for someone, of being "faithful?" What am I being faithful to? To whom? Myself or Cassie.

Or Mark and Cassie? Does something called Mark and Cassie really exist, or does it just exist because I want it to? Is there a difference? And leaving it and "us" behind, I am left with only me, and I wonder. If there is only me, what is it that I am being faithful to?

And the answer seems simple. Me. I am being faithful to myself.

Choices. Decisions. It is easy here. It is difficult here. There is no one. Only me. Faithful to me? What does that mean? Which me? Faithful to the dream, the desire, the moment? My head pounds looking for an answer, but all I have is questions . . .

The thought is finished. I don't need my Walkman anymore and shut it off. Across the sheet metal roof through the leafless trees, stark against the twilight sky there is a silver moon; a luminescent sliver of silver, a gash of white on Prussian blue, a scalpel slash against a projectionist's screen, a bottom wedge exposed, suspended in the trees. A hint of more, but no more is coming.

I've seen this moon before. This moon through these trees. This exact moon, these exact trees. It sweeps over me like an orgasm, complete and directionless. I am supposed to be here. I am supposed to be alone. Solitude has not rejected my destiny. It has defined it. I've seen this time before.

There is not a sound anywhere. A stillness has settled over Kasi. A dark stillness, the light fading without electricity rushing to fill the loss. I'd forgotten it could be like this.

The sky is deep plum, its texture against my emotions like a rose petal. The moon is brilliant, burning insistent through the trees.

Another mouthful of beer. I could only have had this moment alone. In groups I miss the seed of the experience, and forced to share I leave unsatiated. I can't be me with others. Sometimes I can barely be me with myself. Moments like this one are the culmination of what I have striven for: the products of self-trust and belief and perseverance. They are my reward for refusing my fears and instead trusting my beliefs. It is the physical and the spiritual showing me that my goals are elusive but attainable, that I have a destiny that demands this moment, and having allowed the demand, there is a reward.

And so: I was sitting in the Everest Lodge in Namche Bazaar. Namche is the capital of the Khumbu district. Six days from Everest base camp. November 20. The dining room walls were large glass windows, open to the mountains and the evening.

"Warm rackshi," Chatraa offered. "Drink warm rackshi. Rackshi is good. Warm is better."

Chatraa was my porter, a small Nepalese man who, at 15,000 feet altitude carried my bag, Paul's bag, his own bag, smoked—"I never smoked until two years ago," he told me one day. "Some German clients kept offering cigarettes to me, so I tried one."— and who *still* had to wait in forward villages for us to catch up. At least, he said, it gave him time to smoke. "Drink warm rackshi." So I did. It too was a starry night through blackness, a just rising full moon catching the summit tips. From out of the darkness the sound came; a *dhungchen* horn blat, low and guttural, building, a solitary voice added to and developed with *kunlung* trumpet and *buk* cymbal until it grew and built into its full discordant harmony. A Tibetan monastery. Evening puja. Built on the cliff wall above us, above Namche, the letters *Om Mani Padme, Hum* splashed in yellow and red and green paint across the rock face beside. The air was chilling, fresh and clean. Invigorating. Alive. And I shared the moment with Chatraa. I owed the moment to Chatraa. He wasn't with me. He had gone to a cheaper Nepali hotel, already drinking warm rackshi with the porters of other trekkers as I watched the music unfold. It was he who had convinced me to stay in this Namche Lodge whose quiet and calm allowed the moment. If I had looked for the moment, I would never have found it. How do you orchestrate serendipity? I shared it with him because walking in the mountains watching the weather turn and the mountains sit unmoving, what you came to know was that you were tiny, that this nature I returned here to experience had no emotional ties to whether you lived or you died, and that what you had was yourself and each other to embrace and survive it all, and that what I had was me and him. I shared it with him because in that moment, I was open and unspoiled and pure, and in purity, how could I not love. And then it was over, finished, the *dhungchen* blats slowly unravelling into silence until there was just one, and then none. I felt touched by God, child-like. Free. Cleansed. Alive.

Another mouthful of now warmer beer. On the horizon in front of me, the sky is blood purple ending far behind me in black, and I am amazed at the gulf of colour between the two. Quiet. Calm. Cool. The fall into night has been so gradual it is hard to remember it wasn't always like this. I let Cassie go. I let the music go. It is so quiet. I can hear the moonlight moving through the tree limbs.

Out of the darkness comes Tony Orlando and Dawn's *Knock Three Times*. Downstairs in the dining room there is a portable Japanese cassette player running on a large nine-volt battery. Two gas lamps hang from the posts. From across the road, the muffled rumble of a generator. The tape is a collection of twenty mostly forgettable super hits by twenty mostly forgettable superstars of the 70s: *San Francisco, Beautiful Sunday, I'd Like to Teach the World to Sing, Love Potion #9, Stoney, Chirpy Chirp Cheep Cheep, Mother and Child Reunion* and *Stay Awhile* (What a zeit-geist. To think that once Paul Simon, Lobo, The Searchers and Middle of the Road were peers. And *Stay Awhile*? By the Bells? They're from Winnipeg. A Canadian prairie band in Laos? No wonder they're unfriendly.) There is only Vanthong's father cradling his grandson in a rocking chair, a teenage girl cradling my dinner in the kitchen and myself cradling my now empty beer. Who is listening? Vanthong's father taps his foot rocking his grandchild to *O-bla-di, O-bla-da* sleep (How did the Beatles get mixed up in this mess? When was Tony Orlando and Dawn ever their peer?), but he grows tired against the insistent pulling and lets it go into a mutual calmness. Where did Vanthong get this tape? For the second time today I am speechless.

I appreciate the gesture, but if my suspicion is correct, I'd rather have Laotian or even Thai music. Given the choice, I think I'd rather just have the quiet. If we can ask, "What do you want to hear?", is it such a leap to ask, "Do you want to hear anything?" Music was once a celebration of life. Now it is everywhere, a filler instead of a part. In this darkness Kasi is quiet, calm and peaceful. There is no need for music. There is no gaiety to be shared, no dance to be enjoyed. Vanthong's restaurant is a hollow cement cubicle, tonight with no other guests. The music rings false and contrived and I don't need my culture offered back to me. I carry it with me in everything I do. I have come here to escape my culture. That I don't escape it well is beside the point. I have searched out videos in Bangkok and Koh Samui. (I stood with forty other Western travellers on Koh Pee Pee watching *Dirty Dancing* the week Koh Pee Pee left the stone fishing ages and began its descent into the must-see ages. Two weeks earlier it was just "unspoiled". Life.) I have watched others fumble through cassette collections in Chinese guesthouses searching to create just the right mood because after all, what use is a Chinese guesthouse without the right mood? It is all delusion, a mindset that says we need this to exist, that without it the current experience, whatever it is, is somehow incomplete. The delusion of not being able to see the perfection here and now and instead trying to mould it into the perfection we perceive it can be. How bad does the experience have to be for Tony Orlando to be the answer?

One more time: the Khumbu, Nepal. November. A few hours before the rackshi. The air is crisp and fresh. The ridge trail cuts though Himalayan pine forests with sudden, tantalizing views to Everest and Lhotse through the branches. The scent of evergreen is strong. The sky is a perfect blue. Below the ridge, the milky turquoise water of the Imga Khola river breaks and splashes white and silver against the rocks. Gaining elevation, I pass another Western trekker. "Namaste," I call out in greeting. There is no response. "Namaste," I call out again, but still there is nothing. I keep walking. That night I see him in the Everest Lodge. I overhear him talking to his friends. He had listened to *Queen's Greatest Hits* all day long on his Walkman. It was all that had kept him going he says. All that had kept him going.

How bad does your day in the Himalayas have to be for *Fat Bottomed Girls* to be the answer?

Back to Koh Samui. In 1988 I met a Thai-Canadian woman who had been there in 1968. In 1968, she said, to exchange money she had to leave the island. The nearest bank was Surat Thani on the mainland. In the 1970s when an ex-pat Californian Vipassana friend from Japan visited Samui, there had been a single hotel in Nanton, the island's largest town, and but a few bungalow complexes scattered here and there around reached by dirt road. By 1988 the road was paved, there were four major banks in Nanton with mobile money exchange branches in Toyota mini-vans that worked the overflow bathing suit crowd on the main street and made resort calls to the beaches. VD clinics were commonplace rather than hushed, and an airport had been built. The plan was for direct flights from Hong Kong, until someone noticed that Samui didn't have enough ground water to support that many tourists. The airport sat unopened. At least that was the story. It is Thailand, after all. It's open now. They must have found more water. How much can one palm hold?

Koh Samui used to be famous for its coconuts.

Samui is a study in cultural displacement and economic imperialism; there is a Mai Tai bar, a Cuba Libre bar and a Bob Marley reggae bar. The only establishments with *Thai* in their name are followed by *Massage*. Do we sow the seeds or just reap them? Does it matter?

Nature Bungalows is on Mae Nam beach. The sand is gold, not white, and Mae Nam is a fishing village, not a discotheque. Few Western travellers choose it, because who wants beauty and peace when you can have reggae and syphilis. My first time there with American Dan, electricity came from a generator behind the kitchen and the stereo was silent when the generator was turned off. In July 1988, that meant from 11:00 P.M. to 4:00 P.M. By January 1990 it meant until the next banana shake was ordered. Daily came the litany of The Eagles and Bob Marley and Tracy Chapman and fruity milk, until I could no longer Take It Easy, Get Up Stand Up or Talk 'Bout a Revolution, even if I did it in a whisper.

In Nanton, I bought a tape of a Thai musician, Pornsak Songsaeng. Pornsak played a Duanne Eddy-esque twangy guitar with a Johnny Cash lone-man delivery. He was from the northeast of Thailand, near the Laotian border. In the 19th century, the Thai northeast was part of Laos. Today I understand that to appreciate the music is to appreciate the culture. It wasn't always like this. In 1984 I sat writing in a small restaurant in Egypt wishing upon hope the owner would play their even then dated Eagles tape, rather than the Arabic music they insisted on. The Eagles, you see, evoked memories of the Canadian Rockies. Six years down the road, it is the Arabic music I miss. The irony is all too palpable. The scene doesn't change: someone else just moves in to take the vacated place. Only the faces change.

Pak was the manager at Nature Bungalows. "Can you play it for me?" I asked him.

"Look how happy the music makes everyone in the kitchen," he smiled.

Pak was from the northeast of Thailand. So were the two kitchen help girls. Pornsak was "going home." Pak always smiled. So, usually, did they.

"Look," Pak said. And he was right. Their hips re-set, their movements changed. They flowed and were gentle and joyous. Compelling. "This song is about loneliness," he said. "About a man who had to leave his home in the north and go to Bangkok to find work. This one is about a man married to a bad woman. He has tried everything to please her and nothing has worked, so now he wonders if he should try Thai boxing with her."

For the bungalow staff days off are few and far between. Every day is a tourist's holiday, and what is a holiday without a kitchen. Maybe six months without a day off, and then where to go? A taxi to the next beach?

Before the end of even the first side another guest interrupted us to ask if he could change the tape.

Twice now in Laos I have been offered girls. A misogynist society? The world's oldest profession? Simple economics? I have the look? Only twice? Take your pick: there are no right answers. What happens to Laos in the debate?

Is she offered because others before me have asked, or because I am a single man coming from Thailand and "why else do men go to Thailand?" so they, rather than me, initiate the process and descent? (What does it say about Thailand that mere mention of its name creates such impressions? No one ever says, "You're coming from Thailand, you must be interested in Southeast Asian archaeology. You're coming from Thailand, you must be interested in Theravada Buddhist forest wats." Even Cassie had to be talked into it. The first time I came to Thailand, so did I. Maybe it doesn't say as much about Thailand as it does about the people thinking it?) Is the girl offered simply because she is offerable, and it's my naïveté and ego thinking it is about me? And what if I accept their offer? Their month's wages are my two beers back home. Literally. A per capita GDP of $190 US is only $15.80 a month, and $190 US is an average. The promise of wealth in a village economy turned on its head, how many in opposition to their moral and ethical beliefs would consider it? How many Americans would consider a similar offer? How many would if a small, used car otherwise cost fifty years' income and someone offered you a month's wages for one hour? How many would if they didn't have running water? And once one chooses that alternative, how much easier to justify the next? As Laos moves closer and closer towards a capitalist economy, as first Chinese and then Thai and then Korean and finally American and Japanese goods enter further and further into the country and more and more people want the luxuries those goods offer, money will take on a value in excess of its worth, just as it has in North America. And once the process of selling local girls to foreigners by the hour or week begins, where does the culture and the family unit go? The economic underpinnings of the village are corrupted, and in their corruption we assume both roles.

People want something for nothing: a deal. Cheap clothes, cheap jewellery, cheap sex. Soon fake shirts are everywhere and brothels of indentured, numbered females line streets long removed from the integrity of red lights into simply heifer beef under strobing black light and neon. If McDonald's can pre-cook and heat lamp food, why not a Thai club owner? Everyday, people are suckered into the something-for-nothing game in Bangkok.

"Rubies, smuggled out of Burma my friend." Offered from the

shadows of Bangkok parks, offered as you lay on a Samui beach, offered as you pray at a wat. Displayed in old Sucrets throat lozenge tins lined with foam rubber. "They are genuine, my friend. Real rubies. Real sapphires. From Burma."

They are cheap. Very cheap. $5 US. £5. It depends. "Where are you from?"

Rubies "smuggled" out of Burma because the government has taken all the people's wealth, and in desperate poverty the jewels' owners were forced to sell them to survive.

"It is a real ruby, my friend. Look. I can set it on fire. Nothing happens. Nothing can hurt it. It is genuine my friend."

Do rubies burn? I don't know anything. No one I ever talked to did. That it turns out rubies don't burn, that even good synthetic stones don't burn, is beside the point. Fire is dramatic. Jewellers never say "Look. A real diamond. It burns." Everyone knows diamonds cut glass. What do rubies do? No one knows and no one asks, because who wants to burst the bubble? $5 US for a Burmese ruby. A deal too good to be true. A ruby worth $2000 US for only $5 US. That is the point. We will make a fortune, forgetting that if the story is true, it is on someone else's plight. It is our good fortune, our savvy. We deserve it. We blur the ethics to live the dream. Treasure in the Orient. The romance of the adventurer instead of the commonality of tourist. Where is our respect for the culture we have come to see? Where is our respect for our own culture? For ourselves?

I watched an American couple in Bangkok make their way through the Silom Road night market. An orgy of consumerism preying upon the hapless and naïve first time visitors with designer shirts, designer belts, designer bags and designer watches. The illusion of quality and status without the cost: a Pandora's box of desire, opened and inexpensive and in front of your eyes. A designer experience. Just choose your label. That, of course, was the spoken, but unintegrated irony. All the experiences were the same. Only the choice of trademark personalized the event.

In short quick thrusts the crowd pushed through the market to a daisy-chain of shouted promises that each bargain was better than the last. If shopping is sex in the West, it is a *ménage à trois* doggie-style here. The cramped street market emptied into Pat Pong *Hello friend!* and the line between sex and shopping *Hello friend!* was lost in flashing disco lights and white-toothed promises of a "pussy show" *Hello friend!* and "banana in a cunt" and happy hour beer and designer women and *Hello friend!* designer experiences and "pussy and cunt one-on-one" *Hello friend!* and more stalls, more chances to *Hello friend!* buy and "boy on girl fuck-fuck show". More of everything, until you had to buy a watch, you had to buy a shirt, you had to buy a girl. It was watching everyone else do it with nowhere to avert your eyes, until even the most resolute of wills collapsed into the swirl to buy, buy, buy.

Swept along by the crowd, engulfed in the noise and smothered in the pollution, the couple passed a table of cassettes, and distracted by the sounds coming out of the cassette player, stopped. The song that was being played now. They liked it. They wanted to buy it. Where? they motioned. The salesgirl shook her head. "Only these," she pointed.

"No, you don't understand," the couple said. "We like the song you are playing now. The Thai music. It is Thai, isn't it?"

"No. Only one," she said. It was her own tape. "Only these. Twenty-five baht each. Five for a one hundred." Four bucks. She didn't like these tapes. "Only for tourists. Only for *farang*."

In Vanthong's the side ends with *Samba Pati* by Carlos Santana. The song finishes and the cassette deck snaps off. The girl has gone home, the grandfather and grandchild sleep in their chair. There is only me. The generator across the street has been turned off, the dim yellow lights gone. All is calm. The sounds of crickets and cicadas seep in from the night. I get another, now cooler beer, from the Chinese pyramid next to the empty Ovaltine tins, and turn the tape over.

28
North

Often I awake overwhelmed in the wash of a dream. Usually I can't recall the details, an intangible residue all that remains, teasing me with my own emotions while denying me their cause, dangling the subconscious dream as a taunt in front of my conscious self, as if I could unfold the dream and understand with just a clue. Somewhere inside I have already analyzed this dream, its details and their essence, the truth of its content. Sometimes I wake up singing. Sometimes the songs are obvious references to the previous day: songs from the radio, from a cassette, songs that popped into my head and stayed there. Often though, they seem to have come from out of nowhere, and their obscurity surprises me. Is it the lyric my subconscious wants me to recall, or the association? Feelings born out of the night, their rationale obscured, their truth a silent knowing of a reality that in logical terms I haven't yet even begun to codify. I know and I don't.

This morning, I awake and know, in that first instant of thought even before I am aware I am thinking, I know Cassie and I will fail.

Indecision characterizes everything else. Will there be a truck? When? What if it arrives late, as we did yesterday, and instead of leaving at ten or eleven o'clock, we leave at two or three? If the truck takes ten to twelve hours to Louangphrabang, that would mean getting there in the middle of the night. Do I really want to do that? There is transportation back to Vangviang, and from there to Vientiane every day. I could just relax, spend the day here, and return to Vangviang tomorrow. I could get my clippers back. Should I pack? Should I wash up and forget it?

The truth is simpler. I'm scared, suddenly, finally, aware that north of Kasi, there is no public transportation. The reality of danger in Laos is a constant, but heretofore it was a hazy, unreal constant. It was "there", but where exactly was "there"? And so the haze has cleared: "there" is "here", and I am alone and facing it without the support of either strength or reassurance. On the positive side, there is no one's perception of me to live up to, no intimidation to do anything but what feels right. Regardless I will only have myself to answer to and that is intimidation enough. I don't want another failure. I have too many of those already. They create a self-forged chain as long as that of any Dickensian Christmas visitor, and I drag it around as an obligation rather than discarding it as the indulgent trapping of an overworked mind. I have instead tried to shorten it link by link. When successful, in bursts I have stood tall and free, only to add new links in my new-found burdenless euphoria. The chain never disappears. It only stays shiny.

I still feel the uneasiness of yesterday, the sense of aloneness and exclusion. I want to go on in spite of my fears. If I succumb I will forever carry the result of this lost chance and the knowledge that the loss was solely of my choosing. That is a much larger fear than any unknown possibility. I walk and shuffle and kill time and wonder.

Next door, children in ever greater numbers crowd into the school. "Our teacher," says Vanthong, "is a very good man, but he doesn't look like a teacher. He looks like a bandit," and he laughs at his own joke. "The children are scared of him, and he pretends to be gruff. But he is very gentle. He intimidates them with his looks, and he gets them to work hard. He could never hurt anyone, but they don't know that. They work hard. It's good."

About 9:30 a solitary truck pulls up outside the guesthouse. Fifteen minutes later, a second arrives. The drivers sit around an outdoor table for a restaurant stall in the front of a wooden building next door to Vanthong's, a building that turns out to be a second

Kasi hotel. I hadn't even noticed. Vanthong said yesterday there used to be three. This is one. Maybe Vanthong lied. Maybe there's nothing "used to be" about it. The woman innkeeper speaks perfect English: better than Vanthong's, in fact, and his is excellent. I am stunned. I never considered that others in Kasi might know English, yet here is this woman. The irony of association and pre-conception. I never thought it odd that Vanthong was able to speak English or speak it as well as he did. Nor Chantravong in Vangviang for that matter. It is a miracle that here in Laos there should be someone with the ability in English that Vanthong has. A miracle or the CIA. I take so much for granted I don't realize how dependent on others I am.

She asks if I want a ride to Louangphrabang and begins a discussion on my behalf with the two drivers. I watch my future bounce back and forth across the table, the decision no longer in my hands. It is settled. I can go in the second truck that arrived. It will be the first truck to leave. Better to be in front she says. She invites me to sit and passes me a glass of cool tea from a plastic pitcher. There is no place to eat on the way she reminds me, and offers some rice and some sausages with the tea. I feel uneasy, embarrassed by her hospitality when I am Vanthong's customer. He is her competition. Good Western business logic tells me there is no profit to her kindness, and I am ashamed that after all this time I still think this way. I thank her for the tea and the suggestion. Generosity without expectation.

Vanthong's wife has prepared me a lunch: a plastic bag of sticky rice. Through a door in Vanthong's kitchen comes singing. Thirty soprano voices high and loud and pure. The tune is unfamiliar, but not the emotion. I listen and around the door frame, try to peer in without being seen. A Westerner sticking his head into a children's classroom would be disruptive to them and disrespectful to the teacher and I don't want to be either. I just want to listen.

I used to sing as a child. It was what I loved most. It was my life. Singing. Long before I took my struggling natural athleticism onto a sheet of ice and began the long effort to capable mediocrity, I loved music. I sat like the RCA dog in front of one of the built-in stereo speakers in my parents' teak cabinet hi-fi system listening to records over and over, marvelling at the elegance in the teak slat speaker-covers and the impressiveness of the technology. "Why aren't you outside?" was the question, but pointed questions to a four year old are never about answers but about altering behaviour, and so into the sub-zero Toronto weather I went, skating on my ankles without a puck to play with or the ability to be needed by those that did. That one day I had both, I suspect, is not the point. My grade two teacher at Sentinel Drive Elementary told me that if she had a class of boys who sang as beautifully as I did, she'd retire and take us on tour. I was so proud and yet so embarrassed that I never admitted my joy or my skill to anyone. I remember trying once to tell my parents. I even had a theory about why I was good. My complex theory was, in hindsight, that I practised. What I didn't see was that I practised with the natural ability I had been given in compensation for my poor skating technique. A Vienna Boys' throat in a north Toronto suburb. Life. The parental sharing came out guarded, an obscure promise to tell them something some other time, a time that never came for a thing that died. I sang everywhere, to everything; records, the radio, television commercials. My favourite game was singing every single one of my collection of 45s. I had about thirty: The Lettermen (*Turn Around, Look at Me*), Eydie Gorme (*Blame it on the Bosa Nova*), Richard Chamberlain (*Love Me Tender*). Eclectic for an adult. What it says about a six-year-old requires therapy, I fear. I would sing only half of the song before the record "skipped." I was the needle. I would sing over and over the same notes, sing over and over the same notes, sing over and over the same notes until I slapped myself out of it and moved on to the next song, which also skipped, also skipped, also skipped, and so the exercise went. I even sang at a friend's birthday party: a song from one of my dad's barbershop quartet records. I slid off the barstool and belted it out and sat back down again, just like Frank. One day something happened: I got embarrassed; someone didn't react the way I wanted them to; someone thought it was just a dumb kid. I don't know. I don't remember the details, just the effect. I stopped singing in front of people. Later I tried to overcome my fear and sing as I knew I could, but it rarely lasted for more than a song or two, and too often depended on my level of alcohol. The joy in singing comes from the joy in singing, not from overcoming inner unrest and self-consciousness.

And the children soared.

The Bandit stands in front of the class, leading the group in the song. Short, heavy set, a beard over an already dark complexion and scraggy hair, disjointed and sticking out from under his knotted skullcap. His shirt, stretched tight over his belly, is missing a button. Over top, he has a black leather vest. He radiates happiness, contented as he waves his arms to the rhythm. In grade four, my music teacher at Annieville Elementary, Miss Spencer, did the same: one-two-three, one-two-three. Over and over and over we listened to Haydn's *Surprise Symphony* and someone else's *Dance of the Skeletons* or some such thing, which had a "frightening" album cover of dancing white skeletons in a graveyard. It was supposed to scare us by demonstrating how music could create moods and images without written words. It terrified us. The only words more fear-invoking to a grade fourer than "pop quiz" are "classical music": on a pop quiz, you can always cheat, and there's always the hope that everyone fails and the teacher throws the grade away. Classical music just is. One-two-three, one-two-three, her arms cutting through the air in perfect, precise triangles, her arms flapping like turkey wattle back and forth, back and forth. That was 3/4 time. Cursive, loping squares were 4/4 time.

Why can't I find contentment teaching? Why is it that I can't let go of my aspirations? I am held captive by my own perceptions of success and destiny. Maybe I am fooling myself. Fooling myself about who I am and what I want to be and what I think is important. After all this time I am still chasing ghosts, running both away from and after myself. I wonder if I can ever stop. In a few short weeks I will be back in Canada facing all those questions about life and existence all over again. The voices are joyful. The bandit's face behind the beard a study in confidence and serenity. In the music, there is no fear. I have forgotten to be afraid. Lost in the moment, there is only that. It is time to go.

I am still unsure about the rides. Two trucks don't seem so much safer than one, and safety was the only criterion for accepting the rides. Yesterday, Vanthong said that a solitary truck was not safe. If there were only one truck, I shouldn't go. A convoy was better. A convoy was safe. I asked him about two, whether a pair constituted a convoy, but he never answered. Maybe he never heard me. Earlier this morning, he had told me he would check out the rides for me. If he didn't think they were okay he would tell me. The trucks are ready to go. I start to climb on the roof, but I am shouted back and pointed inside the cab, along with four others and the driver. In Vientiane, I was told it was better to ride on the roof, since guerrillas were less likely to attack if they thought a foreigner is on board. Here yesterday, Vanthong told me it was better to sit inside since guerrillas were more likely to attack if a foreigner was on board, and from a distance, it is hard to see inside a moving cab. I don't know which is true. It doesn't matter. The choice has been made for me. I am the stranger here. I climb up onto the foot landing and take one last look around for Vanthong. For the entire time that the trucks have been here, I haven't seen him.

29

North

The road climbs quickly into the mountains. We follow the profile of the mountain, gaining altitude tracing switchbacks until we reach a ridge-top and the road horseshoes below a clear-cut summit. We are fifteen minutes ahead of the second truck. From across the valley I watched it slowly trace our route. My impression inside our cab is power and control, but from this distance, truck number two looks only insignificant and vulnerable. For long moments it disappears behind tree cover, taking much longer to re-emerge into the open than I think it should. At first glance even the road is hard to find. Our partner in security is invisible long enough to be unnoticeable on the roadway to all but those conscious of its existence and looking. If the truck never reappeared, the moment would pass by unnoticed. With no radio contact, how would we know if it were attacked? How would we know if they were disabled? The only clue would be the plume of smoke rising in the rear view mirror. This is security? Being there to sift through the burned wreckage of a transport truck and claim the dead bodies?

Initially it unnerves me that the partner whose existence was the key factor in my decision to continue on should be so far behind. The realized attack, however, comes not from the guns of guerrillas but from the road in an unrelenting barrage of jolts and bumps that exchange the fear and anxiety of bullets for the more practical realities of seating and support. There is too much going on in the moment to be scared of the future.

Then without warning we stop. Improbably there is a line of stalled traffic. Two army transports have blocked the road, pulled across it in a diagonal criss-cross. Four other vehicles are backed up behind them, ahead of us.

The road runs through the middle of what was once a village. The scorched outlines of huts chequer the hillside, the landscape a patchwork of charred, smouldering earth. There must be fifty in all, the image anchored to the earth by a few wooden posts standing desolate like the phantom tree trunks that emerge grey and silhouetting out of a forest fire. Around these ghost huts are large square straw mats, each covered in deep piles of winnowed grain. Some mats are perfect but for discoloured edges, others lay charred and brittle, hints of smoke still steaming through the grain. Whatever happened happened without warning.

Spilling out across the road are the melted, heat-disfigured skeletons of dead vehicles. Transport trucks, I think, but it's hard to tell. All that's left is misshapen, unpainted metal. The road-kill sculptures lack the bulk of both the road construction equipment I saw on the road to Vangviang and the military vehicles ahead of us. Lot doi sans fit the size descriptions, but they don't travel this far north. Neither the Japan-Laos friendship buses nor the road construction equipment could make it up here; the roads are too steep and too narrow. There are no other automotive choices in Laos. It has to be a transport truck.

A group of soldiers using acetylene torches cut the frames apart. I feel self-conscious about my camera and what their reaction might be to my documenting something perhaps better left unreported. I try to look inconspicuous, an absurd gesture in the circumstance. How do I not be white?

I settle in for a long wait, growing less concerned about my status and more curious about where I am and what I am looking at. It reminds me of coming home from that summer job in the Rocky Mountains. Eighteen years old. My first work away from home. It was an eight hour drive from Revelstoke to Vancouver, and leaving after work on a Friday, we had pushed hard along the highway trying to shave as many minutes as possible off the eight hours. A Porsche 914, paintless in red undercoating, Targa roof off and in the trunk. And then, as now, the traffic stopped. There had been an accident; a semi-trailer and its load over a guard rail and down an embankment. It was a warm July night, and as people stood along the highway watching the highway patrol's response unfold, an inevitability settled over us that replaced our impatience with camaraderie. In an hour we were gone, and later in the evening, when we reached Vancouver, it didn't seem to matter so much that it was twelve and not eleven, but rather that we were home. The street-lamped roads on the city outskirts were near empty, the air warm, the Eagles Greatest Hits cassette looping back yet again to side one. Home.

I look for a place to pee. The choices are the exposed roadside embankment on the driver's side or the open expanse of the valley on mine. Not a tree or Porta-Potty in sight, and I wander away from the activity searching for discretion. It is a self-inflicted strain my kidneys do not deserve.

Without warning there is commotion among the drivers. The two army carriers pull diagonally across the narrow road to create a space and the other trucks ahead of us edge to the side. With the urgency of a favour not to be taken for granted, we slide past.

A half-kilometre out of the ex-village, we pass what from a distance looked like rice sacks lying bunched together and dirty along the roadside. They are not sacks, but flattened, dried animal hides. There are perhaps forty, lying in two neat rows on both shoulders of the road. They are a dusty black, the colour of worn pavement, hair still bristling. My first instinct says skins laid out to cure in the sun, but no one cures hides on a road. And they are intact: feet, heads, tails, noses. And they are flat, as if they had been cartoon-style steamrollered. Pigs I guess, but what do flat pigs look like? It makes no sense. Why have they been left untended? Why along the roadside? And the sheer number. To cure one or two, but forty? The information comes too quickly to be processed, too quickly to be explained. Before I can even run through all the questions, we are past them and again climbing.

Fifty meters further, we pass the carcass of a single dead animal, its body bloated and foul in the sun. The stench of the decaying flesh hangs in the air like mustard gas. It fills the cab before any of us can react, clinging to the hairs in my nostrils and the back of my neck, the stench trailing after us for hundreds of meters.

What have I just seen? I am overwhelmed by the stench, overwhelmed by the discordant information. I want to know, to ask what, why, when. To understand. Nothing comes. No one in the truck speaks English. No one will understand my question. The futility of desire in the reality of incomprehensibility. I have known it before and learned its lesson well enough to reject even the attempt. In the cab there is just silence. I sink into my own thoughts, the stench perspiring away in the heat and running down my arm. To the north, the mist hanging on the hills is lifting.

By one o'clock we descend into a small mountain outpost and stop for lunch. The settlement is tiny. There are four wooden and sheet metal huts and a single, curious concrete structure, ten feet high and square. There is no door, no ladder, and no obvious method of entrance from below. Given this morning, if I didn't know better I'd say it was either a defensive position or a bomb shelter, and I don't know better. Maybe that's the point. Maybe I'm not supposed to know. Maybe I'm not supposed to be here. Laos is still full of questions.

The air is cool, the sun lost in the overcast, the shadows that would have fallen across the valley from a blue sky giving it dimension and urgency replaced by a canopy of light that removes the distance and offers in return complacency. The wind over the ridge cuts cold.

Two boys carrying automatic weapons stand as sentries. One approaches me and offers in his outstretched hands four small, warm, new potatoes. I accept the vegetables and hesitate. His hands are dirty. I want to peel the potato, but I don't want to insult him. Will it look like I am fixing his gift? How do people eat potatoes here? He takes a potato back, peeling the thin skin off with his fingernails, exposing the soft creamy flesh inside before eating it. Does he wonder if this is my first potato?

I feel foolish having chosen to acknowledge his uncleanliness over his generosity, especially given my own state. My kneejerk reaction when caught thinking instead of experiencing. It has been me since my childhood. A spoon that in the tasting of the food touched the lips of the cook could not return to the soup if I knew about it. The soup now contaminated, I ate it only if forced, and then with resentful half-spoonfuls past curled lips, always leaving a little at the bottom of the bowl to be sure. I became pickier and pickier about my food until the list of what I could eat was simple and to the point. The "Peanut Butter and Jelly Sandwich Kid" my aunt called me. She couldn't now. Now, schools send children home if they bring Peanut Butter and Jam. Allergies. If only they'd sent the smokers home when I was in school.

At twenty-four, that same child travelling alone on a self-imposed, self-initiated coming of age, understanding that he could not finance the twin pillars of selectivity and exclusivity and still travel for the length of time he desired, learned in Europe and the Middle East to eat and drink what was available and be happy and contented with that.

It was the breaking of the cycle of desires and cravings, a breaking of the cycle of wants and accommodation. A world had always existed outside that child's window, a window he had been too cautious to open. He suspected, somewhere, this wasn't true just for food, either.

Yet it is all learned knowledge, all this that I recall. I am burdened with the requirement that I remember instead of live.

Once I asked Santikaro Bhikkhu at Suan Mokkh about eating meat and being a mendicant and ego. What did he do if while on a morning's begging round, someone gave him meat? Buddhist monks can't eat meat, but having been given the meat, to not eat it is a conscious choice, an act of ego. And he said, "I don't eat meat. Or fish. Or fruit or vegetables. I eat food."

The potatoes are good: their warmth a welcome sensation in this desolate and unpopulated landscape. A third sentry sits above the village on the crest of one of the hills that defines the saddle the road follows through the mountains, looking back in the direction we came from. There is only one road in or out of the village. The northern entrance is easy to guard, the road traversing ridges in clear sightlines for miles. Suddenly, there is a shout and a roar and both sentries turn to face the southern entrance as our convoy partner broaches the hill and begins its descent into the village. We are safe again. As if caught napping, our driver runs to fire up the engine, and jumping into a shaky second gear we pull out of the village in escape from safety.

By 6:30 P.M. when we make our next, and what proves to be last coffee stop, it is apparent that this truck is not one of Vanthong's ten-to-twelve-hours to Louangphrabang type but one of his "whether" trucks. Already we have been driving for eight and a half hours and when I ask how long until Louangphrabang, I am told another six. Maybe. The maybe implies more than road conditions. Earlier I asked how long, and the driver said thirteen hours, which pleased me until I saw how few digits he needed to reach twenty. Patience, patience, patience. After so many hours, the freshness of the air and the fading twilight mixed with the smells of the village feel welcoming and reassuring: familiar. I get a glass of warm drink and walk into the evening.

The village feels different. It is subtle. It is in fact many minutes before I see that it is different, that there is even something here to be noticed. For all outward appearances it is the normal Southeast Asian hill village experience. The place is full of commotion with pot-bellied pigs and chickens and dogs rooting for food and each other; and shoeless, sometimes pantless children rooting for the animals and shrieking in the chase; and the smells of open fire cooking and spices and the damp earth. Then it makes sense. It is the children's reaction to me that is different. More precisely, their non-reaction.

When we arrived at the village, a few of the children, catching sight of the truck, had run up to greet us. Spotting me the greetings turned to whispers and the smiles to stares and stolen glances and then, just as quickly, we were forgotten. Curiosity, then acceptance. Stop. No "Hellos". No "sabadees" or "sabadee Soviets". No shouts at all. No one asked me for candy. Or money. Or balloons, or photos, or cookies or chocolate or school pens.

Forgetting us, the children run off to finish their game: chase the dead rat. It seems a simple game, requiring simple equipment: a dead rat, a piece of rope, and a number of small children, one of which is able to run faster than the others. The rules of "chase the dead rat" are not complicated. One end of the rope is tied to the dead rat's tail. The fastest child, a girl in this case, takes the other end of the string and dragging the dead rat after her, runs off across the village. The others chase after the dead rat. Simple. It is not a game of speed. She does not race to outrun the others. Rather, she just runs fast enough to keep the dead rat dangling beyond the grasp of her pursuers. The dead rat is always about to be caught, but never is. Elusive. The joy is in the playing, not the winning. *Sabadee. Fuck you* indeed. How long before the game is chase the emasculated tourist?

Listen: Trekking guide books for Nepal printed in the early '80s suggest that village children do not usually beg, and those that do are so innocent a simple, unincriminating "no" will suffice. Above all, the books state, do not encourage begging by giving out balloons, candy, pens, money, however well intentioned.

People must read selectively.

"We just want to spoil the children." That's what I heard in the Langtang Valley, north of Kathmandu. "We just want to spoil the children. That's why we give them balloons. It doesn't hurt anyone." And so they gave away balloons as they walked through the villages. I wonder if they heard themselves accenting their subject pronouns? A trekking group from Belgium, Flemish pied pipers of benevolence. At lunch they would dangle the balloons in their fingers, enticing and taunting the children to approach, to ask for and humbly receive. If you snooze you loose and if you're shy, you cry. Other times they didn't even break stride, the withered pieces of uninflated latex pulled from their pants pockets in confused bundles and given away in swinging step-by-step synchronization. The balloons were the remnants of a brother-in-law's now-expired shopping-mall advertising campaign, balloons emblazoned with the mall's name, the in-joke of Himalayan-backdrop advertising and cost-free altruism lost on the children. Photos were taken of the happy, human placards holding the balloons—mall name forward—Tibet's southern peaks in the distance, the trekkers' ten seconds of benevolence warming their own hearts and producing smiling children and dumbfounded stares alike. Personally satisfied, off they walked: the tent pulled down and the miracles service finished. Praise the Lord. Hallelujah. Spare the rod and spoil the child. Unseen in their aftermath were the fights for possession and accumulation by the bigger children, the cries of anguish by those passed over in the latex-manna mania. The loaves had multiplied—Hallelujah brother!—but the basket was gone.

Namaste is the Nepalese greeting. You press your hands together as in prayer, raise them towards your face, and say namaste. It's used like sabadee: hello, good-bye. Namaste literally means "The God in me recognizes the God in you." Whether they really mean that or not (how often do we ask "How you doing?" when what we really mean is "Hello, nice to see you," which is nice, but doesn't require an answer), it's a nice idea. Namaste is how Nepalese in the Himalaya greet other Nepalese in the Himalaya, and with the influx of travellers, how everyone greets everyone. In a land where people and crops and animals come and go, sometimes in an instant, but the mountains never change and never forgive, where what you have is yourself, your neighbours and your Gods: Namaste.

In the world of Hurry Up Materialism, however, namaste is old fashioned. *Hello one school pen? Hello one rupee? Hello one biscoot?* Those are cutting edge greetings. Into what the knife cuts or where exactly it comes from I'm not sure, but I have a couple of guesses and both answers are the same. I know *who* the knife cuts into. I can't imagine Nepalese children acknowledging the Nepalese porters with *Hello one biscoot.*

Worse, if begging did not pay, petty thievery did. Cameras, Swiss army knives, pencils. The absolute value of the object did not seem to matter as much as the absolute acquisition. One child asked me for a school pencil. I had none. He saw my pair of chopsticks in my pack, knew I was lying and knew I was leaving. And then there was only one. I would like to have seen that moment at the pencil sharpener at school.

They have learned well. Pass the collection plate sister, and don't be shy. *Sabadee. Fuck-you* indeed. What a legacy. Our reaction to yet another unrealized Shangri-la. How long until these children leave behind their dead rat for outstretched hands clamouring after money, until they won't play chase-the-dead-rat in front of us until we pay money? How long until the parents encourage and expect begging, themselves joining in the game with dirty, snot-nosed babies clinging to pathetic breasts, their sympathy value realized and offered as a proof of poverty? How long until I am not welcome here? Already this remote coffee stall is stocked with Pepsi and Heineken tins. Already there are television antennae on the village roofs. Already there are white tourists in the village.

The twilight is all but gone now. The sky is cold and indigo, the warmth that moments earlier coloured the village gone. The amber light of cooking fires and oil lamps leaks from the huts. In the shift, the air turns sweeter and more pungent, the smell of burning wood, livestock and spices coagulating in the approaching dew and sticking like a perfume. The aroma of dinner. It feels homey, and I fall back to Vancouver and the comfort and security of Saturday night chilli con carne dinners on TV tables in front of Hockey Night in Canada on our first-on-the-block colour TV, the neighbourhood gone quiet in a cultural self-sequestering, the darkness of winter separating and insulating. I want to stay. When I remember to forget, I think I am still in Canada, still surrounded by the familiar. I want to stay, to throw down my guard and let this feeling embrace me, this security of belonging. I want to say that what comfort those associations offer in spirituality they lose in reality, but I know this is wrong. There are two realities here: a superficial one and a deeper, more significant one. The black pigs and the thatch roofs are the superficial. They are the window dressings, the house paint. The reality of "house" is its colour. The reality of "home" is what's inside. There are dinners cooking, families reacquainting, the safety and comfort of light, and from that light, warmth and protection. It is this reality that reminds me of home, that makes me feel safe and belonging.

I take another mouthful of my tepid drink and the moment is gone. Coffaltine is not familiar. This does not taste like Canada. I throw the rest away.

In the cool purple dusk we leave. We are now alone. We have

been alone, I suspect, since the last village. The second truck is nowhere on the horizon.

We had not been much of a convoy anyway. We were always in front, always out of sight. They were always behind, always pulling up. It was not so much that the other truck could stop an attack but rather, knowing that the other truck was following, it might offer a deterrence. Any attack would either have to be quick or it would have to deal with a second vehicle. It did, I suppose, place the burden of danger on the second truck. At best we offered a first line defence, and our best wasn't very good. A quick clean explosion in the rear without excess would be missed by us, its reverberations lost in the travelling earthquake that we were. There was no protection in our convoy. How would they even know we were two? Perhaps the safety was an illusion. Perhaps it always is.

During the day, the scenery had kept me sufficiently occupied to dispel the fear. Largely the view was disappointing. The road was barren, the clear-cut hillsides stubbled with tree stumps. Nothing inspiring. Nothing compelling. Nothing fear inducing. In between, the villages bustled with energy and commotion, each with at least one Laotian traveller waiting for the truck, bags set beside them, others waiting alongside to say good-bye. It was all too common to be fearful of.

The night is different. What is there to focus on when all around is black but for the tunnel of the headlights? Perspective removed, realities become suggestions, objects shapes, the routine suspect. There is no build-up to the event; objects appear instantly, out of context, racing towards you. The opportunity to contextualize is removed, replaced by strobes of information that startle and confuse. Compounding the uncertainty is my lack of place in time and space. Where are we? Is the dead rat village halfway to Louangphrabang? Three-quarters? Are we almost there? How much danger have we driven through? How much is left?

We fall later and later. Every article lying in the road becomes suspicious. The entire cab sits up alert, leaning forward to see what we pass by and over. Bundles of cut bamboo stalks, tied together and left along the roadside become traps, their design to slow us down, to stop us, to leave us vulnerable without our now most valuable asset, motion. The first time we pass one, so sure am I of guerrillas that I check the bushes for flashes in the darkness. By the fourth bundle the anxiety is gone, the tension developed and lost in the evaporation of unrealized aggression. There are no guerrillas. My reality shifts from fear and anxiety to mundaneness and complacency as the terror becomes first habitual and then repetitious. By the tenth bundle I feel more annoyed and aggravated at having to slow down than scared. Misshapen pyramids and cylinders dot the road, their reality unrecognizable in the jumping shadows of the headlights, threatening until so close that their reality, buffalo dung, becomes apparent. Scared shitless.

Lulled by the repetition of unfulfilled anxiety into a calmness, the cab relaxes. The vigil begun, it runs its course until the immediacy of the fear subsides and is forgotten.

And then there is a glare.

A brilliant, unmoving, white-hot glare in the middle of the road. Reflected light where there should be only mud and dirt and shit and bamboo. Luminescent, metallic glare. A cigarette package, standing on end, cellophane wrapper intact. Perfect. An oncoming train, a brilliance racing towards us, its gleam confirming all our earlier fears. Long before it is recognizable, it startles the cab into attentiveness, and recognized in its improbability, assumes a personality of terror that passes from a product of the mind to a product of the intelligence and in that intelligence, to the reality of our inability to act or determine. Proceed and watch and wait. To pray is to remove myself from the moment and I am too glued to it to leave even for God. More than bamboo bundles or silhouettes of buffalo dung, this does not belong. Its position is too precise to be mere chance, its presence too perfect to be haphazard.

And then nothing. This too is a false alarm, a betrayer and exposer of my fear, fear that only holds the power I choose to give it anyway. The fear is real, a reality that wanes and waxes through the constant, unrelenting harmlessness of the objects. The fear is false, an anxiety and tension created by possibilities that exist as much in my own mind as in reality. Death. Its distinct possibility terrifies me, the belief turned fact that it had happened in the past, on this road, to lone trucks in the night. The fear is real.

At ten o'clock, the darkness and its fear forgotten as the mundane reasserts itself, we make our last stop before Louangphrabang in a village that for the first time since Vientiane has enough intricacy to its streets that it demands real corners. A frontier town without the frontier. I expect to see horses tied to the rails.

It is TV night with what must be the entire male population crammed into and in front of a small wooden house, its doors flung wide open, flooding the street in flickering cool blue. Men wearing undershirts and sarongs and boys in soccer shorts bunch together swarming the set, crowding the doorway and spilling into the street. Across the street the women cluster in small groups talking, their daughters playing in the truck's headlights.

Outside the truck, away from the drying heat of the engine and the cool breeze of movement, the air is hot and humid. The drop in elevation has left the chill behind us, replacing it with cicadas and mugginess. There are no new passengers for Louangphrabang. I curl up against the passenger door. At last a headrest. I am the last passenger. After five minutes, we slip back into the night.

30

Louangphrabang

Wednesday, February 28

4 80 kilometres north of Vientiane, Louangphrabang sits in the middle of the Annam Highlands, a range of mountains that runs through Laos's northern provinces to the west coast of Vietnam. The jagged karsts that characterized Kasi have metamorphosed into softer, gentler karsts of vines and vegetation as though moving from the Rockies to the Appalachians. Cutting through the karsts is the Menam Khong, the Mekong River.

Louangphrabang is tiny, population-wise only one-fifth the size of Vientiane, and on Asian population maps, Vientiane is only mentioned out of cartographic obligation and courtesy as the political capital of Laos. Louangphrabang is not even Laos's second city. By population, Pakxé is number two. Louangphrabang is a village of 44,000 people in a geographical area that counts in the billions. China has bus depots larger than this.

What Louangphrabang is though, is the cultural capital of Laos, its Kyoto or Sukhothai or Pagan. Louangphrabang was Moung Swa, the capital of the Kingdom of Lan Xang, The Land of 1,000,000 Elephants, a consolidation of small independent states and principalities brought together under the rule of King Fa Ngum in 1353. Lan Xang was a contemporary of Thailand's Sukhothai, two hundred years after the height of Angkor in Cambodia. The Kingdom lasted 350 years.

I'm sprawled across the seat half asleep, half conscious, my back rigid against the passenger door for support in the bumps. 11:30 P.M. We're here. The Phousie Hotel. The unfortunate Laotian pronunciation of Phousie is in English "pussy". I lived near a "pussy" hotel in Nagoya. In Japan they're called Love Hotels. It was 3,500 yen to rest, 5,800 to stay and sometimes, the "pussy" standing outside had a man's voice. There was a human-sized plaster Statue of Liberty over the lobby door. *Give us your tired, your poor, your horny?* "Rest" meant just two hours, but after 11:00 P.M., all night and "rest" were synonymous. Calling what transpired at a Love Hotel as "rest" was certainly playing free and easy with the language, but then "free and easy" was what Love Hotels were all about. Most folks brought their own girl, but it was by no means mandatory. Either the bringing part or the girl part. Companionship could be provided by the management, or not, as one's predilections went.

Stumbling sleep-drunk out of the cab, I throw my bag over my shoulder and try to catch up with the driver, already walking up the gravel drive. The dehydration from the heat of the cab has left me delirious and incoherent: my mouth isn't clammy as much as my thinking. The humidity is suffocating, but the sky is clear and the road dry. The night hums, crescendos of sound and then silence. Waves repeating across the courtyard. Crescendos and silence. Questions asked and answered and asked again. There is no traffic. No noise. We are the night's only movement.

Two men sit in rattan chairs on a cement patio in front of the lobby. The hotel seems deserted, the courtyard empty, illuminated by strings of yellow lights like a cheap roadside motel. Sabadees exchanged and the driver paid, the unexpected news comes: this deserted hotel is full. A convention of provincial ministers or something.

I have no map, speak no Laotian and hold no expectation of Louangphrabang apart from the Phousie, a hotel name I have carried around with me as some sort of Holy Grail of accommodation since Vientiane. How could I head off now, on foot, into a city I didn't know to look for another hotel I wasn't sure even existed? How could I get all the way into the parking lot and then be rejected?

There must be room for me here. Somewhere, somehow. There has to be room. A plastic pitcher of tepid tea and two glasses are produced. I slump into one of the chairs with a glass and try to wake up, to re-hydrate myself into a state of logical reasonableness.

Remembering the advice of my long since discarded *Lonely Planet China Guide* but not its absolute failure, I take an assertive tack, refusing their statement, insisting there must be something. My nemesis shakes his head. His name is Sisiry. Pom Sisiry. He is the manager. There are no rooms. Perhaps another hotel will have space? He will go look for me, if that is okay, but the question is more statement than inquiry. Without waiting for my answer, he rolls out his motor scooter.

And there is Good News. There is another hotel. The Nang Noi. They have a room. $5 US per night. Is that all right? It is the same price as the Phousie. Compared to 500 kip it seems outrageous but this is a city and I am too tired to argue. What else can I do? I thank Pom. The truck driver will take me. Pom will show us the way. It is close, he says. Just down the road.

At the Nang Noi, three men sit drinking over a blasting cassette stereo.

I accept a Sprite in welcome, but it is warm, the taste dissatisfying and unquenching, the carbonation burning in my throat instead of cooling. It is like searching for refreshment in Eno.

The concrete cinderblock room is a stale pillbox with three single beds. It smells of must and mildew, like the stacks in a cheap second-hand paperback bookstore. The bed covers lie like a dead weight against my body, smothering rather than comforting, a settled dampness in the cotton, the quilt heavy like a dentist's x-ray bib. Through the concrete, I can hear the music, echoing and hollow. I fall, deeply, asleep.

31
Louangphrabang

I fell asleep last night believing the Nang Noi was far removed from the centre of Louangphrabang, that we had travelled a great distance to get here. I fell asleep believing we were far into the outskirts of the city, perhaps even touching farmland; a sub-urban agricultural place, which given the nature of Laos, meant dirt roads and trees and no traffic. I awake having it confirmed by the scent of fresh laundry drying on a clothesline in a garden, the scent of soapy water evaporating from the concrete washer-room floor and the sounds of aluminum basins being filled. Cities don't smell like fresh laundry. Cities smell like washing machines. There is nothing about clothesline and city centre that rings even remotely true. The smells of the countryside are as much the smells of domesticated human life that the city extinguishes as they are smells of livestock and manure.

The only sounds at the breakfast table came from me and the kitchen. The coffee, baguette and the quiet coolness of the dining room offer no image that suggests anything other than rural well being. The girl serving me is even wearing a frock. That the Nang Noi is on a busy paved street next to a small engine and motorcycle repair shop disorients me. First the Phousie, now this. Will nothing be what I expect in Louangphrabang? How much more mistaken can I be? I turn back to look at the girl clearing my breakfast dishes. Left she points. That's what my instinct told me, but instinct told me that through this door should be a dirt road, a field of grain and a water buffalo. Disorientation is lonely and vulnerable.

The paved road is broken and potholed, the shoulders scattered with broken concrete chunks, motor scooter and bicycle frames and oil stains. Standing alone, it's not so much that left is obvious, but that right is obviously not.

Out of this disorientation appear Andy and Laura. They are walking to the airport. They had stopped a taxi, but Andy thought the price too high and had refused to budge from his lower offer, even in the face of a conciliatory counter. For the principle of a few disputed kip they would carry their own bags, on their backs, the few miles to the airport thank you very much. This is the real world. Get used to it. If you don't believe in God, do you at least believe in karma?

They have been in Louangphrabang four days, and had a great deal of difficulty getting here. There had been no truck through Kasi for two days, and when one finally had arrived, it had taken them only as far as the Dead Rat Village, where they had been stranded two more days.

"You know that village that looked as though it had been burned down, the first big village you reach after you've climbed out of Kasi? Well at the village we stayed in, your 'Dead Rat Village,' we met a man who was in that burned down village when it was attacked. It was attacked eleven days ago."

"He escaped with the children," Laura says. "Twenty people were killed."

"Every time he'd talk about it, or look at the children, his eyes would well up in tears. He'd look at the children and just cry and cry and cry. Did you notice there were a lot of children in the village?"

No. Yes. Not the number at least. Eleven days. That made it the 18th, the day after we arrived in Laos. Legend becomes fact or at least, fact-like.

I want to doubt, to question the date. There are too many language difficulties, too much leeway in numbers and dates. Like attaching blame to vulgarities, the search for precision is folly. Eleven days or three weeks or even January 1st. It doesn't matter. There was an attack, and the quality of rumour and its propensity to danger was observed. We missed it through randomness and luck. No more. Yet we missed it, and unscathed we stand there and talk about it. Another piece of Laotian reality offered up undocumented and untraceable, the store of information built on and validated, the essence more important than the fact. The story is real. The story is hearsay.

In Vientiane, a traveller David had befriended told us over a coffee that in Louangphrabang there was a temple famous for its bimai masks (*bi* as in Opee's Aunt, *mai* as in "When I go to Hawaii I'm drinking a Mai Tai!" and *bimai* as in the Andy Kim 70s classic cover of The Ronettes' classic *Be My Baby*), masks of the New Year's celebrations. The name of the wat was lost on David's now-name-forgotten source, but what was remembered was this: it is "up stairs" and "in the centre of the city". These bimai masks, allegedly, could not be taken out except during the New Year celebrations, but like all good religious observances, there was a loophole. The door of the cabinet could be opened, and the masks viewed without having to be physically "removed". It was, allegedly, an accepted loophole and well worth the effort. Religious loopholes always are. You take guilt-free pleasure wherever you find it. In a temple "up stairs" and "in the centre of town". At least that's what I remember. David's not here to ask. I miss him. Let me guess. The monks "wear orange robes" too.

Tat Phousie fits all the requirements of a bimai reliquary: high on a karst at the end of a long, steep staircase, dominating Louangphrabang's skyline overlooking the Mekong, visible from anywhere in the city. If "up stairs" was the central requirement, this was the place. Climbing the staircase however, proves that ingredients do not a dessert make. What loomed so white and large from the distortion of the street below is impressively small and dirty at the top. The door into the Tat is sealed shut, and the remaining summit is small and cramped and rocky. The Tat is a Tat, and no more than that; there are *no* bimai masks in the Tat. Next to the bimailess Tat, invisible from the street below but surely common knowledge, a lone uninterested, acned teenage soldier mans an equally uninterested rusting gun emplacement covered in camouflage netting. A badly grammared sign says no photography is allowed from the summit's eastern edge, the same direction as the gun's emplacement. In the 1975 civil war that brought the Pathet Lao to power, Louangphrabang was the eastern front for the National Government. East is the direction of the airport.

At the bottom of the Tat Phousie karst is a large, sprawling, sunken wat complex, Wat Mai Shuvan na Phuma Ram. It fits none of the requirements of a bimai reliquary. Still, there are stairs. Maybe "up stairs" meant when you left the temple? Remember, life is nothing if not perspective. The obvious was a failure. How much more can the obviously not be?

Wat Mai Shuvan na Phuma Ram is sunken under the weight of its own elaboration. An enormous gold-leaf façade depicting stories of The Ramakian rises and falls in relief along the viharn's portico, the gold both absorbing and emanating the light, alive and vibrating. Can plaster and metal be sentient?

From this beauty steps a novice monk, standing before the wall, his hands at his side, one dangling in the varadamudrā gesture of charity, the other clutching his Lao-English dictionary in the gesture of friendship. His body curves and bends like water around rock, his chin chiselled, his scalp a halo of black stubble, each muscle and bone radiating eloquence and creation. Uncovered by his orange uttarāsanga, the lines of his shoulder and back conjoin and disappear in curves and shadows at his neck and underarm, his exposed nipple surrounded by flesh, his feet fashioned as if pulled Michelangelo-esque from Italian marble, like a bodhi tree extruded from the earth, immovable and heroic and pure. His voice is soft and gentle, the disassociated words and phrases he has lifted from his dictionary's pages dangling lifeless and misunderstood. Understanding, like beauty, however, is not about words. Language is the concern of words. This conversation is not about the grammar of linguistics, but the grammar of substance and honesty, of intimacy and innateness. I say bimai and he smiles and responds lost to the words, lost to their meanings. The moment is here, the moment is now. For minutes we stand just looking at each other, seeing, being. What we both wanted we found. Even without articulation. There is nowhere to go, nothing to do, no one to be.

He opens the padlocked door into the sanctuary. In the darkness of the viharn, a towering golden Buddha image, hands nesting palm in palm in the dhyānamudrā position, one breast exposed, uncovered by the shimmering drape of an orange silk uttarāsanga, sits meditating into the emptiness. Huge crescent eyebrows catch the light, turning the Buddha's eyes forlorn and plaintive, searching instead of finding. They are the same eyes as young monk's. Tens of smaller gold and bronze Buddha images surround it on the altar. Two rows of tall, thick cedar-like columns rise up through the darkness, red and gold lotus stalks moving from light into dark in the zebra beams of sun and dust and God that cut the darkness and splash onto the floor. A bell. Lunch time. And still, in the darkness, the Buddha sits.

At the base of Tat Phousie is the Phousie Hotel. That makes sense—churches in Canada are invariably on Church Street, near the 24 Hr Church Convenience store, and across from Church Drycleaners—but recollection tells me the Phousie should be in the middle of the city, that it has no business being here. Logically then, that should have made the Denny's across from Tokugenji Denny's-ji, or ji-Denny's. Then again, it is Western logic, and while Denny's is certainly Western, Tokugenji is certainly Eastern. It is all too strange to contemplate. Recollection is not serving me well. In the courtyard at the drink bar is the manager from last night. He reintroduces himself, Pom Sisiry, and repeats his apologies for having no rooms. Today he does, if I would like to stay. He will take me to the Nang Noi on his scooter to pick up my bags. It is tempting.

Pom is a hotbed of information; there is a large encampment of Vietnamese soldiers just outside the city; there is a Soviet-operated munitions factory at the airport; the Chinese-Laotian border at Muan Sing is open. I am taken aback at his openness given Laos's geography, political inclination and the associative repressiveness I felt in China. Given Laos's alignment with the Soviet Union, that things are changing here is reasonable, but China's proximity, size and the military autocratism that prevailed in even the assignment of Beijing youth hostel beds leaves me decidedly unsure of what to say and believe. I'd feel a lot easier about it all if Laos were next to Romania. Free flowing conversation is not my impression of communist Southeast Asia.

Some of Pom's rumours ring truer than others. The munitions factory explains at least the sign, if not the grammar. The Vietnamese backed the Pathet Lao—which means Land of Laos—when they overthrew the Royal family in 1975. 1984 reports suggested 50,000 Vietnamese troops still in Laos. That there should be a group nearby is believable. That the border with China is open is a tempting revelation in the afterglow of Tiananmen Square. Pom says without a visa, there is no hope and I have neither a visa nor the time to search for one and be disappointed. Still it is seductive, stumbling through one door on one journey only to find other doors of other journeys opened. The "falling domino" theory of determination? That is, after all, how I met Cassie. Maybe Eisenhower was right?

Mr. Phommanila owns the Nang Noi. Pom, in the guise of "we," explains the situation, and Mr. Phommanila seems to understand. Mr. Phommanila insists we join him for lunch, and in spite of our protestations opens a bottle of banana sherry. It has been a long time. Once, in a misunderstood emulation masquerading as friendship, sherry was a nightly, and briefly morningly, part of my life. I even purchased a cut-crystal decanter and glasses. After a short, exhaustive indulgence, both adventures ended. The memories are instant and disquieting. It was not with this particular past that I had expected to commune in Laos. The dichotomy is uncomfortable but not surprising. After all this time I still expect, instead of marvel and accept.

As we move past the introductions the conversation grows disjointed in the manner of a non-native speaker armed with children's English and adult ideas. What he wants to say, most of the time, Pom translates for him. He feels affection for the West, in spite of his government. "The 'Sisterhood' with Vietnam and Kampuchea," he says, "is nothing. It is the idea of the government, but it is not the truth. Laotians do not like Vietnam or Kampuchea. We like Laos. There is no 'Sisterhood'. America," he continues, "is not our enemy. Our government tells us that it is, that the three of us must together fight America. I do not agree. I like America."

It is difficult to find people staunchly pro-American in Southeast Asia. There always seems a hesitation, some disclaimer to discrimination. *I like the people. It's the government I don't like. Some Americans I have met are nice, but some are just too American*, and everyone nods in agreement, the characteristics of "too American" left unspoken, everyone knowing in his or her own mind what exactly that means. The tyranny of unspoken consensus. Canadians are accepted unquestioningly and unconditionally, generosities extended as though in an effort to make up for the distrust of Americans. The delineation, at best, is not national but individual.

And so: Koh Samui. Mae Nam beach. Nature Bungalows. Act IV. On a day defined by a piercing blue sky, metallic pastel palms and magic mushrooms, American Dan and I are approached by an Indian fortune teller. Three Indian mystics in long slacks and turbans work the beaches looking for near-naked fortunes in straw hats. "Where are you from?" is the question, as it was in Bangkok, still missing the self-irony of a mystic having to inquire. Identities established, ignoring American Dan for Canadian Mark is the answer. As soon as the words are out of Dan's mouth, the mystic turns his attention to me. Dan, for all the insightful one's interest, could have been a bar-b-qued chicken. Two hours later, a second spiritually advanced one appears looking for business. You'd think a mystic with a turban would know we weren't good for business, or at least that Mae Nam was not a good business beach. You'd think they'd at least have a secretary: there are plenty of beaches to go around without doubling up. "Where are you from?" is the same uninspired question. It's as though they went to the same mystic school, and India is so large country and so diversely spiritual, what are the chances of that? "America," I say, cutting American Dan off.

"My friend here is from Canada." And so ignoring American Mark is the new uninspired answer. The perception becomes reality. And so children, the lesson is . . .? That Americans are cheap? That Canadians are gullible? That Indian mystics are nationalistic assholes? That you get what you pay for and they went to an unaccredited school of mystics? Maybe it's just an odd coincidence for Dan and I to have experienced while looking through the eyes of God.

Mr. Phommanila's hobby is the Voice of America broadcasts on short wave. We talk about the changes happening in Eastern Europe, of the burden in Asia that China's retrenching has created. I want him to know he is not alone in his courage and conviction: that the status quo can change, that popular dissent exists in others as well, that that dissent has been heard. He nods, but then looks to Pom for help. Pom looks to me. Somewhere we have broken down.

Call me Ira. Call him George. He says *tomayto*, I say *tomawto*, and pronunciation is our problem. Once we establish how each of us pronounces what we're talking about, it is clear he is more aware of events in Eastern Europe than I am. Voice of America is going to discontinue their Laotian broadcasts he says. He asks me why? He loves VOA. What can I say? I am not even American.

1:30, and lunch has stretched to three empty sherry bottles. That's a bunch. Pom has other commitments and I have to pass out from the heat and an over-indulgence of sweet banana alcohol. Come Mr. Tallyman.

Paul left too soon. When you search for what you desire, what you find, if you find anything, is what you searched for. Everything else passes by irrelevant and unobserved because it is and so it isn't. What Paul craves is here. It is here because it is accessible, because it is less publicized, because it is now. It is serendipity, and how do you dismiss that? Serendipity doesn't need justification.

The essence of rumour doesn't change from place to place. Fact is rumour substantiated. Rumour remains elusive, an equal fact unsubstantiated, the grain of truth unseized. But that is the appeal of rumours. They contain that grain of truth. They have a believability because they have an inherent claim to integrity.

They come from something. There is too much smoke here for there to be no fire.

Paul left too soon.

Across from the Phousie is Louangphrabang's main market, the Talàat Dala, a combination of Vientiane's merchandise and Kasi's charm. Where is the sun? Where is the warmth? From stall to stall my reception ping-pongs from respect to condescension. It is from the soap and household goods sellers that my respect comes, despite my having no reason to purchase from them. That I do not buy seems irrelevant. However fleeting, there is a connection. There is no economic sense to their kindness, but then economics never made much sense to me and what did make sense had little to do with kindness. Perhaps it is not that there is no gain to be made as much as there is no loss to be incurred. The social aspect of the economics versus the monetary. Would Soviets buy soap? Am I wearing a red Polo shirt? Is my belly really that big?

Where the Talàat Sao in Vientiane had jewellery dealers, the Talàat Dala has coin dealers. Handwritten lists of Française Indo-Chine Piastre, half Piastre and quarter Piastre de Commerce coin mintings from 1880 into the 1930s are stapled to posts all over the market indicating years available and price, as well as silver George V King Emperor Indian Rupee and East India Company Queen Victoria Rupee coins. The lists mean that someone knows these have value to someone else. It doesn't mean the sellers value them, at least not necessarily numismatically. When you ask for a year, kilo-heavy sacks are produced to look through. The coins are mud encrusted and stuck together, but at least they are real. In Bangkok's market, the coin of the realm is Piastre knock-offs. The only giveaways are the clink of steel instead of silver, the mis-shapen face on the face, and the year: every single coin was minted 1888. A bad year for noses, apparently.

In the dark, back corner of the market, one stall sells bootleg cassettes of Thai pop music, the colour cassette liner replaced with a photocopied black and white reproduction. The Thai is translated into Laotian on the back. The irony is laughable. The laughter, however, is more directed at people than life. A group of hill tribe people is in the market, dressed all in black: heavy stovepipe pants, jackets buttoned to the neck and hats. There's a lost tribe of Pennsylvania Amish? None wander alone, choosing instead to browse in groups of three or four. Pom says they are from the "other side," far beyond the banks of the Mekong. Indeed. Taunts and smirks fill the space behind them as they move like a collapsing hole in water. For all my "Sovietness," I am not at the end of the respectability continuum. They are. The line is not between Laotian and tourist. It is between Laotian and foreigner. And they are not Laotian either.

32

Louangphrabang

I have an image of W. Somerset Maugham in the Raffles Hotel in Singapore. I don't know if the image is accurate. I don't know if it's even reasonable. It doesn't matter. It's mine. It is an image of heavy, dark polished mahogany bar tops and ruddy brass railings; of languid ceiling fans and arched plaster of Paris ceilings stained with the smoke of Dutch tobacco, of the creak of rattan chairs and the reflection of daylight caught on polished hardwood floors; of the musky pungence of Star Lilies and the delicate sweetness of orchids. It is an image of calmness and order, of waiters in starched white waistcoats waiting and drinkers in white linen suits drinking. It is the romantic colonialism of gin and tonics and the elegances of home mingling with the exoticism of the foreign. I have seen it in the crumbling French architecture of Vientiane and Pakxé and the grimy shuttered two-story pensions of Nong Khai; in the mustard yellow walls of Kunming in China; in the traders' houses in Kobe and Nagasaki. It is here in Louangphrabang, in the approaching rain, the building moisture and suffocating humidity. I fill my lungs with it and in my breath, the romanticism is not outside but inside and we are one. Incomprehensible and welcoming, coddling in its foreignness because in spite of its foreignness, it is familiar.

The Phousie and Louangphrabang have swept me away.

My solitude here surprises me. Except for five minutes with Andy and Laura, I've been alone since Vientiane. The notion of being alone, of being the "only one," is romantic at best and wistfully pathetic at worst. Everywhere I go is someone else's yesterday, my today someone else's tomorrow. Lost in the uniqueness that this is for me is the understanding that this is in fact the totality of its uniqueness. Events this day are unique to the time but of no greater significance than those equally unique happenings tomorrow for someone else's eyes and camera. Everything is unique. Nothing is. In 17th century Japan, Haiku poet Basho wrote:

> Surely there must be someone crossing
> The pass of Hakoné
> On this snowy morning.

And tomorrow and tomorrow and tomorrow, creeps in this petty pace. Life. Even the most seemingly inaccessible places play host to travellers far removed from my own reality. Yet it still exists, this idea of uniqueness, as does the reality of its non-existence.

Regardless, alone my experience goes uncompromised by my lack of a peer group. In many ways, it is better for not having one. There is a Zen parable of the pearl and the pond. The mind, goes the parable, is like a small pond. On the bottom of the pond lies a layer of fine, soft mud and silt. Each time we have a thought, each time we shake our mind, we create waves, movement, and so stir that soft mud and silt until it lifts off the bottom and floats suspended in the water, obscuring all that lies below the surface. We think thoughts all day long, often the same thoughts, and so the pond exists in a constant state of murkiness. We see the surface. We see the cloudy thickness of the suspended mud. We see no more. But if we can calm our thoughts, calm our mind, eventually the water calms, the ripples abate, and in the abating, the soft suspended mud slows and then settles, leaving clear water to see into. And finally seeing into the water, we see resting on that fine bed of mud, a pearl. It is not new; it has always been there. It has just been obscured by our thoughts, by our ripples. Our job is to pluck that pearl from the bottom of the pond. For this task, we are given a pair of chopsticks. It is a difficult task at the best of times, lifting a pearl with chopsticks. Each unsuccessful attempt stirs the mud around the pearl, each swish of the chopsticks through the water stirs the calm. Sometimes we get half way and the pearl slips, falling back into the mud, billowing it up in a cloud that rains down on the pearl, partially obscuring it again from view. But eventually, if we work at it long enough, we catch the pearl, we do not drop it, and it comes to the surface.

Without the burden of a peer group to live up to or defer to, without a peer group to suffocate me with their support and demands, my thoughts clear.

I know it will not always be like this for either me or Louangphrabang. Too often I forget and take myself, this place and this time for granted. Too often I stir the water, and miss the pearl that is there.

My room looks out over the gravel inner courtyard. I have a half-length mirror, and it has been a while since I have seen my image in that extreme. My thinness surprises me. At home the adjective would be gaunt. Here it is alive.

It is the look of Asia, of co-existence instead of excess. Man made in God's image instead of his own. I do not need to survive in North America. There is no rigor, no acceptance of sufficient when everywhere is enticement to excess. Here, there is only this, therefore this is all I need. What is it I require to survive over? What is it I believe I do? What is it I have been told I do? At the Vipassana retreat in Kyoto, we were instructed to fill our stomachs three-quarters full and use our energy and time to understand the reality of ourselves instead of digesting our food. Is this why I eat so much at work? To see one's self as true, offer sustenance, not opulence. Monks exist on one meal a day. What do I need? What do I think I need? What am I told I need? Who is it that's telling me?

There is a Western toilet and shower. The white ceramic bowl has no seat. The shower nozzle works, but next to it in the stall is a large rusting oil drum cistern full of water, a pink plastic scoop floating on the surface. The cistern and a pool of water belong in Laos. It is certainly more participatory. Where the cistern involves, the showerhead accommodates, and in its accommodation, the essence of the experience is lost. When the essence of the experience is lost, when the desire for beauty and expression is sacrificed because the act is mundane, then eventually all is lost to the mundane and we exist instead of live. We succumb instead of participate.

In Ayutthaya with Cassie, I squatted naked in a wooden washhouse as she doused me with dish after dish of cool water scooped from a huge ceramic cistern. I scrubbed and washed and she doused and rinsed. I was clean. I was refreshed, and when dressed, I knew that I had lived every moment of that shower. Our lives are nothing if not a series of moments fitted together into days and months and years and finally lifetimes. We take the beauty out of the mundane, and in the act of removal, we create the mundane ourselves.

From 7:00 A.M. to 7:00 P.M., Louangphrabang is without electricity. This creates the absurd juxtaposition of being able to get a cold Sprite (a Sprite in and of itself in Louangphrabang is absurd, but I digress) on the rocks at 7:00 A.M., while at 1:30 P.M., in the wilting heat of the afternoon, there are neither fans to take refuge under nor cold drinks to slip into. If a cold Sprite quenches thirst, a warm Sprite begs for redemption. By 11:00 A.M., an entire night's work by the refrigerator has gone to waste, "iced tea" what Pom calls the beverage in the pitcher because "lukewarm tea" won't sell. With the cool of the night and the return of the overhead fans, Louangphrabang is comfortable. Sleep comes easily. To awaken after 7:00 A.M. however, is to awaken in lethargy and a body-sweat outline across the sheets, dreaming of soft drinks.

7:01 in a hot sweat. That's the time for a cold Sprite.

I ask Pom where to go to find a truck going south. Having gotten to Louangphrabang, getting out is now the goal. Do I always live in the future?

There is a football field stadium near Tat Luang he says. I can walk. Pom assures me I will have no trouble finding either the field or a ride to Vientiane.

On the first point at least, he is right.

Two trucks are parked on a small asphalt lot near the grandstand and a reviewing platform/band shell. An enormous Laotian flag has been painted on either side of the stage, a Hammer and

Sickle over the centre. I may not know what I like, but I know art. One of the transport trucks is going to Vientiane in two days. He's leaving at 4:00 P.M. Tomorrow it is going north to Xam Nua. If I wait, I can ride then. Pom was right.

I'm basking in my success, indulging myself with a warm Sprite at 5:45, when up the Phousie's gravel drive "Hello stranger!" climb George and Margaret. They're at the Lao Tourism hotel. They are in Louangphrabang for two days. They arrived yesterday. They're on their way to a film at the theatre. They've heard that instead of being dubbed, movies are shown with the soundtrack turned off and a person at a microphone reading the dialogue. They were supposed to have flown to the Plain of Jars on the Xiang Khoang Plateau today, but George had heard too many stories about helicopters in Laos. "I once booked a plane in Africa. I went out to check the plane out before it took off. One of the tires had a worn spot in the outer tread. And in the worn spot was another worn spot, which was worn away to another worn spot, which was worn away to another worn spot, which was worn away to the inner tube. We said no. After what we heard here, we decided we didn't need the Plain of Jars that badly."

He wants to know if I tipped the driver and guide in Pakxé, and in my explanation I feel bad. David and I had struck a conclusion logically consistent with our environment and experiences. The effect we desired was the effect we achieved. It had been quick and forgotten. I never considered an alternative. "Besides, you told us it was free, so when they came to our room, that's what we were thinking, that they were trying to pull a fast one."

"Yes George," said Margaret. "It was free. That's what Lao Tourism told us. Remember? Free."

He remembered. Free. He still thought a tip would have been nice.

He was right.

Sometimes the box I'm trying to break free of looms awfully small.

33

Louangphrabang

Last night a truck arrived at 7:30 carrying a Canadian I had met at the Sailom in Vientiane before I left for Vangviang and a French couple I hadn't. He is at the Nang Noi, the French couple is here. None of this seems to mean anything to him. Laos, Thailand . . . is there a difference? He has been to Canada and Australia, one by choice and one by birth, although I think he would argue that Choice and Birth were both Australia. Where that leaves Canada is a question I understand completely. Where that leaves Canada though, *is* the question. Australia is all he can talk about. His heart longs for Sydney. He was there for two years. He just left. Six days ago. I understand longing. Now he's on the way home, but where exactly home is for him seems the problem. Australia was about discovering himself, about living and learning and loving. Whatever Canada was for him, he left it behind once. Why go back? What did Richard Bach write about periodically asking yourself where you were born and watching the answers change?

Maybe his Australian longing is just the tenderness of the separation, but I don't think so. Some things imprint on you and never leave, no matter where you run. Why indeed go back to Canada? What moves a person's mind to force the return? Maybe it's like being here. He wants to travel but he can't explain why or what. Maybe it's just the thing to do, the expected culmination: no one "just goes home". To have come this far . . . But whose expectation? His or his peers? Do you fight against the norm or accede to the expectations and make them your own? A tumbling of demands.

A lot of people talk about taking a year off from their lives to travel. What does that tell you about where those people place the experience of travelling? Been there done that, that's where, except it begs the question: where exactly do you have to have been to have "been there," and how much do you have to "have done"? If I spend four days in Los Angeles, how many "been there done that's" do I get? The city? California? The whole damned country? And four days? I guess if we reduce a place to the tourist highlights, then four days is plenty, but is that all a place is? The sum of its tourist highlights? How about one day?

Living in Japan and travelling was the most alive I have ever been. They are why I'm here now, why I met Cassie and Paul. They're why I met myself. Europe wasn't a year off from my life. Japan wasn't twenty-seven months off from my life. Those events defined my life.

And so: In Nagoya I worked with a couple from Australia who had been travelling in Asia before settling down to earn some yen. In Brisbane before they left, their uncle told them not to work in Japan after their travels, but to come home. "You'll fall behind," he said. Is that what I've done? Fall behind? What kind of a society says that working in a branch plant office, wearing a three piece Korean-made blue pin-stripe suit, buying the chocolate chips and flour and raisins for cookies and paying off a new car loan is valuable, but travelling for a year in Europe, discovering art and archaeology and architecture and music and language and religion and history and geography and culture and people I would never meet at home who expand my horizons in ways and shapes I could never imagine and discovering *who* the real me is and *what* the real me is doesn't count because it's "a year off".

How long do you have to be away from home before it isn't home anymore? How long do you have to be in a new place before it becomes home? Are there standards? Rules? Can you ever look at home the same way once you've seen someone else's home. Once you've seen yours from their perspective? Once their perspective has become yours? I'm not the first to ask this. In World War One they sang the musical question, "How ya gonna keep 'em down on the farm, after they've seen Paree?" I'm just the first to ask me. Or at least, I'm the first to ask me that I actually heard. Fall behind whom? Listen: In 1968, our neighbour across the street in Delta, the man who had built the sub-division we lived in, who built the house my father scraped a mortgage together to buy, entered federal politics in the mania that was Pierre Elliott Trudeau and was swept into the ruling government and the backbench in Ottawa. At age nine I was already behind his son Tom Jr. who was three years younger than me (actually he was Tom III. His father was Tom Jr., his grandfather Tom Sr., but Tom III in North Delta in the late 1960s didn't quite fit the fishing village/riverbank settlement roots of the place. Kids got teased for less.) In 1973 my neighbour left parliament and was elected mayor. I fell further behind. In his 30s, Tom III (or Tom, as he called himself in an thankful acknowledgement to simplicity) lost both his parents to cancer. In his 40s, Tom himself died. Can you fall behind a dead man?

The Canadian-Australian got his Laotian visa in Australia. It took him two days, cost him $15, and he got three weeks. Booked his ticket and he was here, without build-up, without continuity. Just like that. An accelerated progression of the senses.

At Pom's suggestion, the Can-Aussie and I take a long tail boat across the river. The ride is 50 kip. "There is a village," he said, the "over there" from the other day left implied. On the western shore of the Mekong, ten more boats are anchored to rickety stilts plunged into the thick, gooey mud flats. There is a dirt path cut into the river bank, leading up and away. The others from our boat take it. Pom offered no directions apart from "over there," and we are already "over there".

"Sprechen zie Deutsch?"

From a hut at the top of the bank, a brown face sticks out of a second-storey window, the drape across the window pulled back. "Sprechen zie Deutsch?"

"English."

There is a mumble, and the drape falls back across the window. This is most definitely "over there".

The "over there" village in question is a community of weavers. They produce a rough fabric chequer table cloth popular in the Talàat Dala. The twenty-odd village huts are elevated on thick, rough-hewn logs, the looms underneath the huts in the still, hot shade. At a loom, a buck-toothed woman in a mangosteen sarong sits whisking the shuttle back and forth through the shed. Back and forth she throws the wooden needle, back and forth her arms flex and release, flex and release, flex and release, the thread rubbing across the weft making a whispering swish, until another inch is done and her triceps pump against her skin, dancing through a shimmer of sweat, reaching and pulling, pulling and reaching. Separated by a row of beams, a younger black-haired woman in a rust sarong paces the length of the hut barefoot, running cotton threads from a birdcage of eight bobbins onto a series of spindles and bamboo pegs set into the beams, siphoning the threads through her fist trailing behind her back. Over and over she walks and turns, walks and turns, walks and turns, her brown eyes and black ponytail dancing in her pace, loose hair strands falling across her face. Her abandoned blue rubber thongs lie in the dirt, the skin across her calves stretching and pulling, her feet arching and planting, planting and arching. How susceptible I am to beauty. How susceptible I am to dignity and integrity. How easily romanced I am.

On a veranda on the side of the village across from the looms sit a group of men, the ground beneath and around the veranda stained bloody in betel-nut spittle. The smell of laokao and tobacco hangs around them. Their cheeks are hollow, their faces wrinkled and suspicious. How susceptible romance is to reality.

On the path back towards the Mekong and our return boat from "over here," a bamboo-slat drink lounge that was closed on our approach is open. There are six drinking: two men, and two couples although something tells me the two women couple more actively than discriminately. Maybe the two single men just got here second? The wall of big-bamboo slats behind the bar-counter is lined with three shelves filled with full bottles of white liquid. Plastic bags of loose tobacco tied up with cellophane string hang from the shack's ceiling like see-through piñatas. The two escorts are military men, or at least, the top half of them is: olive green caps with red squad buttons, pressed, clean jackets, Hawaiian shirts, casual slacks, and sandals. The red-faced women are bloated and blotched in their afternoon's diversion, hanging all over the two soldiers. Hawkeye and Trapper got lucky.

Two sabadees are tossed out by the men at the bar, and two quick shots of laokao are offered and accepted by us in exchange for us taking their photos. This "money for photo" exchange I can live with. The camera shutter is snapped, my throat burns, and we are forgotten. Then a quiet belch. This will not be a repeat of Vientiane.

The army boys want a photo too, and a second quick shot is poured for us. With the women, but one of the women is shy, or drunk, or otherwise married, and refuses to pose with her face towards the camera, despite cajoling and tickling and loud, slurred words. The shot repeats hard into my throat, and there is no quiet belch. No more. A toast by the four, and there is a photograph: Sgt. Pepper does Laos.

And I loved the show, thanks.

One of the long tail boats is loading as we crest the top of the riverbank. We start to run but a fat ticket seller waves us off and we fall back to a walk, still reaching the shore before the half-full boat pushes off. Neither of us understand. "When does the next boat leave?" is the question, but nothing is the reply. English. I repeat the question, less structurally, more gesturingly. We can't swim. Language notwithstanding, our context should be obvious. It is, but every context has two sides. The first boat pushes off, and "500 kip," and a hand pointed at another boat is the new, less structural, more gesturingly answer. He joins his friends on a deadhead and laughs, but context is on our side. Shortly others arrive and a new boat loads. 50 kip, and he smiles.

On a stone porch around the base of a thick bodhi tree, an old bhikkhu sits quietly, surrounded by a group of pre-adolescent novices playing a board game. I offer a sabadee, raise my hands together prayer-like in a wai, bow, and point towards the viharn. At my mention of bimai the boys laugh and then are quickly back to their game, ignoring me. The old monk smiles without replying. Again I wai, motion at the viharn, and ask: "Bimai?" Stopping their play, the children huddle together over words, neither directly deferring to nor acknowledging the bhikkhu, and a single novice leaves. The old monk sits still and voiceless, without focus. The novice returns holding a key. With a slow wave the old monk shuffles into the viharn followed by a few of the boys, doddering a few steps before sitting onto the polished white stone tile floor.

The floor in front of the altar is scattered in dead and dying bees from a hive high in the rafters. Barefoot, I don't want to step on one or kick a clear pathway. It is a delicate tiptoe. In the Katha Upanishad, it is written that the path to enlightenment is like walking along the thin edge of a razor. There is no mention of bees. Insects are more Biblical than Upanishadical.

The main altar image is a slender, golden meditating dhyānamudrā Buddha, a brilliant tangerine uttarāsanga across its breast. Flanking the meditating Buddha are a pair of mirror-image standing Buddhas, each with one arm downward, palm forward in the varadamudrā or charity position, one arm with the hand extended from the elbow, palm forward in the abhayamudrā, or reassurance position. In front, the altar is filled with smaller golden nāgas, gold and bronze standing images, gold dhyānamudrā images, votive tablets, candles and white lotus flowers.

Tens more Buddha figures stand at the rear of the wat, some like the altar images in single abhayamudrā, some in a double varadamudrā. A Buddha with white eyeballs and piercing black irises stands in double abhayamudrā, both hands extending outward from the elbows, demanding STOP! The worn gold-leaf face offers a calmness the hand gesture does not suggest. STOP! is not a command as much as it is a reassurance, not so much STOP! as stop. Become quiet . . . Stop. Iconographically, a double abhayamudrā represents the Buddha calming the flood waters of the Niranjanā River, but the symbology seems self-evident to me. It is not only the river that is raging. Crowded, jumbled corners filled with images and messages of kindness and giving. I am not alone. I am never alone. And yet, I is all I have. The contradiction of comfort.

What I desire is to sit and become quieter and feel instead of see. What I feel is discomfort at inconveniencing the old bhikkhu. My wonderment is already prolonged I tell myself, or at least one of my Selfs. It fights hard, the agitated Self winning the struggle for Selflessness. The bhikkhu showed no enthusiasm at granting my request, but neither did he show unenthusiasm. He simply was. It was my choice to see one over the other. My respect falls the only way my Self knows: I wai again, bow deeper, and offer cash. He points to a red collection box near the altar. Three hundred kip. It doesn't seem much. Maybe he sees through the money. Maybe he sees through me. My Self fights hard, but the mirror of a struggle is sincerity and awe. What else could it fight against? The mirror images on the altar are me. I am my Self, and yet I am not my Self. It will take longer than today, longer than here and now. And yet, all it takes is here and now. And it has nothing to do with bimai masks.

34

Louangphrabang

In the long, warm amber light of late afternoon, I try again for a ride to Vientiane. Upon reflection yesterday's success has left me decidedly uneasy. The driver's first language isn't English, it is Laotian. My first language is the same as my second. What I assumed perfunctory in the driver's tone could have been no more than simple first language interference: is a solitary "Yes" abrupt or just the answer you give when a full grammatical sentence is too much of a struggle? Or just the answer when you only know two words, and "hello" doesn't fit? Maybe the driver's perfunctoriness is no more than my anxiety? If I am wrong about his tone, then how confident can I be over the content? I would feel better if the truck were there now, if there were a substance I could touch and see for myself. There is already too much on which I am blindly running on faith. I have to find a ride. It has become an urgency and I need definitive assurance. A ride is my only avenue left and an over-stayed visa in a communist country is a road I haven't walked down yet. Nor do I want to.

I overhear the French couple saying they had been to Air Lao to book their flight to Vientiane. There are now no seats available until Wednesday. My plan never was to fly, but hearing them in one statement both consolidate their plans and slam shut my door of option leaves me anxious and panicky. It is classic. I make a plan, and then in honouring the commitment and achievement, panic in the anxiety of its non-conformity.

I always planned on overland. I didn't want to deny myself

the experience, to compromise this event. I already did that flying out of Pakxé. The logic of flight in this constrained timetable was undeniable, but it left me feeling removed from the land, disconnected from the reality of Laos. Instead of a journey, it was a trip. The airplane insulated me and created an experience that reflected my culture instead of Laos's. And even that is misleading, because it is my Culture that flies, not *my* culture. I don't fly. North Americans fly. Every compromise detracts, every opportunity to remove myself from Laos a step away from the reality I desire.

Today two trucks are parked parallel to each other at the far, eastern end of the soccer field. Two husband and wife teams are sitting on the grass between the trucks eating their dinners, cosy behind their trucks. The first group is going north, to Xam Nua. At least that's what I think they say. It was their immediate response, and they repeated it individually and then in unison. This reality is not the same as yesterday's. These drivers speak no English. I still speak no Laotian. Our conversation, in whatever form it takes, is entirely dependent on three things: their understanding my hand gestures, their ability to process my pronunciation of Laotian village and city names, and their possessing my Western-derived intuitive logic. This is the reflection that has led me back to this field today. Still, they seem insistent. There is another chance yet. Fifty percent.

I smile. Sabadee. "Do you go to Vientiane? I want to go to Vientiane tomorrow."

The second family smiles and sabadees back. A good start. Then they look at each other and take another mouthful of food. I repeat. "Do you (I point at them) go (I make the 'yellow pages' walking gesture with my fingers, the figure *clearly* walking away from me, which in this instance *clearly* represents them driving, since no one is going to be walking, they are obviously truck drivers, and since we are *here*, any movement must be *away*) to Vientiane (spoken as the walking figure reaches its climax position, emphasized by a jabbing motion into the palm of the hand the figure is walking on to indicate destination or completion. The jab represents the arrival at the place, in this case, Vientiane, confidently and accurately pronounced, needing no further explanation)?" To emphasize that it's a question, I shrug my shoulders and raise my eyebrows. Subtle, but effective. There's no point in belabouring a point and insulting them. "I (pointing at my chest) want to go (repeat the walking gesture for go, *want* effectively realized by a clenched fist showing possession, a holding on to: I want this) to Vientiane (again, perfectly pronounced [see above])." There is nodding, smiling, words offered back.

Total bewilderment. Blank. No comprehension. Nothing. Remember the *Far Side* cartoon entitled "What a Dog Hears"? In the drawing there is a picture of a man talking to his dog, and out of the man's caption bubble comes "blah blah blah blah blah blah Ralph blah blah blah blah Ralph blah blah blah". For all the good this is doing, I might as well be speaking English to them. Again I ask, quicker now, since I am repeating myself, "Do you (again I point at them, but now also their trucks. The addition of the trucks will clear up any possible confusion, although here is not where I feel the confusion might derive from) go (I repeat the 'yellow pages' walking gesture with my fingers, the figure *still* clearly walking away) to Vientiane?"

"Yes," they nod.

I should learn to trust myself more. *Who's the man? Who's the man?*

"When?" I ask, knowing even before the thought finishes that this will be lost to them. Even the creative logic that suggests a Laotian truck driver whose language bears no linguistic relationship to mine whatsoever should understand *Do you go to Vientiane* falls flat with *When.*

Do you go . . . rides on the assumption of the universal gesture, and it all begins with *you*. It is not until here that the logic of this exercise begins to fall apart. In Canada, achieving the gestured concept *I* is as simple as pointing at one's chest. In Japan this means there is a spot on your tie. In Japan, *I* is achieved by pointing at the tip of your nose. Assuming this a pan-Asiatic gesture I learned to point at my nose whenever I wanted to express *I*. In most of the rest of Asia, this means you have a booger.

The belief that has gotten me through Asia, that has gotten me here, is that all English can be communicated to any non-English speaker if only the right gesture accompanies it. The Marcel Marceau approach to language and communication. If you mime it, they'll understand. If they don't, just mime louder.

Two experiences should have told me that this was not so. One was a column in the *Japan Times* about the life and times of being an American ex-pat in Japan specifically and a Westerner in Asia in general. The story was about an American woman who moved to China. Shortly after arriving in Beijing, she went to her local store, took out a pencil and paper and drew two rolls of toilet paper. She held up the picture, held up two fingers and smiled. The Chinese clerk nodded and came back with two pads of drawing paper and two pencils.

The other was watching a Japanese back-packer at a bus station in Chiang Mai, Thailand. Securing his ticket, he too wanted to know *when*. Similarly burdened by an initial success, he had continued headlong into the confirmation, his carefully pronounced *itsu* producing, in retrospect, oddly familiar smiles and nods. He changed his sentences from long to short, from formal to colloquial, but all in Japanese, all for only smiles and nods. There was no reason for me to believe in the inherent logic and universality of my *Excuse me. When does the bus leave?* any more than his believing in the inherent logic and universality of his *Ano ne, kono basu wa itsu ni ikimasuka?* And that's the English version. On what planet would the Thai bus station attendant have understood あのね。このバスはいつに行きますか?

Especially on planet Louangphrabang.

I think that given the number of Chinese in Laos, perhaps the drivers will recognize the Chinese character for *when*. I take out my note pad and begin to draw the character, realizing halfway through I have forgotten how. My scattering assortment of stroke patterns and half-finished ideas confuses the drivers more. Giving up on *when*, I ask *tomorrow*, and immediately grope for an identifying gesture. What does *tomorrow* look like? A grand half-dome sweeping gesture, accomplished with the right hand, palm up, left to right, not un-reminiscent of the *The Price is Right's* "A BRAND NEW CAR!" is the answer. I draw an imaginary line of horizon in the air, with the sun, my hand, rising in the East, passing across the horizon, until setting in the West. Then I motion sleep. Then again, from the East, the sun, my hand, rising. I wake up. Tomorrow! Easy. Obvious. They all nod. Yes. They understand. Tomorrow. Tomorrow at 7:00 A.M., they will leave for Vientiane. I will come back then.

I thank them with a slight bow and a smile. The bow means nothing to them. A knee-jerk Japanese convention to civility. Absurd. Yet I continue to do it and feel embarrassment and confusion after the fact at the non-response it elicits. At least everyone smiles. I confirm 7:00 with seven fingers raised in the air and leave.

Even seven is uncertain, George Costanza notwithstanding. The Japanese show it one way, the Chinese another, myself yet another. If the concept of a number is difficult how can I arrive at a contentment over sentences? The sinking knowledge is that their smiles and laughs have served to hide embarrassment and that their *yes's* are a gesture on their part to make me happy, rather than convey an answer. Perhaps they think I was busking for meals. The more I play with these notions, the more uncomfortable I feel. Well after twilight, I ask Pom to return with me to confirm my ride.

I am wrong. Totally wrong. Completely wrong. For all my time in Asia, for all the communicative devices I've learned travelling and as a teacher, for all the successes I have had in Laos, for all the assurances to self-intelligence I have made, I grope blind in the dark, fumbling through successes and failures with only luck and providence to guide me. No one is going to Vientiane tomorrow. Tomorrow, all the trucks are going to Xam Nua. They have come from Vientiane today. In perhaps three days they will return to Vientiane. They could take me then, if I want. Three days means Tuesday. It is impossible.

Pom sees another truck at the top of the bank under some spotlights. It is an army vehicle, leaving for Vientiane tonight. The man in the white T-shirt working on the engine says it is too dangerous to ride with them. The last trip, he says, shots were fired. Blue trucks are better he says. Green trucks are dangerous.

Commercial transport trucks are blue. Army transport trucks are green. This truck is exactly the same shape and size as the others. It fooled Pom. In the darkness, you don't see colour. In a fire, the paint is the first thing to go, and after the fact, burned, bent metal does not give away its origin. I will try again tomorrow, and hope that the other truck shows up.

Pom parked his scooter on the road next to a cigarette and coffee vendor. Before we head back he stops for a cigarette, and in the glow of the warming basket of coals, he apologizes for there being no trucks. The sky is a deep, deep plum moving to black, a crescent moon rising up, the same crescent moon of Kasi. Hundreds of stars salt the sky, defining the solid hill ridges against the night. The street is quiet. After dark and unlit, there is little traffic but for bicycles, and three minutes from the Phousie by scooter, we are too far out of town for bicycles. Cicadas rise up and fall away, a staccato of electrical surges, like current pulsating through a bulb in a Bombay brown out. I ask and Pom gives me a cigarette. The evening is warm. I feel dizzy. Today is Saturday. Tonight there is a dance at the Phousie. Since this afternoon, they have been putting up chairs and tables. Pom says something to the coffee lady and they laugh. We finish our cigarettes and get back on the scooter. In the summer of my childhood, I felt this comforting warmth, and in the street-lighted darkness of my suburbia, I walked barefoot in frayed blue jeans cut-offs and felt neither conscious of myself nor anxious over my future. The moment just was and so was I. Summers later, when I realized that neither would return, I cherished it as the glow of my youth, the innocence of childhood. Here again I feel it. In the dark, in the warmth with Pom, so far away from that summer, so far away from that me. And I think about Pom, so soft, gentle, his words and manner so caressing. I feel lulled and submissive. He is wonderful. I wonder if his fullness towards me is that of a concerned hotel manager or if there is more. And again I think of Maugham. Could I make love to this man, this Pom? And of course, the answer is no, but I wonder why I answer so quickly, why the emphatic "of course"? The reasons are obvious: out of learned beliefs and moralities, beliefs and moralities which seem so questionable here, so removed from the environment that created and sustained them. I can feel his closeness on the back of his scooter as we ride, and I wonder again if I could hold this man, if I could make love to him here, so far away from everything, so near to everything, and my answer is maybe. Would I turn him away if he came to me, and my answer is I don't know. To be true to the moment. To be true to myself. The evening's sensuality cannot be denied. It is enveloping in its grasp, and in the breeze that the bike generates, it sticks to my body and wraps around it, pushing my clothing against my skin, forcing it to be acknowledged. I don't know why I took the cigarette. It felt right, it felt necessary: a shared moment together in the quiet resignation of a failed encounter. I didn't want to watch. I needed to participate, to step inside the circle, included in the moment. Somerset Maugham. Pom.

We pull into the hotel driveway, the gravel grinding against itself below the tires, flatter and heavier now under the weight of two. The outdoor lights that ring the courtyard in Christmas festivity have been turned on, the bandshell prepared and waiting for the dance. There is no one to be, nothing to do, nowhere to go. Only me, only this, only here.

35

Louangphrabang

The pastel-pink bandshell is below my second-floor window: a giant headless stucco nāga rising out of the gravel,
the back of its seven-ribbed hood turned towards me, the decapitated serpent king fanning his protection out over the courtyard,
refusing even in death to abandon his duty. Whatever this faceless Muchalinda protects is hidden from my view. It occurs to me
that the perspective is identical to my view over the nāga at Wat
Upumong, but the dimension has shifted; not between myself
and the nāga, but between myself and the nāga and the world. At
Upumong, the nāga introduced a dominant temple landscape. At
the Phousie, the nāga and I dominate the landscape. In Thebes,
in ancient Egypt, the religious logic of the temples was to create
on earth a representation of the realm of the Gods: the huge sand-
stone columns represented lotus stems, and worshippers walked
between the base of the stems, staring up to the heavens to the
world of towering Gods. Here it is the nāga who towers over its
world, and I who tower over the nāga. Here, it is others that walk
through my realm. At Upumong, Muchalinda's job was to protect
the Buddha. Who is Muchalinda protecting tonight?

The pearl inside the scallop shell is a five-piece local band.
Their act is a three-part repertoire: traditional Laotian music,
Thai pop hits and American "golden oldies". That part of their
play-list reads like the cassette from Kasi: *Samba Pati, It Never
Rains in California*, and the ever ubiquitous *Beautiful Sunday*. Is
there just the one tape in Laos? Can only rubies be smuggled?

The Thai and Laotian music plays with grace and dignity. Innocent rhythms and delicate vocals, the music floats across the courtyard in perfect complement to the humidity.

Couples circle the dance floor as if tethered to a maypole and tied to each other, commanding their partner's attention as though each held a secret urgent to the other and that only by making and maintaining this connection could it be coaxed free. Side-by-side each couple steps and then turns to face each other: slide, slide, turn, slide, slide, turn. A courtship of gestures; hands suspended chest-high in mid air as if being manipulated by a puppeteer, each dancer creating small alternating circles with their hands, turning the palm first away and then back, the left countering the right, the right countering the left. A physical ying-yang, the seed of each opposing movement in the originating gesture, each gesture a reflection of its complement. Musical Tai Chi. Fluid, effortless, unrestricted. A sleight-of-hand seduction. Slow motion grace.

The evening's fall from this divinity is the band's interpretation of rebellion and teenage angst. Effortless grace and Geisha shuffle do not translate well into 4/4 time on the downbeat, bubble-gum emotions and Brazilian sensuality. A hanging moon burns deep into the sky behind the stage. Four days older than the moon over Kasi, still hinting a crescent, it is fuller, more demanding, more masculine. Against the moon, the indigenous movements to the imported rhythms look awkward and out of place. The influence of colonial Christian missionaries never ends.

What the rock and roll loses in beauty, it makes up for in caricature. The presentation is an awkward, embarrassing blend of decontextualized rock clichés and Laotian gentility. It reminds me of a hotel house band I once saw in Long Beach, California on Grand Prix weekend. I walked in just as the lead guitarist was dedicating "the next number" to George Harrison, who was in the audience. Out stepped *Rock 'n Roll Music*, out of tune and missing lyrics, finished with the lead guitarist karate-kicking the high-hat cymbal. When the house lights were turned up, George, to his credit, was long gone. So goes the price of unbridled admiration. To ease the tension of George's departure, the band started up Redbone's *Come and Get Your Love*.

Indecipherable pronunciation doesn't help their cause either. Apart from the choruses, themselves identifiable through repetition alone, the words are gibberish: mimicked sounds gleaned from second-generation bootleg cassettes and Don Kirschner 1970s videos. *Samba Pati* is Brazilian and *Beautiful Sunday* by a poly-syllabically challenged Netherlander. With lyrics like "say, say, say" and "hey, hey, hey", how can it lose? For *It Never Rains in California*, even the chorus is indiscernible. Like an unearthed pottery shard, only a fragment mistakenly played correctly betrays its otherwise anonymity. Musical archaeology. Sometimes having a musical memory is a curse. If the band weren't so serious, I'd wonder whether they weren't sending it all up. Adding insult, as the songs sputter and dribble in their hard-won mediocrity, the dance floor fills hesitantly; the dancers aren't sure how to respond either.

A single Western woman sits alone behind a bottle of beer at a table, far removed from the dance floor and the tables that surround it. I haven't seen her before. I play eye tag with her for a while, but later I turn around and she is gone. I had thought to go over, but shyness and pre-emptive self-doubt put it off. Even here, even now, I insist on getting into the way of myself. To travel alone is to experience the exhilaration of yourself, the exhilaration of a country with as few externalities as possible, and the exhilaration of serendipity and experience. To be alone at a dance is to just be alone. She looked awkward in her solitude, as if she hoped the beer bottle would draw her into the crowd instead of acting as a wall of separation. I had thought to go over, but I didn't know how to approach her without becoming a caricature myself. *Hi. I'm white and alone too. Can I join you?* Like my Russian friend said before, to think and to not act is to not yet know, and I think way too much. And so she has left, alone, in the midst of this celebration, choosing to exile herself from the night. The conversation we might have had has become a moment we never will. I had thought to go over in this illusion of an Ontario Hot August Minesing Night. I had thought to go over. Does the band know that *It Never Rains* isn't really about the weather?

Why isn't Cassie here?

I look again at the empty table searching for her face, but it has not returned. There is no answer. She is not coming back, and I fear neither is the other. I have lived for the one-way mirror too long, observing, listening and thinking that that was safe. How do you get hurt when you can't be seen? I want to cast it aside, to jump into the fray and participate. I want to be seen. That is what I touched with Cassie. Without judgment I touched it, and allowing myself I could allow her too, and so we did. We were and we flew, the sum of our two greater than the sum of the individual. It was not our unions, but the way we chose to unite. Having experienced, I want it to go on forever. To stop thinking and instead to feel, to touch, to sing and yet even in those moments of abandonment, there was still this self, still a part of me looking and protecting. It fights hard.

The table is still empty, our isolation solidified. On a Hot August Laos Night in winter under a starry sky. It is a night for romance, a night for touch. A night for a couple.

Pom invites me to join him and some of his friends at his table near the dance floor and orders a bottle of banana wine. At 11:00 P.M., it is too hot and muggy for sweet wine to quench my thirst. Then I see her standing at the drink bar. A figure that is familiar, a physiology that I know: round face, long black hair—the way she moves her head. Without my glasses on, I am sure that it is Nakayama-san, my long-removed girlfriend from Nagoya. The image is overwhelming. With my glasses on, the image is clearer, but still too distant to be sure. Logic tells me she is in Japan, that even if she weren't, Louangphrabang is not where she would be. Logic tells me it cannot be her. Logic never beats emotions. The image defies in its insistence, and I walk towards it to confirm in my chest what my brain is trying to tell it, in spite of the messages from my eyes that insist into my pace. Within ten feet it is obviously not her. The girl is not Japanese. Even remotely. She is not even familiar from the hotel. A trick of the night. No more, no less. A trick of the wine. An undigested piece of potato. I share another wine with Pom, and asked by one of the girls from the front desk, dance.

The dance floor is unlit, the stage washed over by a smattering of red spotlights. The rest of the courtyard is in Christmas light yellow. The drink bar is lit in green fluorescent brightness that hurts in the darkness. It is easy in the darkness. Darkness turns questions to answers and possibilities to certainties. First a Western song, then a Laotian song. Round and round my hands move, asking my partner and being answered, being asked and answering. And still, my eyes seek out the familiar form near the bar, squinting into the harsh light looking, looking. I tell myself it is not her—I *know* it is not her—but I am not listening and my glances grow longer and more frequent as the songs continue. It is not her. Even the shape now seems wrong. Still I look. Still I look.

At midnight, I have grown weary of the party. I get a bottle of tepid water from the over-worked bar refrigerator and retire to my room. I would prefer the party to end for me aurally. I do not need to see the last dance.

On my bed, unmistakable against the hard whiteness of the fitted sheet, there is a single long black hair. A fissure against white, a crack of surface tension against stillness. It is not mine. My hair is short and brown. A maid's perhaps, except that a maid with even the most casual of glances would have noticed a long black hair on a hard white cotton bed. It is a synchronicity I am uncomfortable with.

And so: In Japan, I left black-haired Nakayama-san in a fit of cultural and Self reclamation for golden-haired Amie from Indiana. After showers, golden-haired Amie wore only a white terry-cloth bath towel around her hips, leaving her breasts free. They were perfect and firm and young, and in their bounce reminded me of Gauguin's Tahitians, and I always felt her more exotic for the allusion. Coincidence and fate too had brought us together that first night: her to the wrong choice of two bars to meet a friend waiting at the other, me searching for a familiar face on a night when my legs again refused my brain and found their way past the haunts of my neighbourhood instead of to home. Golden-haired Amie was beautiful and intelligent and I didn't have to choose my words to talk. A fellow gaijin that neither of us knew sitting at the next table struck up a conversation and asked if we lived together. I said "not yet," wetting myself with a boldness I usually denied. I just felt free.

From our first meeting, the non-language barrier and our familiar cultural icons created a barrier that we could not but leap over, and jumping, where we landed was bed. Together we had slept, first like children outside on her apartment balcony, then as lovers. Uncomfortable days later, black-haired Nakayama-san found a single long golden hair on my pillow.

So many miles away from Cassie, so many more away from Japan, in a perfect Asian room on a perfect sultry night, there is a single long black hair.

36

Louangphrabang

By 11:00 A.M. the electricity has been off for four hours and the walls of my hotel room are wilting in the heat. I feel hungover: who needs beer for a hangover when you can have sweet banana wine and dehydration. A knock. Pom is at my door. There is a picnic today near the river. Twice already he has invited me. I tell Pom I'd rather stay around Louangphrabang and be sure of my ride, but he assures me that I will be back in time and insists that I come. Against my better judgement, in the companionship we have developed, I agree. We ride together as far as we can on Pom's scooter and then walk, leaving the bike at his house. Just the two of us. "I am," he blurts out "married. With two children." It is not the revelation I had expected.

The worn asphalt leads up a hill towards a wat. "Only a little while," he says, but the grey glares white in the sun and my eyes squint and tear in brightness, and even "a little while" is too much. Worse, the wat is not our goal. "Soon," he repeats, but without a point of reference "soon" seems interminable. Why didn't we take Pom's scooter?

An hour later the road crests a ridge and at its base we leave it behind, veering sharply down a steep trail leading off into the trees. Lost behind smooth granite boulders and thick bamboo undergrowth is the river.

It is last night's dance all over again. The entire Phousie staff is here and I get recognitions of familiarity I naïvely thought didn't extend beyond Pom. The band is back and they're still bad, but the songs less disturbing without the burden of a Saturday night expectation. Today the musicians get a bamboo and canvas tent. Nāga-hide. The music is lost without conscious effort in the enveloping rumble of the river, and it is too hot for effort. Nakayama-san's ghost is nowhere to be seen.

A portrait photographer with a Russian 35MM camera is standing fully-clothed mid-thigh deep in rapids, his studio an exposed boulder in the middle of the river. There is no bridge, and the only stepping stones are on the river bed. These smaller, dry-challenged rocks make the river jump and break in burning white crests. It is a beautiful studio, if not to everyone's taste. His customers ford their way through this current to pose in soaked and squinting affection on the dry, grey rock, the dry top increasingly wetter with each pose. I can't imagine he does much wedding photography.

Upstream, a group of clothed teenagers—heavy jeans for both the boys and girls, mid-thigh length T-shirts for the girls—wade into the middle of the rushing water towards a smaller, less special exposed boulder. Downstream, five naked nut-brown boys fight against the current towards the same stone.

Pom secures us a hiding place in the shade of a small bamboo thicket on one of the sandbars. He has squirreled his "girlfriend" away from the group, a short, plump, blotchy-faced woman in a purple blouse. She has brought two tepid, well shaken Pepsi in gritty, worn glass bottles—one for each of them—and herself, just for Pom.

Only in Roman Catholicism is three not a crowd. Pom may have wanted me to come to the picnic, but he doesn't want me here. He's married *and* he cheats? This gets stranger and stranger. On my way back through the sand and bamboo to the dance area, it is apparent Pom is not the only squirrel on the island. This is "make-out" sand bar? Can a land-locked country have submarine races? Worse than not knowing the way is interrupting others while I prove it. Could I have misjudged Pom so badly?

Through the underbrush the group of now-damp teenagers appears. A beautiful, longhaired girl in sopping, clinging jeans and a T-shirt wet from the bottom up deserts her group to sit next to me. Through the soaked T-shirt I can see that she is wearing another full torso shirt underneath. Nothing says erotic like two heavy layers of wet cotton over more layers of wet cotton. In alternative gestures she points to herself and to me, to herself and to me. A hint of a smile. To herself. To me. To herself. To me. *Sabadee. Fuck you?* My heart races with the possibilities.

She wants our photo taken, with her camera. That was not one of them. Behind me, I can hear the river laughing.

I am asked to dance, but in the harshness of the daylight, my foreignness looms too obvious and I feel too easily stared at. My self-consciousness stifles whatever grace I possess and exchanges it for just clumsy. I feel more at ease dancing Laotian style, the search for the grace of hand gestures easier than the obligation I feel to fluidity and competence and my own culture when the band resurrects *It Never Rains in California* from last night's grave. Isn't there some statute of limitations?

At 2:30 I remind Pom of my truck. He re-assures me it is not a problem. The hotel caretaker will take me in the hotel jeep as soon as he returns. That's where he is now: gone back to the Phousie to get more soda. Soon he will return, Pom says. Soon. By 3:00 it is still not "soon" and the anxiety I have tried to rein in explodes. In delirium I panic, pacing the grounds and up the bank to the road looking, looking, looking. 3:15. He is still not back, and I calculate in my head the minutes left before it will be physically impossible to return by 4:00.

I feel furious. At Pom for jeopardizing my truck, at myself for letting it happen. At Pom for not telling me the caretaker was leaving, for not ensuring there would be a way out for me, since it was at his insistence I came. 3:22. At myself, because I heard Pom talking to the caretaker moments before he left, and despite intuiting that he was returning to the hotel, I never pursued my suspicion with Pom and I just let the caretaker go. At myself because I acquiesced to someone else's wants in spite of my own needs. 3:30. Do I never learn? I can still make it by 4:00 if I leave now, but "now" is impossible. It has been at least sixty minutes since the caretaker left: thirty each way. Minimum.

Pom tries to comfort my anger, but I feel furious and helpless in my fury. Fury still has no logic. Fury still just *is*, and helplessness doesn't calm it. 3:35, and minutes take forever. How can so much adrenaline and so much energy consume so few seconds? Einstein was right, but proving a scientific theory is no comfort. Most infuriating though, most distressing, is not the stupidity of the action and reaction but its familiarity. It's not the first time I've been here; here just hasn't always been Laos. 3:36. I will arrive late. To look and find nothing. Another lost opportunity.

3:40. The caretaker arrives with two flats of warm, shaken Sprite in his arms. For this I have lost a ride to Vientiane?

The road back is longer and bumpier than I remember. Each attempt at speed rings jolts through the cab, forcing us to slow almost to a stop to regain our stability. 4:00. We are still on the gravel access road. I cannot even see the city from here.

I have lost.

37

To Thailand

Sunday, March 4

4:12

With the jeep still rolling, I jump out and grab my bag from behind the bar counter. The French couple, writing at one of the patio tables, shouts out "Hi." I grunt back an abrupt, breathless return, already walking towards the gate.

"My ride...said...he was...leaving... at 4:00. The only truck... to Vientiane...for two days."

"Good luck," they shout back, but I am already gone.

At the field there is no sign of my ride, and at the three new trucks parked at the east end of the field, no one speaks any English or has any idea what I am talking about. My adrenaline-fuelled sign language means even less today to these drivers than it had to the drivers yesterday. Even their acknowledging nods for Vientiane seem only to accommodate me: one moment a "Yes" offered, the next a "No." Whatever I want.

I have no patience to either explain or accommodate. It is not their fault and I rail against my emotions, but panic and self-derision rail back and the fight is two against one. I know my "thank you" is too harsh, my skin too flush, my eyes too burning. I am just mad at it all, frustrated at them, frustrated at Pom, frustrated at myself. I sit on the grass and look at my pack. There is nothing I can do, no one I can blame, no second choice. It just is. The tyranny of Zen.

A woman from one of the trucks startles me in my stupor with a wicker basket of sticky rice. I thank her and offer a wai, but my anger and defeat isn't hungry. After a few handfuls I return the basket, offering another wai and as reverent a Japanese bow as my Self will allow me.

I look all around, searching the streets, searching the driveways. Somewhere. It must be somewhere. It must be. But it is not. It never is. It is always gone. The looking is the refusal to accept, the denial of the truth because its acceptance is too painful. It is my defence mechanism, my safety net over the madness. What it is designed to achieve it always does. What it desires never comes.

The truck isn't at the Phousie either. No one has seen it, and again I pace the street, looking off towards the post office and down the steep embankment towards the river, my pack back at the bar where it had sat quietly waiting only half an hour ago. Again the nervous twitch, my nails bitten one by one, my hand pushing backwards through my hair. The helpless pose struck against a fence, looking somewhere because I have to look somewhere, I have to do something.

I'll go back to my old room, I think. One more night. The trucks from yesterday are going to Vientiane tomorrow. No. The day after. No. Tomorrow. No. I forget. *Fuck it*. My visa expires tomorrow. I can't wait. *Fuck*. What will I do? *Fuck!* And again I get up and walk, pacing the sidewalk, looking, looking, looking. Again I lean up against the fence. There is nowhere left to look.

The moment is broken by the screech of metal against metal and the scrape of brakes. A pale blue door swings open.

"Where are you?" he shouts.

My truck. My body tingles in relief and I unconsciously check the front of my pants. Grammar mistakes notwithstanding, I can still make it out of Laos by Monday. Tuesday for sure. Monday is still one late, but I can argue the border is closed Sunday. How was I supposed to leave? Tuesday is two days late, and there isn't much to argue about. But both are "out". Both are safe. My contingency plans evaporate before I can even fully codify them. In the sudden success I realize how exhausted this has left me, my adrenaline reserve bankrupted in the worry. He wants to eat first, then go. About an hour. I buy a one kilo bag of peanuts for the trip. Too late do I realize the confused look on the saleslady's face was because the nuts are raw.

There are seven of us in the cab: the driver, his wife, a second younger woman, two boys, myself and a middle-aged man. Seating is by rule of LOWS: Last On Worst Seat, and I am last. My seat is in the middle of the front bench, between the driver and the middle-aged man, the stick shift ball bouncing with each gear change into my left knee, my right leg immobilized by the insistently spacious demands of my neighbour's middle-aged testicles. I will be knock-kneed for most of the trip. What about my testicles? There is no back support. The bench seat has two backs: one for the driver, one for the passenger. I do not belong even in the truck's design. There is however, a worn seat cushion. Life. I'm thinking Kasi tonight, Vientiane in the afternoon tomorrow, and complete physical deformity right now mixed with fleeting thoughts of castration.

The sun is low over the Mekong as we make our way out of the city, and in the tangerine light the broken and patched plaster of Tat Luang's massive asymmetry of greys, spires and domes radiates the colour of uttarāsanga robes. Dwarfed beneath the monastery, the three huddled trucks look desperate and frightened alone in the empty soccer field. Down fleeting, narrow lanes the Mekong appears in staccato bursts of blue and gold and black and silver paisley ripples. Then the clotted-cream pastel of the Vietnamese temple spire, scattering Matisse-like colours in a game of 52-pick-up played with a deck of paint-store sample chips, the nature of the spire reduced in the camouflage of hues to its essence. The now-silent morning market, late in its aftermath without the congestion of sunrise taxis and rickshaws and bicycles and tricycles is reduced to a scattering of soiled cabbage leaves and plastic bags.

Down a treeless street away from the Mekong is the Lao Tourism hotel. Behind a high black gate and thick whitewashed walls, the dusty grey gravel courtyard is empty, the tall hotel institutional white. A protected compound—except, protection for whom? Us from them, or them from us?

Another turn and we are in the hills again. The road is good, the pavement smooth and steady. There is no treachery here, no allusion to terror. Village life scatters the roadside, the reality of the moment hungry farmers and water buffaloes and wooden-wheeled cartloads of grass and straw. The bundles of bamboo dragged behind the smaller children are more protecting in nature than intimidating. These are not bundles of danger. They are bundles of security, of warmth and insulation. A procession of mundanity. Their reality is not the inspiration of fear their mystery was.

The fear was never in the bamboo anyway. The fear was in my mind, manifested out of stories and possibilities and events. The unknown. Were there really events? I doubt my own reality now. There were possibilities. There were stories. Which came first? I slur the vocabulary into a ball and without differentiating create a reality that doesn't exist anywhere else.

Of course guerrilla activity exists. Of course the rumours are a reality. And I wonder how I know, why I say of course?

It becomes a question of correlation, of energy expended versus possibilities entertained. How much do I give what? How plausible does plausible have to be to truly become plausible? How tangible are my fears if I acknowledge it is all conjecture?

Listen: A warm July evening. The town of Saint-Malo, the west coast of France. Bretagne. Early evening. I am alone, walking away from the pensions of *centre-ville* to find a youth hostel marked in my handbook and confirmed by one, small road sign that at that moment seems too many steps ago to still be right. Some of the handbook-listed-hostels no longer exist. Some dates of operation are wrong. Sometimes I don't discover that until I arrive at the locked door and boarded window. In daylight, the errors are more annoying than consequential. In daylight, the unknown is less relevant than in the darkness. In the daylight, I have options. The road follows the edge of a small harbour: perhaps fifteen boats are moored stern first. From the deck of one, a touring houseboat, comes a British "Hello" and an invitation to board. There is a son, a daughter, a wife, and a husband. A perfect British family. The conversation travels from the size of my pack to where we are from and where we have been. They are from southern England. Food and drink appear. Suddenly I am not alone. Serendipity. Early evening slides into twilight and then night. I have not forgotten my uncertain path, and steal glances in the direction I had been walking, following the row of dim lamps that light the harbour-walk and these moored boats. There is an end. Then there are only woods. The sun has disappeared into the trees with disarming quickness. There is only darkness and uncertainty, and I hope, in this exhibition of hospitality, for the offer of a place to sleep. Already in France it has happened twice, the second time just days earlier. Why not again? Then I had been hitch-hiking. My ride had been a single woman in her thirties. She had taken me home. "*Veux-tu de doucher? Te doucher?*" she repeated, miming shower with her free hand the second time, acknowledging the confusion of my rudimentary French that had wondered if "*doucher*" were more inviting in nature than cleansing.

On the boat, the husband announces the end of the evening and of the five of us, only I am not where I belong.

"You really should think about hitching a ride on a houseboat like this," he tells me. "It is very easy. Quite common." He would have offered me a ride, but they are going in the opposite direction. I don't think he knew which way I was going.

That is the problem with optimism. The question is as easily "why again?" The acquaintanceship of holidayers is deceptive.

The unlit path to the hostel is a sudden right-turn into deep, absolute blackness. I feel my way blind, placing my feet in ignorance instead of simply moving and knowing. Sharp, unseen snaps and creaks follow my footsteps, coming from my left and filling the pathway with sound. The day before, three German Shepherds had charged me as I walked along a country road in mid-daylight, a charge stopped only by a high, chain link fence. Then, in instinct I had grabbed for my knife. Then I could see my escape. Then I could see my safety. In daylight I have options. What dogs live in *this* blackness? I search for reassurance and find it again in my small Gerber knife, flicking it open as I walk. Five minutes? Ten minutes? My pupils dilate, and instead of solid darkness there are hints and shapes. And then, ahead, the darkness breaks, my space opens, and I see the hostel. There are no fences holding dogs. There are no sounds. My hand breaks its grip, releases the safety, closes the blade, and slides the knife into its sheath.

In the morning, leaving, I retrace my steps. A soft, sweet dew dampened the earth. Loose clovers and grass stems and flakes of soil stick wet to my shoes, the moisture beading against the leather. The air is cool and fresh with the promise of warmth. Godbeams of sunlight dapple the coffee-coloured path, breaking through leaves and branches, the forest canopy moving in evaporation, fluttering the light on the still earth like reflections on moving water. In a meadow on my right is a small flock of sheep and lambs.

Two paths diverged in a French wood.

Well into darkness, our truck reaches the television village. It is eight o'clock. The driver is picking up sacks of rice for Vientiane. He is already carrying a load of 70MM brass mortar shell casings. Cloistered in darkness, TV-town's narrow unlit streets jut and turn at improbable angles into new unlit streets impossible to see even as we accelerate into them. And then a third street, and Coleman-yellow and semen-white kerosene light seeps through open doors and windows muddying the edges of darkness into a warm, hazy twilight. Neighbours mill about in the heat in tufts of conversation. Children shriek past playing hop-scotch tag, stirring the dry dirt into pillows of cloud, and the bouncing throw of our headlights catches the players through the earthen fog in staccato flashes of movement. Without a moon to illuminate and give depth to the shadows and cut the darkness into sections of brightness and definition, the spilled lamp light creates only a façade of awareness, a suggestion of form without the integrity of substance. It is a tunnel of life.

We stop in front of a two-story warehouse, the gable of the roof jutting above the truck. A double shutter under a gabled peak is thrown open from the inside and a block and tackle lowers sacks of rice to the ground, picked up and ferried to the truck.

The sounds of insects fill the silences between the scruffs and scrapes and grunts of sacks being hoisted up on knees and then shoulders and then over the truck's wooden railing, falling onto the empty brass cylinders, the maraca of settling rice calling and answering like cicadas. Only a fraction into the journey, my back feels disfigured already. We'll never make Kasi tonight. There is a narrow workbench at the edge of the street. It is just wide enough to lie back on and straighten my spine. A clear, northern Laotian night sky. It seems hyper-focused, less absolute in its distance. The tail of a shooting star traces an arc low over the horizon. A million stars. I could touch them if I tried. I could touch this. There is no separation, no me and them, no me and it, no here and there. I am part of the whole. They are part of the landscape. From here, it all seems so obvious.

From the opposite direction comes a murmur of voices, a rumbling. Sounds. I follow them to a blue nylon tarp erected in the centre of the street in a disjointed circle, a TV flickering violet light over a crowd of children sitting mesmerized in the dirt. A corral of television watchers. A "walk-in" drive-in. Entrance is 50 kip, but I'm just passing through.

By 11:30, my Kasi wonder is justified. There is no way. On the up side, even though we are alone on the road, the fear that had choked me on the trip north has refused to reappear. My only interest is to stay comfortable within the awkwardness that passes as my seat. At fifteen minutes past midnight, we make the dead-rat village, rolling to a stop in front of the coffee hut.

The silence in the cab is deafening. Absolute stillness, absolute quiet. Thick. Heavy. Vacuum-like. It sits like black tomato soup, slowing movement and stopping time. Like swimming in ice cream. Not even the bark of a dog intrudes upon it. The deafening din of the cab never annoyed because there was no alternative. It was not intrusive. I was never even aware of it. It just was. In the travelling disturbance that we are, I forget the silence and peacefulness that surrounds our bubble.

The five men will stay in the coffee hut. The two women go to another hut on the opposite side of the village circle. On a straw mat there is a small dirty pillow and two heavy quilts that feel damp and smell of mould. I wonder about bedbugs or lice. A

Canadian friend in Nagoya got lice while trekking in Nepal before coming to Japan. In Nagoya, Japanese doctors carefully explained to her that in Japan lice did not exist. Since they had no problem, they had no cure. There was nothing they could do. Then they bowed. Ethnocentrism does not negate politeness. She slept in a bathing cap for six months. The Japanese at least appreciate dry hair. Try explaining that to a one-night stand. *Where did you ever get a condom that big,* and *isn't it supposed to go on my head?* I got lice at the youth hostel in downtown Toronto. The disinfectant soap I bought worked better on the label than on my body. I don't look good in rubber and while shaving ultimately proved to be the best solution, contrary to Gillette's insistence, smooth down there is not the "best a man can get."

I am too cold and tired to really care. It is a passing concern, a fancy, not a threat. Fully clothed I crawl under the coverings, and still wondering, fall asleep.

38
To Thailand

S ix A.M., and there is already a fire in place biting into the chill. The cold moisture of the night weighs the room down, the covers warm and comforting but claustrophobic in their weight. It feels more like a winter coming than one going. I need a piss. At the edge of the village, a small mound of dirt next to a tree looks out over the valley below. A cotton mist robs the surrounding hilltops of their dimensions and in the deception they assume illusions that tower. The fog catches the sun and diffuses it. A young girl hurries by bouncing empty cooking-oil tins across her shoulders. A rooster crows, then another, then a dog barks. Hut roofs steam through the haze, breakfast burning off the night's dampness.

"Coffee," the driver shouts, but even the mention of the sweet pungence is too much for this morning. This morning is not about differences. I don't feel like Laos today. This moment, this place, these mountains, feel like familiarity. I want reassurance. I am hungry. I want what I know. Floury pancakes and bitter coffee and sweet syrup. "Coffee," he shouts again. He squats beside the fire, hands extended, catching its warmth before it can escape into the roof. My drink is already poured, on the end of the table. It is warm around my hands. Breakfast is sticky rice, but I refuse. I don't have enough kip.

Today I am out of the cab, riding on a rooftop of rice sacks on shell casings. The bed of the truck is filled, the sacks reaching to the edge of the side wood railings. Either the other driver was wrong, or conservative, or all the guerrillas have been killed, or this guy just doesn't like me. The "roof" isn't even a question. He just waved. It occurs to me that that job in Revelstoke was clearing a mountain-side of unexploded mortar shells for a to-be-built snow shed. All we ever found was shrapnel. Life really is circular. There are two of us on the rice-sack roof: the remaining young man and me. We lost one of the boys last night at the TV village, so now with the two of us elevated upwards, the cab is a free-and-easy four instead of seven. The roof is open and alive and surrounded by landscape and sky and air and room. Room enough for even the largest testicles. Watermelonless, we head off. Just the two of us.

Familiarity returns quickly. Villages recognizable from last week are approached, passed through and left behind in instants that last week seemed hours. Mysterious five days ago, they lie condemned now as merely part of the drive back.

The landscape is devastated, orphaned trees and logger-mal-practiced stumps the only suggestion of a forested past. Who is responsible? Does anybody know? Does anybody care? Laos is the capital of Nigeria, right?

Thailand's deforestation is internationally famous. Indigenous recognition of the industry's zealotry however has come only recently, in the wake of devastating floods previously uncom-mon. To right the wrong that for so long was only smart business, Thailand's government introduced a moratorium on logging. Weekly however, the *Nation* and the *Bangkok Post* fill with details of new logging scandals and new illegally logged forests, with only innuendo and knowing eyebrows offered, accusations hidden in a subtlety that acknowledges a military government, a history of political coups, regional instability and entrenched cronyism.

In response to the moratorium, legal Thai log merchants sim-ply began to import the teak forests of Burma.

In another two hours we reach the dead village. In five days everything has changed. The carcass is gone. I anticipate the stench, for my nostrils to fill in its bloated foulness, but the stench never comes and instead, without warning we are at the skins. Only half remain.

The truck skeletons are gone. Not a remnant, not an over-looked bolt or fender. The charred wood is gone too, cleansed with bagfuls of charred grain. There is no smoke, there is no smell. It is a slate wiped clean, the ghosts exorcised, packed up and gone home. No questions. No answers. No history. No problem. We speed through the cleansing unobstructed. On the hilltop above the road is a single wooden hut I don't remember seeing before. Had it really been there on the trip up? I doubt my own memory—Maybe this *isn't* the right village. Maybe it's still coming?—but that is after all, the whole point of cleansing and history manipulation, and so in my doubt, the village never was. It had never been there, the carcass had never been there, the skins had never been there, the piles of grain taken away had never existed and the guard hut had always been there. Orwell was right.

And then we are gone, dipping below the ex-village. Even we no longer exist. I trace the road across the valley with my eyes as it descends the facing ridge into the valley towards Kasi, as I did the week earlier searching for the second in our convoy. Soon we will be dipping behind tree cover, for periods longer than another anonymous observer might think we should. An armed guard rides with us to the bottom of the mountain. Where did he come from? When did he get on? Was he always with us? And I don't remember. Wasn't it always like this?

Two o'clock. At last Vanthong's. From the north, he is the start of Kasi. From the north he is the signal to safety. Beyond Vanthong's everything is known, everything is safe. Last week, he was the end. Last week he was fear. Beyond Vanthong nothing was known and everything was suspect. Does nothing change but perspective? My heart pounds in familiarity and success. This is home. I feel drugged in anticipation and relief. I want to jump down and embrace it all. Except Vanthong is not here.

We are eight hours from Vientiane: fewer in fact, since we will gain the time the northbound bus lost picking up passengers. Perhaps I will have my dinner after all. That's all I crave now. Vientiane and a last night to seal this journey: a steak at the Santiouk, cake and coffee downtown and a cold beer at the Ekalath. To bask in the satisfaction of success, in my belief in myself. The lesson of the Savanakhét cravings didn't sink deep.

I tell the driver I will need to stop at Vangviang to get something

I left in the guesthouse. I am embarrassed to say the something is nail clippers, but he seems satisfied to leave it at something and nods.

Will Chantravong have the clippers? Will the bus driver be there? I work the bus schedule backwards in my mind, but it is lost in the permutations of dates and scenarios I have been carrying. Today is Monday. I know that much. My visa expired yesterday. I know that much. More than that my brain can't handle right now. Anyway, whether the bus is there or not doesn't matter. The driver could have, like Chantravong said, returned the clippers on the next trip. As equally, perhaps they are just gone.

I feel foolish and embarrassed for my anger at Chantravong. It was a misunderstanding that was no one's fault. I shouldn't have vented my frustration over the situation towards him. The circumstance of my life, repeated over and over. Incident. Anger. Reaction. Regret. Remorse. Repentance. Incident. Nothing has changed. In spite of Vipassana and Suan Mokkh and Tokugenji, in spite of all the reading, in spite of all the reflections. Nothing has changed. My journal entries and confessional letters to friends and lovers written in self-sacrifice to the God of self-knowledge in the guise of correspondence wasted. Nothing has changed.

I know how I *should* act. I have even found the wisdom to see how I do, regardless of should. It is all intellectualization. All an understanding of Self that, combined with a miniscule Pali vocabulary, wins me admiration over coffee at the Hello Guesthouse on Khao San Road from the spiritually naïve and the enlightenment-seeking voyeurs that flock to the inhalation of the self-sacrificing mendicant-wannabes like the vultures of Varanasi waiting for the corpses to cool. When I look in the mirror, I know that the wisdom and compassion and understanding and answers I have searched so exhaustingly for still elude me. The hip bone's connected to the leg bone, the leg bone's connected to the Self bone.

The pattern repeats. The river laughs and I laugh too, but I laugh to elude it and it laughs at me. Perhaps the patterns have dulled over time, their frequency of repetition reduced, their severity softened. Perhaps this is all I can ask for. But I don't think so. As equally, perhaps I just don't want to know. In their occurrence my reactions seem justified, the logically reasonable rebuttal to the self-observed self-righteousness of self. After the fact, they are simply painful, the memory of the ends eclipsing those of the rationalized "means". More or less, it seems the same to me. I should apologize to Chantravong. I will. No more shoulds.

Just out of Kasi we slow to pick up a new traveller waiting on the roadside. We have already picked up a few men travellers along the way, but only for short rides: this rice-sack roof experience is nothing like the roof experience of the lot doi san. As soon as we reached Kasi we became peripheral to the transport network. From Kasi to Vientiane, it is safe. Travellers don't *need* transport trucks. They don't *need* us. People waiting now are only going a short way. There are no seats inside the cab, no conductor. It is roof travel and the driver's discretion.

Over the side wooden railing a small Lisu woman struggles, a baby strapped papoose-style across her back in a soiled black cotton sling. While she is still struggling to hold her balance and find a place among the rice sacks and us, there is a slap on the cab roof and we jolt back into motion. There is no offer of help, no voice to temper the truck's urgency. The male banter that in clusters had filled the roof is swallowed, the male eyes that looked everywhere and nowhere now awkward and shifty, confined to their male neighbour or the sky. I steal glances at her, as much to see this Lisu woman so close as to wonder why she is up here and not inside. I feel invasive and shifty and let her go. Halfway to Vangviang, when we are waved over by four soldiers, I steal another glance and she has already slipped away.

The soldiers are in black-and-olive camouflage pants, rubber thongs, black muscle shirts and brown, hard muscles. They find a place for themselves and their weapons against the railing, settle, and my roof buddy slaps the cab roof. All over again I am worried about being here. A ride to Vientiane secured and my now-expired visa out of my control, I am back to caring about the trivial. I hear the soldiers say *Soviet* and my roof buddy reply *Canada*. One of the soldiers offers me a cigarette. I hesitate my no, splitting a second to weigh the pros and cons and force a choice that should be obvious. It is no problem. My deliberation is his nonchalance.

In less time than my decision to indecisiveness, he has decided for me and his attention is back to his friends. Again I give philosophy where only reflex is required. No wonder I wallow lost in insistent questions. I wouldn't last a day in a war.

Vangviang village is longer than I remember. All my landmarks are backwards. I wonder if I will even recognize the guesthouse when I find it, if this even is Vangviang. Everything is turned around, everything less familiar than the memory I thought so entrenched. Maybe the dead village really did never exist.

"Vangviang," my roof buddy says, but I repeat it back out loud to make sure, and he repeats it to me. "Vangviang." I nod my head. I'm still not sure.

The driver stops in front of a food stall. "Guesthouse," he points. In the sun, the guesthouse is much less impressive than I recall. Were there always this many people on the road? Was there always this much commotion?

At the front door I call out but there is no answer. That Chantravong might not be here never occurred to me. On the wall at the back is taped a slip of white paper. A note I hope, foolishly thinking me and my clippers command some place in Chantravong's existence.

I'm right. It is foolishness. The note is Andy and Laura's tour recommendation. The restaurant description has been carefully folded over and taped hidden out of sight.

Chantravong's stumbling restaurant-ignorance a week ago makes sense. I had been right. I feel abused all over again. The burden of responsibility removed with each departing bus, by chance he has been exposed. I wonder now about the reference. How many times did he suggest the note before Andy and Laura volunteered it? I feel betrayed for them too. I fold out the restaurant recommendation and reattach the note to the wall.

At the food stall a fat woman tells me that Chantravong is at home, but the people recognize me and motion with a squeezing action. I am "Clipperman". Someone goes to get him while I paint a C in the middle of my shirt and put my underwear overtop my pants.

Chantravong appears on his bicycle. Out of his front pants pocket he pulls the clippers, wrapped in a yellow tissue and cellotape. Others from next door and across the street stop to watch.

"The bus driver brought them back the next trip. They are okay?"

He apologizes for my having to come back, and I thank him for his efforts. They are fine. Then we do it all over again. "Four hundred baht," I hear him tell the onlookers that have started to mill about. I told him four hundred baht to impress my anger upon him. In their recovery, it is again their cost that makes the impression. The illusion of importance becomes dollar credible. I was right. I feel ashamed.

We smile and shake hands and laugh, but it feels faked and artificial. A sales call. A business transaction. He is not doing me a favour. He is clearing his good name. "Helpful" Chantravong. "Good-for-business" Chantravong. I wonder how he describes the incident in my absence. I should apologize to Chantravong. My promise to myself. I should apologize. I should. I say nothing.

In the falling dusk a few kilometres outside Vangviang, the road crosses a shallow stream into a small village. "Bath time!" the driver shouts, and the four in the cab head off towards water: women to the left, men to the right.

In the younger of the two women in the cab there is a quiet, undeniable sensuality. The boy-voyeur in me wants to look, to follow her with his eyes, her femininity draped about her and nat-ural: an exposed shoulder, a calf glistening in the beads of fresh water, the roundness of her hips clinging wet to the fabric, the lines oblique and suggestive. Like a crescent moon over Kasi. A hint of more, but no more comes. The essence of the body rather than its stark wholeness. Sensual Zen.

I watch her walk towards the edge of the water, but even in acknowledging my desires, I feel violating and sheepish. I look away, but my pointed non-looking feels contrived and uncom-fortable. Instead I look around at everything, a look that suggests nothing and violates no one. It is a lost cause, a singing in the wind. I can see my caricature and it is unbecoming. I lie back into the rice sacks and look at the clouds.

My roof buddy picks up my camera and turns it around and over, trying to open the case.

"Here," I point, and I gesture how to hold it, how to focus. Immediately he waves it around the horizon looking: the mundane framed in isolation and seen suddenly for the first time. He points the camera at me and trips the shutter with as much curiosity as design. Tilted out of sorts, the horizon forgotten in the vision, it is not the image he desires but the joy.

Immediately he turns for the two women bathing and takes a picture. Two brown women in wet sarongs, Gauguin-like too. With a shout he tells them and they shout a reply, and it is done. With no intrusion intended, there is none taken. *Look! I've got a camera!* With a smile full of teeth he hands it back. He is happy.

Just a boy, he is captivated by boyish delights that are excusable and achievable through his youth and innocence.

That is my problem. In too many ways I am still a boy trapped inside a man's body, unable to indulge the whim and forget, unable to move on and let go of the unfulfilled remnants of my childhood.

It is perhaps the curse of being the only child, of the anomalous upbringing that only children face. At least it is the curse of being this only child. I was always in the company of adults, expected to learn the subtleties of grown-ups, rushed into a pre-maturity while siblinged friends were busy in basements or bedrooms or backyards playing games and screaming in the depravity of companionship.

By high school, the maturation process had reversed. Denied the skills of pre-interaction with my now adolescent peers, I stumbled awkward and defenceless among the hormonally elevated mass of my chronological equals, avoiding through a proven and reinforceable ineptitude conversations with the girls I would have plotted and succeeded in kissing in grade two, justifiably excluded from the high school-group of "cool" and the group of "in" because I had never known how just to be a child and then just a teenager and I didn't fit "in" and I wasn't "cool".

Relationships and events and maturation passed me by. Things natural, things accepted and expected from adolescence I hid, self-conscious as the attention centre of both myself and parental-pride, my skin burned crimson under the spotlight so expectantly trained on me, with no sibling to deflect its glare onto and away.

Inside I went, protected from the scrutiny of others until introversion became my battle cry and the seeds of struggles now fought took hold. At thirty-one, I fly between the knowledge of adulthood and the desires of childhood, feeling regardless of my choice, deprived.

To look or not to look? To satisfy the unfulfilled urges of irresponsible youth, or to let go into adulthood and risk again feeling as though "the right thing" has let a little piece of life pass me by?

There is a Sufi story in Idres Shaw's *Thinkers of the East*, the parable of the "Ceremony of Gifts": There is a ceremony of honour for the Master. All attending bring gifts. Some gifts are offered without names, some with names attached. The gifts with names, the Master returns, telling his followers that "These [gifts] represent the lower conduct, the conduct taught to children. It is done to teach the pleasure of giving and receiving. It is preparation for adulthood." The unnamed gifts the Master accepts. "These [gifts] represent the higher conduct, the conduct of giving without attaching obligation. Whoever continues to take his refreshment from the lesser will not rise. You cannot receive payment in satisfaction on the lower level as well."

I stand in front of the Master, a nameless gift in my right hand, an empty eager nametag in my left.

And then it is over. The driver shakes his head, smothering his hair in a powder blue towel. Behind us, the eastern clouds have turned a deep charcoal with fiery, burning edges, the riverbank dull and brown, the individuality of the grass and reeds lost in the reflection of the sky.

This is comfortable. There is no fear. There is no danger. Nothing new that I feel obliged to observe, nothing left that demands accomplishment. Old and familiar and welcoming. This is coming home.

The struggle to get around Laos has been hard, my body and mind exhausted in the effort.

Relax.

Feel the breeze. Smell the land. Touch the air. There is no more worry. There are no more decisions. Everything to Thailand has been determined. Some would just say "everything". There are no choices, no alternatives. No needs.

Relax.

To our backs it is growing darker, the karsts of Vangviang muddied and ill-defined, the road ahead slowly disappearing, indistinguishable from the ditches and the fields and the landscape.

My roof buddy can't speak a word of English. Together we have sat on the roof now for almost twelve hours, never more than five feet between us, our destinies lifetimes apart, our current realities mutually dependent and determined. An entire day together in a common goal whose achievement is out of our control, communicating only through unintelligible mumbles, hand signals, smiles and laughter. The bond of the roof is unshakable despite its improbability.

He is slim, with dark, deep-set eyes, a small puggish nose, high round cheekbones and a pockish, acned complexion. He is young: maybe in his early 20s.

I don't even know his name, where he is from, where he is going or why. Those are the first questions addressed with another Westerner. He knows I am from Canada, but I wonder what Canada means to him except "far away," and I suspect that "far away" is how he describes the journey between Louangphrabang and Vientiane. What does he think of me?

What does he see when he looks at me? I spend my time looking out on the world around me and in on the world that is me. Does he do the same? In the differences I compare and contrast and judge: *he is like this, he isn't like that; I'm like this, I'm not like that.* Yet most obviously, when others look out at their surroundings, it is me that generates the comparisons, the contrasts, the judgments. What am I "not like"?

What does he see when he looks at me? Do I meet his concept of Westerner? Am I just another rider, the differentiation of "Lao" and "Westerner" long since forgotten? Or was it even considered? Perhaps there have been others? What stereotypes have they left for the unsuspecting followers to fulfil and overcome?

I never know what others think of me. Not really. I guess, I create assumptions; self-assurances that this person likes me, this person loves me, this person respects me, this person hates me. The reality is I never really know. If they were honest, I wonder if they could ever admit to knowing either? How much of my impression do I control? How much is in response to what I give or don't give? How much is what I want to believe and how much what I don't want to believe. Even the truth is dichotomous: this is mine, that is theirs.

Of support, we get friendship; of friendship, we get support; of love, we get love? But if another's response to me is determined by my response to them, where is the validity behind those emotions that are expressed towards me? Are they genuine or merely reflexive, determined through some complex weighting and not simply "felt"?

Do I love because I really love, or do I love because I am loved? Or do I love because I want to love, or is my love simply a response to physical gratification? Do I love because the sex is good?

Would my roof buddy like me more if I smoked? If I could offer him a cigarette?

I feel embarrassed having stopped the truck to retrieve my nail clippers. Nail clippers. They are not very substantial, and they certainly aren't very rugged. They were mine, they served a purpose and I wanted them back. Fair enough. When he looks at them, what does he see?

He overheard Chantravong gloating the four hundred baht cost. That represents almost five trips between Vientiane and Louangphrabang, assuming 4500 kip is the real and not the tourist rate. Five trips, wrapped up in a little yellow tissue for cutting my nails. Then there is my camera, my Walkman, my backpack. He has a small plastic Adidas gym bag and a thin vinyl windbreaker. Both are held together with safety pins.

The Talàat Sao in Vientiane is full of Walkmans and radios and appliances. He must know their kip equivalent, as well as their status. How does he see me? Does he even care about any of this?

At 7:00 P.M. we re-enter the leapfrog village. From inarticulate shadows and outlines, rigid yellow and orange beams cut into the street from windows and ajar doors and gaps of construction. The yellow light concentrates the moment, demanding attention, offering in its precision the promise of comfort and warmth and home.

The street is a flurry of activity, as mostly adolescent girls busy themselves with tins of water, piles of vegetables, firewood and the business of rounding up younger siblings. Ahead in the blur of fading distinction, others play to maintain the village's identity, leapfrogging in the purple road, dogs barking and yapping around their jittery, shrieking movements.

The atmosphere is the offspring of Phil Spector and Julia Child: "a wall of smell," a confusion of many intermingled into one: a distinctive, marbled, layered wall of odour, a bouquet of interdependency. It is the smell of settling fresh dew on raw earth, of smoky thatch roofs and the scent of dried hay stalks, of cooking fires and the thick aroma of frying oil and chilli peppers and soup stock. It is the sweet and pungent smell of Southeast Asian hills. The fragrance of the village fills me as I breathe it in and so it becomes me and I am this Southeast Asian village.

The driver orders us a large plate of food and a tureen of soup, a decision reached communally by the other five, myself relieved at the language barrier to let someone else decide my meal.

Tacked to the wall is a 24x36 glossy pin-up poster of Momoko, an unknown, interchangeable Japanese pop idol. The poster is pink in colour and sexual leaning towards paedophilic in sublimation. In Japan, "pink" clubs are feel bars and hand-job joints, a barker standing in front of the flashing lights and pink neon enticing friend and foe alike to enjoy the night with a not-so-subtle jerking motion made with his fist. What is the point of learning the Japanese phrase for hand-job when some things just lend themselves to physical comedy? Momoko's pubescent cuteness is glamorized with the culturally demanded frosting of make-up and the ridiculous fashion of Japanese schoolgirl innocence.

Why be a woman when you get so much more attention being a little girl? The culture is mad over surreptitious toilet viewing too, although it seems more restricted to paper publications than in-person clubs. Talk about a wet bar. To Japan's unending credit though, I never once walked past a "yellow" club. Or maybe it was just my inobservance. When your mind is set on a Denny's BLT, there is much that can pass you by. Momoko's smile is immature and forced, an ill-aligned incisor protruding proud and angular through cherry lips the proof of her beauty. She might as well be from outer space for her relevance to life here. And I can't imagine wanting a hand-job from her.

The restaurant owner is trying to hook up a television antenna. In bursts of snowy reception he is successful, his success met with shrieks of delight and pushes of anticipation by the children already sitting in front of the set. The owner is unable to maintain the TV connection, and the children scatter back to their puzzles and games and toys. To much renewed boredom, the set becomes operational, and in its initiation rite, is forced to show a Hong Kong Kung-Fu movie, the cloud of shouts and grunts turned as loud and obvious as possible.

The driver pays for us all. He paid for us last night as well. And for lunch in Vangviang. Now dinner. For everyone. I offer him some kip. I changed 100 baht with Vanthong's wife. He insists.

It is dark now. Cool as well. There is no way we will make Vientiane for dinner tonight, but a coffee and cake are still possible. We've been on the truck for twelve hours.

39

To Thailand

Side-by-side the two of us sit in the centre of the roof, falling back against the sacks of rice like astronauts in lift-off. There is nothing imploring me to see, nothing imploring me to look, nothing imploring me to be. Only the stars, shadowy wisps of horsetail clouds teasing below them like lingerie across a pale breast. Only myself.

To lie back is physically uncomfortable. Emotionally it demands submission, the acceptance of lost participation. It is easier to sit up and support myself. The road is good and we drive quickly, shooting a numbing wind over the cab straight into our faces. My buddy pulls out a wool blanket tucked under some rice sacks and covers himself up.

He gestures me to get under but I'm not that cold. It is good to feel the wind and chill slicing through my shirt collar, the pounding numbness on my forehead. I don't want to rob myself of it by retreating. In the dark, I am freer than ever. The one-way mirror has faded with the daylight. It is not mine to control it seems, only mine to accept when offered.

In the blackness I dig for my Walkman, stumbling blindly with my fingers searching for the headphones and volume. Chris Rea. *On The Beach.* Barely audible through the wind and engine rumble. I turn it up full, but it distorts to the clarity of plucked rubber bands. Dying batteries. The music says Koh Samui to me. It says Cassie, that I wasn't always alone. He is her favourite, from a time in her life when she needed a favourite to protect herself.

Against all odds it found us in the market in Nanton amongst the bootlegged Cream and Doors and Eagles. We played it over and over and over, lying beside each other in the warmth, and I allowed myself to think of the walls he sang of as hers, and our love as freeing. We lay there stealing the sun, turning our skin first the colour of young teak, then tea, then nut-brown, diving into the turquoise water, stripping off in secret our bathing suits, swimming innocent and pure in the amniotic water. In the heat of the afternoon we would retreat, first into vodkas and then the bungalow and then each other until we were one and there was no other. The intro to *Fool If You Think It's Over* is missing 13 seconds, erased Nixonally by Cassie. She pushed the record button by mistake. Every time I play it now I hear her fumbling fingers and her breathing and feel the sunshine and think I have captured her and that forever she will be there. Over and over. Each time she pushes the wrong button. Each time I hear her. Each time I have captured her. I want to go back. I shut the music off.

Numbing wind and longing is not Koh Samui.

The obsidian night sky goes on forever, the stars burning silver through the sky unresisted, and in the distance, low on the horizon, a treeline we never seem to pass. The stars never break the sky, never shift the blackness into shadow. It is always just the road and the truck; the truck and the road. The blacker delineation of trees. The Vancouver sky in my youth never went on forever. It was always broken by mountains, by buildings, by hesitation. There was always an end, always a boundary. Japanese visitors to Vancouver marvel at the sky. It is *so* large they say. Perspective, perspective, perspective.

I pull the blanket up over my legs and waist. Sharing this space with my roof buddy suddenly feels too much close, too much sensual. Like sharing a bed with someone for the sake of sleep rather than love, I am unable to dissociate the emotional from the practical, the ill-at-ease from the accepting.

Is this something intrinsically me or something I've learned? A by-product of society or birth? Whose society anyway? I create my own reality, regardless of the environment, don't I? And inside, I know I must, that if I couldn't what would the point of it all be? What is it about Asian culture that allows for a physical closeness between men to exist and not have society call into question that man's integrity or sexuality? What is it about mine that doesn't? Where did I learn to think like this? Have I just been too closed off to see the possibilities? Why do I associate integrity with sexuality? Which is it I'm afraid of? Am I really so far removed from Louangphrabang?

For Chaatra every Nepali woman was his sister, every Nepali man his brother, and touching and holding were so commonplace as to go unnoticed: as much the measure of his existence as drinking, playing cards and the holding on to our past was Paul's and mine. In Japan communal bathing is the norm, the public *cento* as much a place of community as bathing. Or at least it once was. Perhaps that is the answer. Community. The bathing re-enforces the group, the bonding not individual but societal. In the West, in my West, under the cherished banner of individuality, the bonding is one-on-one. Possessive. One individual washing another in mutual and exclusive bonding. The sauna I shared at "Let's Sports" with my colleague Martin in Nagoya, I shared with a friend, not a co-worker. It is all too close to Cassie pouring water over me in Ayutthaya.

Too much of *my* culture can't touch or embrace or share without being left awkward and self-conscious in the exchange. Yet to hug a friend, to be held myself, is simply to express the respect and friendship and love that is the sustenance of the relationship, regardless of the overt acknowledgment. It is absurd that I should experience hesitation now, alone here on this truck, in this darkness, my peer group so singular, so far into this shared journey, so far into this journey that has held up life to me and forced me to acknowledge in it my successes and failures.

I can take no more of the cold and slide underneath the blanket, pulling it tight around my shoulders and neck. The blanket is not built for two who are separate but rather for two that think as one, and together we have to snuggle to keep the edges tucked away and deflect the wind over instead of into the blanket.

The warmth is immediate: a good warmth. So is the rejection of the distance and the acceptance of the closeness; the fulfilled longing for physical touch I didn't even know I had. He is warm beside me, his side and leg pressed close against mine, our shoulders freely mobile against each other's. A silent bonding between us that I wonder if he even considers.

The stars are brilliant. There is not a single compromise to the night, no distant lights, no city glow, no smell of pollution. Brilliance on absolute. I am living out a dream and in its realization it is even better than in its conception. I am in Laos, alone but for the circus of memories I insist on entertaining, riding through the night on the top of a transport truck, the wind swirling.

There were times in my life I never thought I would achieve my dreams, times when I couldn't even articulate that I had dreams. There are still times when I think I will never achieve those dreams, when I am still ashamed to articulate them. They were innate, sometimes inane desires and emotions I miscommunicated to friends and family through ill-defined, vague ideas and situations, too often characterized more by non-committal stammerings and romantic Hollywood depictions than by concrete descriptions of the idealized moments inside my head.

Here I am living one and I still don't know how I'll describe it to others when I get home. I can describe the events. I can describe the places. And the question isn't whether I can describe them. The question is who will hear the descriptions? I understand these idealized moments now. They are moments of Self, of a oneness of body and spirit and time. The images of mind dictate locality, adventure, events. They are the crucible, not the catalyst. It was me I longed for in those vague descriptions: a me as ill-defined as the dreams.

Sometimes I wonder what the point is, trying to describe to friends at home experiences that have confronted and seduced me into who I am, trying to describe experiences that those same friends, consumed in their own existence and their own search to articulate their own dreams, are incapable of understanding because understanding requires dreams and desires and knowledge and history that is not theirs. Empathy and knowledge are not the same.

If they were here right now, would they experience what I

experience and understand any better the emotions and revelations that move me? And intellectually I understand no. They would be aware of their own moments, and caught up in that discovery they could understand only those realities of mine that intersected with theirs, at the oscilloscopic cross-overs that bond in recurring familiarity friendships and loves and mutual appreciations without either compromising or exposing the core of the individual.

My friend has fallen asleep: his head tilts towards my shoulder, eyes closed, mouth fallen ajar in the wind. I can hear him breathing through his nose, reacting to the bumps that shake his calm. I feel a warmth that cannot be explained away as simply the sharing of body heat. It is an embrace of partnership. Is this how brothers feel? Lovers?

I cry out for a closeness beyond mere proximity and find it infrequent. And in that infrequency, there comes a self-consciousness and an eagerness to gratification that devours the tenderness in a suffocating embrace of desire. Human touch, human tenderness. To play with the emotions of life in full rather than in the piecemeal offerings I learned to accept as an adolescent. Curled half-foetal, his legs and shoulders press without suggestion against mine, still warm, still comforting.

There are red lights ahead. Vientiane? I am excited at the closeness, excited at being back. But the lights never grow and the city I anticipate never breaks the horizon illuminating the sky. Neither do the lights seem to pass by: They are just there, a constant hovering in the night sky, insistent.

I recognize another village. We are a long way from Vientiane.

The village is the start of a massive road construction, and the road bursts into four steam-rolled lanes of red soil. Monstrous Caterpillars and dump trucks sit motionless, illuminated under yellow compound lights. There is no evidence of paving. Without blacktop, the smoothness will be gone in weeks: days if there is a rain. I wonder the point.

At 10:30 the driver makes a bathroom stop and my buddy retreats into the cab. I am alone now, huddled against the wind under the blanket. The lights in the distance have crystallized into enormous hydro pylons, stark in the landscape against the cast of the moon. I am sure they signal Vientiane, sure they mean it is a matter of minutes instead of hours, but still we pass them by, still their images disappear into the blackness until in the distance the faintness of new red beacons appears and grows brighter and on the horizon more pylons appear.

There is no possibility now for coffee and cake or even a beer. Vientiane rolls up its sidewalks at 10:00. I even wonder if the guesthouse will be open. There is nothing I can do, and with the possibility of a night gone, I lose my anxiety over time and fall into sleep.

It is warm. Too warm. Everything is Halloween-sucker green. The whining tires tell me we are on pavement. My mouth is gluey. Huge amber tree trunks line the road, surreal against the Lime Rickey sky. I feel tied down, my addled brain trying to fight lethargy and having no weapons. Vientiane. 11:30 P.M. We are alone on the street, the rumble of the truck replaced with a whirr.

And cicadas.

In the trees lining the street, high above the blacktop. Near my ears. A clicking hum that races in madness towards ecstasy. My body is languid, as though my muscles have been disconnected from my skeleton. It is too hot under the blanket, too sticky, too condensed. My eyelids have been anaesthetized. The truck rocks in sympathy with the pavement and my body rocks in sympathy with the truck. Anything to recapture sleep. I throw off the blanket. There are no familiar landmarks. There is no one. Far into the distance the road, the lights, the emptiness.

Cicadas.

A hum of electrical current rising and falling, falling and rising. A hum of rubber, pulling.

We enter a flood-lit compound. A junkyard. Still. Quiet. The cab doors creak open, followed by voices and two metallic slams. The air is stagnant, the cicadas reverberating across the compound. The stars are gone, hidden behind the Ray Bradbury sky.

A smothering sky. I sit up and try to focus, but my eyes refuse. The driver shouts something up to me. I respond unintelligibly, understanding neither the question nor the answer. More voices. I fall back against the sacks of rice and the shell casings.

The cicadas whir, the pitch rising like a motorcycle straining to shift gears. Crescendo. Ecstasy. Climax. They fall away into silence. Asleep.

40

To Thailand

The passing *psssht* of air brakes breaks the silence and I open my eyes to a cloudless robin's egg sky tinged with gold. I feel alone. Seven A.M. From the top of the truck, lying on my back, there is no one and nothing. Only me, only the sky. The junk-yard is silent, the road quiet. No one else is up. I *am* alone. Not empty alone: complete alone. As a child, my best days were the days I awoke before my parents. I was alone and the world was mine, unwatched and unjudged and full of potential that required no explanation. There was no better hour, and regardless of its content, it always ended too soon. Like those childhood-summer days in Vancouver, I thought these too would come often. Here, now, I am enough. Now and then. I am, and I was. The sacks fit my back. My back fits the sacks. I am comfortable. And clammy. Like stew simmered too long.

7:09 A.M. It is already too hot.

I need to pee. The searching for a tree and angle that will hide me from the road is futile. Every angle leaves something exposed, something facing someone. In the shade it's cool. The sun streaks through the trees, leaving the edge of the compound mottled in shade. The two women appear from the rear of the compound, awkward, running their hands through their hair, straightening themselves. The driver and my buddy from the roof are up too, crouched together in the dewless soil examining the front driver's side wheel. Now I get it. Roof buddy works with the driver. That's why he knew about the blanket. Was everybody awake but me?

Do I want a ride into town? I look towards my roof friend to say good-bye, but he returns no eye contact, and the driver is in a hurry. I give him the 2500 kip and follow him to the road anticipating a taxi, but instead it is the first transport truck by he waves over. We shake hands and his grip is warm and firm. I search for a last glance at the woman but I can't find her. Life. "See you next time," he says. The door scrapes shut. *Yeah. Next time.* And I am gone.

The morning commute is sprinkled with trucks, taxis, sāam láw tricycles, tuk-tuks and bicycles. A food vendor pushes his food cart along the shoulder, the stainless steel gleaming in the sun. We pass the airport and then the Soviet Hotel, even in this morning light grey and depressing. Then Wat Bang Long, the Vietnamese temple. A right turn past the cake shop, around a second corner and the driver pulls over.

Instinct tells me right. This isn't Louangphrabang.

The lane is lined with cafés and bakeries. I had only walked this road at night, and in the uninviting green fluorescent light these concrete boxes had looked depressing and sterile. In this amber, awakening light they are full, the front façade a window thrown open to the fresh air, couched in the murmur of voices and the shuffle of feet as baguettes are served and coffee glasses refilled in an inviting waft that says morning. The street breathes with the scent of warm bread and strong coffee. It hangs in the road seductively, a meandering advertisement to life. It has worked.

A black Nissan taxi pulls up across the street, stopping in front of one of the cafés. From out of the back door two ladies of the morning emerge, smelling of Lilly musk and dressed in black stiletto heels and black seamed stockings. A quick word through the window to the driver and they vanish through a doorless passageway next to a patisserie. The Nissan pulls away. The moment is over.

I miss the morning ritual, the pre-work camaraderie, the passages of civility. I witness it travelling, but it is a ritual denied. The essence of the mirror and the demands of a traveller create no place of belonging, no place of identity. The basic prerequisites of the rite are lost: there is no job to complain about, no friends to nurture, no sense of play and work. Rather it is me they watch as the anomaly to their existence, the stranger looked at through the security of their mirror. The traveller is always going somewhere else, the self captive in the demands of travel that negate the routine and promote the surprise. Today I have nowhere to go, and in this gentle re-injection into the city, I envy their belonging and security and feel out of place and weary slouched and determined under the weight of my pack.

The Sailom is just waking up when I get there, two elder women the only ones in the dining room. After an Abbott and Costello exchange of "sabadee" and "good morning," one asks if I want a room, already turning towards the reception counter. I explain no, that I want to leave my bag here while I go next door for coffee.

"You go Nong Khai? You leave bag here now? How long?" and she looks at me like she's seen this movie before and didn't like the ending. I explain my visa situation. Again. I have to go today.

"Okay," she dismisses, returning her attention to her companion laying out cups, teapot and a wicker basket of rice.

The coffee shop is full of customers only half as well dressed as those further up the road. There are no women. Only men, tobacco, newspapers and coffee. A working men's place. There is no exuberance, no animated gesturing. Just calmness. I saw the same calmness in Varanasi: rituals without haste, without exaggeration. The moments exist simply in the purity of self. The River isn't going anywhere. God deserves the few extra seconds it takes to reflect on the moment, to experience instead of do. If God is us, if we are God, then so do we.

Rings of smoke curl from behind a newspaper, backlit against the front window, the hard scrape of chair legs over ceramic tile floors. I have never seen the café this full, always arriving in the lull between meals that saw the staff in the kitchen, sitting around a squat table with their own coffee, forcing them to come to me instead of being there. This morning there are three behind the counter.

At a table for four against the back wall is ex-pat Bill, the American from Bangkok, an empty plate and a half-finished coffee in front of him.

"So what happened to Paul? Did he get his visa to Kampuchea?" I'm not sure Bill will remember me. The face yeah. There aren't many Westerners here. It's more the circumstances of who I am. He talked a lot with Paul. Paul was here a long time.

"No. Never got it," he says. "Left for Vietnam a few days ago. Had no money. A real tight budget, but I guess for two weeks he can survive. No, the guy never came through. I didn't think he would, ya know. Anyway, it was a chance, right. Said something about hawking his clothes or something. Black market stuff. There's a lot of that, ya know?"

I explain my visa situation, the calendar roulette I'm playing, that I don't want to leave, that I like it here. "Thailand'll just be the same old Thailand. Noisy. Dirty. Crowed with tourists. Even one more day would be good."

"Don't go then," he says. "Stay. Look. You're already illegal, right? You going to be any more illegal tomorrow? Any less if today? Two days, three days. Does it matter?"

He makes sense, or rather, telling me what I want to hear, he makes sense to me.

"Are you flying or going through Thaduea?"

"Thaduea."

"If you're going Thaduea, don't worry," he says. "Look, I was five days over in December and they did nothing. They're supposed to fine you 100 baht per day. That's what I heard anyway. So I'm five days over, and I had my 500 baht ready, in my pocket right? I wasn't going to tell them if they didn't ask. That's not my job, right? But if they asked, I had my 500 baht ready. And I gave them my passport and they stamped it, no problem. They didn't even mention it. Just stamped it and I was through.

"If you're going from the airport, then maybe that's different," he says. "At the airport, they've got you, right? There's no place to go. You've got your flight booked and waiting, your ticket paid. But at Thaduea, they don't care. I mean, Nong Khai is right there, and you're already at the border. What are they going to do? Throw you in jail? It's not like they caught you in Louangphrabang or Pakxé or something. Then there's trouble right? But in Vientiane, no one is ever going to stop you and ask for your visa, and at

Thaduea it's no problem. At worst, 100 baht per day. So you leave today, it's 200 baht. Tomorrow 300. It's still cheap compared with what you paid to get in. But I went over in December. Five days over and they never mentioned it. And they won't throw you in jail. It costs too much.

"I got thrown in jail once," he says. "Just for a few hours. Years ago. I wanted to go to Cambodia, so I went out to Aranyaprathet. Paid some Thai guy to take me in, smuggle me over the border. We got in and walked to the first little village no problem, but in the village the police picked us up right away. As soon as we got there they picked us up. Threw us in this Cambodian jail. But it was too expensive for them and they didn't want the hassle of a foreigner. They don't want you there if they don't have to, right? So they deported me. Took me back to the border and put me in Thailand. I was terrified, but no problem. They just gave me back to the Thai's. 'Let them handle it,' right?"

He makes a lot of sense. Not about jail. Jail is far too plausible given the unknown quality of Laotian justice, and unlike the Englishman, there are some things I don't need to experience. But about the fines, about immigration not wanting to lock you up. About being found out at Thaduea, how it's a show of good faith, although the airport doesn't seem any less good faithful when I think about it. It doesn't occur to me until much later that his story makes no sense. His story is that he has a multiple-entry business visa. How can you overstay that? Worse, he never mentioned what happened to the Thai guy. Something tells me "letting the Thai's handle it" is not what *he* wanted to hear.

But I do want to stay. To relax. To do nothing but wander about. No plans, no objectives. Just wander. My reward.

Fuck it.

41
To Thailand

The woman at the guesthouse is confused. First I don't want to stay. Now I do. Foreigners.

There is a single woman already in a double room. The old woman wants to put me in with her. "She is Canadian too!" I don't want to share, and I don't care where she is from. It is only 9:00 A.M. There is no obligation to double up yet. A week ago this place was half empty. We strike a deal: if another single man arrives and the hotel is full, I'll share.

The Canadian female in question is sitting with a Japanese male over a coffee. That we are talking about her is obvious. I introduce myself and explain the proposal. Her name is June. She is from Calgary. His is Toshio. They met at the guesthouse yesterday. She is a business psychologist, an emotional sounding-board for the corporately mobile. "The tacit acknowledgment that there are pressures to business that just don't go away," she says. She doesn't want to share either. Toshio is in the golden limbo of post-university pre-career life. This vacation is the freedom carrot dangled in his face for sixteen years during his stay in the paramilitary institution known as the Japanese school system. When he returns to Japan, he will marry into Toyota or Mitsubishi or Sony or Toho Gas, take the surname "salaryman" as his own, and live happily ever after. There will be no divorce, no separation, and no unsanctioned extra-curricular indulgences. It is an *omiai*, an arranged marriage. *Congratulations. Would the groom like to meet the bride?* This is his bachelor party.

There is a problem with June's visa. Like the rest of us, she did her dirty work with the Mekong River View Guesthouse. Like the rest of us, she hadn't wanted the tour. Unlike the rest of us, she worked out a deal where she would pay only 3000 baht for the visa without "the tour".

At Vientiane immigration, however, she was told she had only a transit visa, not a tourist visa and transit visas were not extendible. There was nothing they could do. They were sorry. Three days. Only. Next.

The only possibility was to return to Thaduea, find the immigration official that had originally stamped her passport, and plead her case. If the official agreed, she could have two weeks. There were no other options, and Vientiane immigration acknowledged it was a long shot.

She is beside herself with anxiety. She had worked hard to get to Asia, paid a lot of money and waited ten days to enter Laos, and now couldn't stay.

I tell her I am late, that my visa has expired, that I am worried too. If she would be illegal after tomorrow, I am illegal now. She isn't alone. If her dilemma is hopeless, it is at least shared.

She is travelling alone. Independence forces you to deal with all the struggles, all the downsides, individually, without confirmation, without solace, without the security of reassurance. At the best of times, it is yet another opportunity to rise above, to prove with character what your mind craves in philosophy. At the worst of times, it is a fusing of desperation and desolation that in the synthesis reduces logic to nonsense and character to indecisiveness and panic.

Worse, if her preconception of The People's Democratic Republic of Laos is at all the stereotype that prevails in the expectant ignorance of Nong Khai conversations, it is a preconception that instills neither faith nor security. Communist. Alien. Unknown. The defining characteristic of decisions and choices taken and made in Laos. There is nothing to work from, no benchmark of behaviour that, however wrongly extrapolated, offers at least the security of the tangible. For information and assurance we relied on a man who made money by saying "yes" and nothing by saying "no." It is only a matter of a few hundred feet between Thailand and Laos, but the invisible wall that divides the Mekong, exciting and anticipated from Nong Khai, is solid and defended and enormous from here.

I tell her about ex-pat Bill's 100 baht solution, that they don't care at Thaduea, that they only care at the airport. She is flying out, to Vietnam. Her flight is next week, booked on the assumption of staying. She would have left early anyway. I open my mouth wide to change feet, and she says that that is the whole point. She doesn't want weeks and weeks and weeks. Just a few days.

Toshio has lots of time. His problem is less bureaucratic. He has heard all the stories of violence, all the rumours of danger both natural and man-inflicted. He has heard of the internal passport, that you need one to travel within the country, that you can't get one and so you can't travel.

For every traveller, there is the tacit acceptance of an increase in uncertainty, over and above all the problems of language and culture and self. Unless insulated in a tour, stepping off the plane re-establishes your priorities squarely on the bottom of the hierarchy: Where do I sleep? Where do I eat? How do I stay safe? Why did Stallone make *Stop or My Mom Will Shoot*? In my life in Canada, there are a thousand actions I take every day I never think of. Once I did, but quickly they became routine knowledge locked into my subconscious, never acknowledged as decisions because they long ago passed from observance into reflexive repetition. Where to buy food? Where to walk? Which direction to walk? Where not to walk? Where to get a good hamburger? That's why places like McDonald's thrive.

For Toshio, it will be even more extreme, for if the West exalts individualism as the ultimate ascension of humanity, in Japan it is the observance of uniformity and conformity that defines the culture and moulds the individual. *The nail that stands up gets pounded down.* It has nothing to do with sex.

Used to having his life ordered and pre-determined, suddenly for Toshio nothing is known, and in reflex action, he looks for rules and regulations, both defined and implied, for help along his way. Laos is dangerous and regulated. Those are "the rules". For me, the regulations are a concern, the danger a concern, but my own desires and goals, and the intellectual understanding of the schism between reality and possibility, force me to acknowledge instead of an absoluteness, an unpredictability whose propensities I can accept. The reality of face value is what Toshio spent his whole life being taught.

He is from Shikoku, the smallest of the four main Japanese islands. He is impressed I lived in Nagoya for so long, and stereotypically impressed that I can speak some Japanese. He is easily impressed. In Japan, the sad reality is that we non-Japanese achieve "some" with *konnichi-wa*. Twenty-seven months is long if you're having a baby, but I have friends in Nagoya that will stay in Nagoya their whole life, and what would be *more* impressive is if after twenty-seven months, I couldn't say anything in Japanese. His English is much better than my Japanese ever was, but his reinforced politeness won't allow it.

"How did you like Japan?" he asks. "I think you must like Japan very much to stay there over two years."

I did. I liked Japan very much. I didn't. I hated Japan very much. In the end, I just couldn't cope with it anymore, and my inability to cope had nothing, in the end, to do with Japan. When I arrived, it was all new: Torii gates, Shinto shrines, Buddhist temples, sushi, indecipherable menus, grown women dressed like little girls, magazines devoted to photographs of women peeing, drunken men in blue suits throwing up into subway garbage containers, toilets where the only seat was your own. People ate raw fish and raw beef and rice and "taco" meant octopus and coffee was $5 a cup and it was an all-day event to find shirts that fit and the condoms fitted tight. Everywhere I went, there were people who called me gaijin and stared and pointed. Bus loads of children, all dressed in perfect black shorts or skirts, with perfect pressed white shirts and tiny little perfect yellow or red felt caps, spotting me through moving bus windows as they passed by, pressing their faces tight against the cracks in the open windows screaming *Harro! Harro! Harro!* until their faces turned purple and the glass fogged up and they couldn't see. And I yelled back *Hello!* to them, and waved and laughed and called myself gaijin. Old Japan-hand gaijin colleagues thought I was crazy to allow "them" to get away with that, to allow "them" to degrade me and perpetuate the myth. I thought my colleagues were crazy: over-reactive, burned out personalities with no sense of humour or life. Those old Japan-hands were the myth, not me. But one day after about a year, instead of laughing I too railed against the *harro*'s and the gaijin's and the stares. I had never noticed before. I had been taking pictures of vegetable stands; gazing at the will of motionless Zen monks on the street corners collecting alms; running after and trying to take photos of the processions of Zen monks that found their way through my neighbourhood; laughing at the fashion trend of knee high socks and broad brimmed hats and the crazy English signs. But that was before. Now Nagoya was my home. I lived here. Over there was my apartment, over there my bar, over there my coffee shop, over there my coin laundry. I had a subway pass, a bicycle, an office, a girlfriend, secrets. I had a life. I wasn't a tourist. I wasn't some object of display or wonderment or curiosity or deification. I wasn't a gaijin. I was a human being. I lived here. But still, from everywhere I heard the gaijin's and *harro*'s and I saw the pointed fingers and felt the stares and the averted glances when I caught the perpetrators and suddenly, it wasn't fun any longer. I asked Nakayama-san to teach me what I needed to say to tell people to stop staring. She taught me, "*Sumimasan. Gaijin o minaidei kudasai.*" I told my friend's wife. She was Korean-Japanese and had spent her whole life fighting back. "That means 'Please excuse me, but please don't look at the foreigner,'" she said. "Not only will they keep looking, but now they'll laugh too." She taught me what she said: "*Miruna bakayaro?*" It means, "What the fuck are you looking at, asshole?" Loosely. Direct translation is ephemeral. It's really all in the eyes. So I stopped calling myself gaijin, calling myself instead Mark, or if pushed, Canada-jin. I called it my "zoo threshold," in honour of the monkeys at Nagoya Monkey Park. They were locked inside glass cages, over-fed and under-exercised into demented obesity for amusement and mock-deification by the Japanese. On weekends Japanese crowds oozed by the display cells, their faces inches from the glass, distorting in the closeness, rapping their knuckles with impatient demand on the windows, mimicking primate sounds and actions, throwing grunts and eeks back through the glass at the monkeys for sport in a pathetic attempt to elicit retorts from our ascendants, all for the cause of smiles of approval from their ill-incisored girlfriends or wives or children. I was white and Canadian and wore a blue pinstripe suit, but I was just another monkey. Hell, with my body hair, one class jokingly called me *saru-chan*: monkey boy. (You want to stand out? Be the only white guy, the only person with any body hair, in a public swimming pool filled to overflowing with black haired, smooth chested Japanese.) My inability to be Japanese was my glass cage, my students mimicking my English body language instead of learning it, all displayed for the approval of self and classmates and company. So began the reacting, the fighting against life instead of the living of it. But how do you fight 120 million people who all think the same way, who all act and react predictably and uniformly, who individually see you as a person but collectively see you as gaijin?

"No, you don't understand," Toshio said. "Gaijin is not insult. It is only what we call foreigner. It is not meant in disrespect."

But the reality is that gaijin doesn't mean foreigner. It means white Westerner. And even gaijin is slang. The correct word is *gai-koku-jin*: the three Chinese Kanji characters literally translate as "outside country person," except "outside country people" from Korea and China have their own individual terms, black-Africans of all nationalities another, and sub-continental Indians yet another: "outside country person" is not the broad-stroked generality the Kanji suggests. Once I asked my class as an exercise to describe me. In a blaze of mass individualism, they all said tall, blond, blue eyed. If it were only so. I am 5'8¾", brown hair, green eyes. Fortunately the myth of body parts extends to my penis.

"Yes, it is true. We mean Westerner when we say gaijin, but it is not disrespectful. All Japanese study English in schools, but they never speak to foreigner, they never meet foreigner. In Japan, everyone is the same: black hair, yellow skin, black eyes. The foreigner is different, and so we look and stare. I know it is wrong. We all know it is wrong, but we do it anyway, because we never see a foreigner before. We say gaijin *san*. It is very polite. We don't know what to say. We don't know if you are American or German or Canadian, so we all think American. To us, it is all the same. So we say gaijin, but we do not mean bad things. The children stare, but they are children and they don't know."

And of course he is right. My problem with Japan was exactly that: *my* problem with Japan. The subject of the grammar is me, not the country. It was not up to me to change their behaviour. It was my job to change the way I react to that behaviour. The lessons of Zen: learning to act instead of react. What I had done in Japan was learn to react, or rather, to hone an already well-developed skill. I had allowed my happiness to be dictated by outsiders, rather than by me. Because the truth was that while I demanded to be seen as a person, I insisted on seeing them as Japanese, and so ultimately I was rebelling against myself as much as I was rebelling against them. I was demanding from them behaviour I could not accede to myself. Behaviour thrown back in my face, except that I wasn't able to see that face, or perhaps more precisely, I didn't want to see my own face. With my eyes turned outwards, I didn't have to look at all.

Interestingly, Japanese eyes aren't black: they're brown. The colour black is an optical illusion. Yet every Japanese I met in Japan, or have met since, insists that Japanese eyes are black. They can't all be wrong.

I don't know which was the truth and which the possibility. I'm a person. I'm an object. You tell me. Truth is too elusive to be so easily discovered. Truth was what I had gone to Japan looking for, remember? Not truth in so many words, but rather a making sense of all that left me empty and unfulfilled when by normal convention it shouldn't have. An unquantifiable goal searched for without any blueprint for its attainment. How do you search for truth? Is it as simple as learning how to believe? Or is it believing how to learn? Aren't truth and belief mutually exclusive? How do you know when you have been successful? There is a universal truth, a truth that is absolute and once found, able to be held forever in the grasp of the palm. I know it, just from the tidbits I have experienced, the morsels I have taunted and exalted myself with. That's not the problem.

I wanted truth but more I wanted answers, the solving of

problems superficial and their Band-Aids rather than the solving of the central problem and letting that solution solve the superficial.

From behind our conversation comes an Australian voice.

"I heard you talking," he starts. "You say you've been north? We want to go north too. Is it safe? Difficult? We've heard lots of stories, you know. Talked to different people. Nothing really concrete. Is it okay?"

Two men. Maybe in their late twenties. I tell them. It is easy. The danger is real. Then I stop. Is the danger real? I don't know if the stories are true. Nothing happened to me. I saw the aftermath of something. Dead animals, a dead village. I had heard one explanation that seemed questionably reasonable, but nothing had happened to me and that one explanation, Andy's "eleven-days ago" story, was also reasonably questionable. I had been safe. There had been no trouble. And it had been easy. Even the transportation connections, the anxiety of Louangphrabang notwithstanding. "You don't even need a map," I say.

"We don't need one here!" shouts the other. "Been here twenty-four hours and already seen it all. Been everywhere, done everything. How tough can the country be?" and they laugh and I am expected to laugh as well.

Goodday mate. Fuck you.

Vientiane wasn't Bangkok, but neither was Bangkok Vientiane. There were no strip clubs here, no bars with pounding music and mirror balls and chatteled women in numbered bathing suits gyrating in boredom under coloured spotlights, available for an hour or the night or until you passed out and they stole your wallet. Vientiane was special. It had a sublime grace that wrapped itself around you and took you back to your childhood if only you let your guard down long enough to allow it. It was a grace that did not feel the requirement to shout in neon to arouse your attention. True enough, in many ways it was the literal ruin of a city; crumbling sidewalks, peeling façades, grass varicose veins running through the streets. Bangkok too was the ruins of a city. It deceived better though, hiding its decay behind the speciousness of economic prosperity and skyscrapers and sex.

In this attitude is the transformation of Laos from being the first Laos into the second Thailand, a transformation that will see the pride and the integrity of the people compromised and sold to placate the demands of a tourism weaned on the accommodating wet-nurse nipple of Thailand, by operators faced with only the obligation to emulate to achieve wealth. The Talàat Sao is already filled with Thai consumer goods, and the market stalls of Nong Khai burst with the profit-margined Laotian exports. Daily the boats from Nong Khai carry the Thai nouveau riche across the river, the entrepreneur/used car sellers with fistfuls of money and the aggressiveness born out of and fuelled by accumulating bank reserves. Perhaps it is already too late. The hotels charge in dollars and baht. The Sailom in baht exclusively. Lao Aviation in US dollars. Only the tourists, the contented and the poor want kip.

"Well then, you don't need my help do you? I'm sure you can figure it out all by yourselves. I mean, how tough can it be?"

And that isn't what they mean. They just mean that Vientiane is small, that it is poor, unmodernized. It isn't Bangkok, you know?

Vientiane is all of those things. And they're right, it is easy to see in a day, but then Bangkok could be seen in a day if your palate was undiscriminating and undemanding. To degrade Vientiane in fun is to impose our standards and our contexts onto someone else's standards and context, and as a tourist in a foreign country, we have no right to do that. That we all do it is no justification. Why else would Thai restaurants serve French fries, Nepalese guesthouses chocolate cake and apple pie? We have no right. We should be looking, understanding, experiencing. Not judging.

From New Zealand. They aren't Australians.

People think the Nepalese poor. In patronizing compassion they explain this to their faces. And of course, they are. But there are different kinds of poverty, and our standards judge their society and their haves by our criterion. That our values are absolutely skewed towards monetary gain and consumer maintenance and acquisition is never questioned. The Nepalese suffer from poor water, poor medical care, poor education, and it is almost impossible to get a good cigar. But they have a strong sense of family and a strong sense of village and place and religion. They are happy.

Those same Westerners that so carefully explain to the Nepalese their monetary impoverishment are themselves poor in those other qualities of life. Indeed, many have come to Nepal specifically to search for those same qualities, even if they don't know it, or can't admit it, at the time. That those financially capable foreigners feel these voids in their lives is rarely expressed to the Nepalese. Only to other Westerners, only to those also looking for that inner peace of mind they hope lives in the rarefied air of the Himalayas. And in our eloquence and sincerity, we soon convince the Nepalese that they *are* poor, and suddenly it is money that is important, acquisitions, status. Instead of folk music and instruments it is Japanese Walkmans and Michael Jackson cassettes.

I influence just by going. Seen as rich, advanced, equating both to "better," my influence exaggerates the misconceptions and my apparent wealth confirms them. To comment in judgment is irresponsible, damaging and immoral. I do it subtly and tacitly. When I talk down to someone speaking English poorly, considering them slow and stupid instead of a second-language learner. When I buy the Indian equivalent of Coke or the Chinese of Pepsi and complain neither is as good as the original, the real thing, as if some universal truth demands American soft drinks be available everywhere.

I explain the way to Vangviang. The times of the buses, the location of the bus station. Even about the guesthouses. It's easy.

42

To Thailand

The journey to the centre of Vientiane by sāam láw pedicab is 250 kip. The route heaves and moans past the high cement walls of the stadium, past the French colonial governor's residence, past far in the distance and down a cross street Lao Aviation and the Soviet bookstore; past memory-clouded colonial residences of ice blue window sills and dangling white shutters and red tile roofs pockmarked in lost tiles; alongside concrete slab sidewalks five feet wide and five inches thick, the slabs broken in precise and jagged fissures, blood-splattered with shrapnel shards of fallen roof tiles; alongside earthen road shoulders pushing into the appaloosa-grey pebbled blacktop, breaking the asphalt into thick oily chunks that fall away and bleed into the soil like crumbling coffee cake, stalks of grass and weed sprouting through the cracks. The sāam láw's rubber wheels are thin and hard, and the whole vehicle twists and creaks in the rolls, the ripped vinyl bench seat bouncing in the speed, throwing me back and forth into the scrolled metal sideboards.

The main road into the centre of town is almost vehicleless, but still we take back streets, passing only a few pedestrians and lonely children's street games. Twice we pass other sāam láws, the drivers shouting breathless greetings in their approach and then gliding click-click-click-click into each other, slowing click... click...click...until past and then hard, jolting strokes at the chain, forcing the peddles through grunts to reclaim the momentum lost, smooth brown calves straining in the effort, tightening and pulling, pulling and tightening.

An English couple at the Sailom recommended the Vietnamese restaurant next to the cake shop for rice paper spring rolls. At the front of the restaurant is a polished glass display case filled by purple cabbage, lettuce, green onions, thin near-transparent rice noodles, Chinese cherry pork rounds strung together like Christmas tree popcorn, and pork sausage. Under two flat lids are stainless steel tureens of broth and boiling water.

Two old women dressed in black sit hunched over one of the tables talking at the rear of the restaurant. The room is unlit but for the muted light that seeps in from the overcast outside and the milky-green throw from the narrow fluorescent lights in the display case, the soft imprecise shadows the light creates at the front of the restaurant deepening into the heavy, imprecise outlines of the women, outlines that bleed into the background and without squinting to see are lost in the darkness. Once I too am seated in the back darkness, the light is easy, calming, reflective. Does nothing change but perspective? The backlight bends around the display case's edges, the shapes still imprecise and soft, but with more detail in the mirror of light that bounces up from the tile floor. Looking into the light is not the harshness I assumed it would be. The metaphor is not lost on me. They appear in the oddest places. On the wall above my table is a *Rambo II* movie poster. *First Blood* (the first Rambo), was filmed in BC, just miles along the highway from where I grew up, in a town called Hope. A different kind of metaphor. The poster is a Stallone sweaty and intense, red bandana around his forehead, fierce blue eyes peering out, green anti-aircraft missile launcher in his hands, the grey smoke and orange flames of burning Vietnamese jungle in the background. Tell me they see the irony. Tell me it is not just me.

At five o'clock, the rain that has threatened all day finally arrives, exploding against the guesthouse like an applause of semi-congealed paint pellets, lifting the dust from the surface and smothering street noise in its own crescendo of acknowledgment. The scent is thick with the smell of moisture on gravel. I still have no roommate.

Out of the unlit wooden hallway comes a female voice singing, soft clear and resonant to a guitar. June. She is still alone too. The dark corridor catches her echo and stills the distance. A whisper of a voice, except it is strong, sure of itself. Joni Mitchell? Delicate. What kind of confidence does it take to sing out loud in a hostel? Or is it not a question of confidence but beauty? Bob Dylan. That's what she's singing. Dylan. Not Joni Mitchell. Once I sang out loud in a hotel. It was in Ayutthaya, in a time before Cassie. All singing took then was joy. I was another man: nut brown and slim, singing because of who I was instead of who I wanted to be or thought I should be. I was sure then, without questions of women or love or future. Just happy. The proximity of time has nothing to do with dates. Dylan. Yes, I'm sure. The lyric is familiar. I know the tune. And then stillness, the rumble of drops splattering against the balcony deck, against the wooden shutter, the room turned cold and confining in the quiet. A melancholy rain. I open the shutter, and the street is empty, deserted, sounds muffled. The song is over, finished. There is only the sound of the rain. And then again June begins; again it is summer, again the rain welcomes, beginning shyly, in a whisper, like a falling feather. Not Dylan this time. Joni Mitchell? Or do I mean Buffy Sainte-Marie? No. It can't be. Joni Mitchell. But the texture is Crosby, Stills and Nash. The emotion. At least it is to me. Crosby, Stills and Nash. Joni Mitchell. The symmetry of it all makes me feel warm, makes me feel like a part of something larger, like I belong, like I am not alone. Crosby, Stills and Nash, the tape I have played to death here, the tape I found in Bangkok with Cassie on my own private search for the 60s. Crosby, Stills and Nash: three men in jeans and boots on a couch on a veranda. Music that I knew, but didn't know. Music that I found here in Asia. A zeitgeist that passed me by and then let me find it. Music that every time I hear it now, I feel Cassie because the lyrics, the emotion, the texture, is her. I can hear *Helplessly Hoping* with all my body.

June. Down the hall.

Cassie. So far away.

It is only a matter of days now until my questions are answered. Letters in a Bangkok post office. A unilateral paper reunion. How many? Three? Ten? None? One? One that starts "Dear Mark," and ends "I'm sorry"? I wonder if I don't prefer the certainty of unrequited love to the possibilities in the knowing. In the fantasy I can express my love. *This doesn't happen every day*, and I fear in realising the fantasy, I will deny it.

Does she still want us? Has this time apart shown her that she misses me, or has it shown her that I was the right man for the right time in the right place and that that time and place have passed and so too therefore must the man? And I realize I've enjoyed being alone. It sweeps over me discomfortingly. The life of an only child is a life alone. How do you change the reassuring resonance of an upbringing? Can you change? Do I still want us? And still I crave company, crave attention and people around me, and yet I feel most comfortable alone. How to live in the paradox? How to find someone that understands.

Too often around others, "Mark" is lost in the group and, in the losing, "Mark's" purpose in the group as well. A fear of failure? Of success? Of being exposed? But which? Another paradox. Only children have no older siblings to watch develop, no younger siblings to teach, no siblings period to discover that we are all alike. Only children grow alone, discovering in other, often painful ways their sameness in society. More paradoxes, for we learn that sameness while clinging to our uniqueness. We are, after all, the only one. And so life. Maybe it is the case for all children. Maybe Cassie wonders and struggles over the same issues, except her position is different. She is the middle. Between. Maybe that is all that there is: a different preposition.

Does she still want us? Do I?

But who are the two? The symmetry is not simply between musicians and Cassie. Maybe everything is symmetrical.

The rain has stopped. So has June. I heard her door close, locked behind her. Tomorrow I leave. There are no more decisions. Tomorrow.

We meet in the lobby, June and I. Because of the rain, it is more full with travellers than I have ever seen it. I had no idea this many

Westerners were in Vientiane. We want to talk, and the tables are all more open than the intimacy we're looking for: there is an empty bench built out from one wall and a few cushions. Our own space, our own corner. We are alone.

Her Thaduea visa question hadn't worked. In spite of her pleadings and the Sailom's de facto intervention, the answer at immigration was quick and simple and monosyllabic. No. Tomorrow is her last legal day.

And so the Laotian dominoes fall; one decision begets another. She will go to Vangviang tomorrow morning, perhaps Kasi the next day, and then return for her flight to Vietnam. Whatever the fine at the airport, she will pay it, and if asked, simply explain what happened, that she couldn't change her pre-booked flight, that it wasn't her fault. So too has fallen the domino of anxiety. Finally she seems calm, finally she seems at peace.

She has been to Suan Mokkh for the ten-day Vipassana retreat with Buddhadāsa Bhikkhu. I did the same retreat a year and a half ago, discovering that like Christianity, there is more than one true way. I should have known better. John did, but George bought it all, and he was always my favourite. The external paradox of life. Suan Mokkh was June's first time doing any meditation and she's glad she did it, but she didn't really understand it. That was one of the problems at Suan Mokkh. The farang bhikkhus who ran the retreat weren't that good at explaining to an uninitiated Western mind what exactly was going on. I understood the concept, the basics—at least partially—as I'm sure others did, but many didn't; one fellow was held back at the end of the ten days to de-program him from his belief that he had indeed in those ten days reached true enlightenment. He never slept but walked around in circles smiling, his eyes dancing, *insisting* on his transcendence. I didn't believe him, but I didn't blame him either. He may have felt like Jesus, but he looked like the lead in *Helter Skelter*. What we had done at Suan Mokkh was powerful, but it wasn't a game, and too many ten-dayers saw it that way, as a "thing" to do, as an event to be experienced, a "Been there. Done that". The farang bhikkhus were too long-term-committed to Vipassana to be effective in a short-term, one-off. In Japan I thought Zen was the true way, until searching for reasons to attack the internal paradox of the fulfilment in my practice at Tokugenji and my feelings towards all things Japanese.

At all zazen sessions at Tokugenji there is a *jikijitsu*. The jikijitsu is a monk whose Zen practice is to watch the zendo and other meditators during their zazen practice. Some would call it patrol. Some found worse descriptors. A zazen cop as it were. To fulfil his duties, he slowly, deliberately, walks the aisles between meditators in his own meditation, feeling his weight fall onto the heel of his right foot, then the outer edge of the arch, then the ball touching and finally the entire foot planted, the weight shifting through his thigh, the knee taking the pressure until he is firm and then he lifts the left foot. Slowly he progresses, lifting and planting, planting and lifting, planting and reaping. Slowly he progresses, looking and watching, watching and listening. And we sit. Resting across his shoulder the jikijitsu carries a *keisaku* in a two-fisted lazy baseball bat grip. A keisaku is a long, narrow oak stick, flattened out into a paddle blade at one end. It is with the keisaku that the jikijitsu enforces the zendo. Sometimes the enforcement is a gentle nudge with the keisaku. Sometimes the enforcement is by being hit with the keisaku. Zen is not for the weak of heart. The Zen practice at Tokugenji is Rinzai; meditators face forward into the zendo and towards other meditators. Because Zen, unlike Vipassana, is done with eyes open, meditators can see peripherally the jikijitsu's approach and their own pending doom. At least I could. The trick, of course, is to be so purely concentrating on your practice that you will not be slouching (and therefore not deserve to be hit), you will not be too proud (and therefore not deserve to be hit), or you will notice the jikijitsu and let it go (and therefore not deserve to be hit) because the jikijitsu has nothing to do with your Zen practice. Except of course that he does, in the same way that everything in the zendo has to do with your practice, whether that everything is physical, or emotional, or psychological. Or you will simply be hit, whether you notice the jikijitsu or not. Because everything in the zendo has to do with your practice, and whether you deserve it or not is moot: there is no "deserving" in zen. Seeing the jikijitsu is like hearing a sound: you acknowledge that it happened, and you let it go. At least that's how I saw it all, and given the dearth in my 27 month Japanese language base, native-speaker linguistic explanations were short and sweet and wholly inadequate. Watching the jikijitsu gives a whole appreciation for what a Thompson Gazelle must feel like on the Serengeti. The jikijitsu slaps meditators with the keisaku eight times across the upper back, four from the right, four from the left. I understood the number. Eight represents the Buddha's eightfold path: right speech, right action, right livelihood, right effort, right awareness, right concentration, right thoughts and right understanding. I understood intellectually the keisaku: it kept meditators on task, it helped meditators who were off task, it represented Self and not-Self. Thwack! It hurt like hell too. Thwack! Right through the shirt.

During one sit, the jikijitsu hit everyone. It was simply a wake-up thwack. Thwack! *Be alert! The time for Zen is now!* Thwack! I understood. Thwack! But then, a rin-jong bell sounded calling all those meditators who had been given a koan out of the zendo to meet with the roshi, the master of the temple, and the zendo emptied but for three of us: two meditators and him. Twenty minutes into an hour sit I realized I was sitting wrongly, that rather than my back supporting me, my muscles were supporting me and they were tired. I moved. Slowly, so as not to be seen. *Be the Thompson Gazelle grasshopper.* Not slowly enough. And so for the second time the keisaku. Thwack! Thwack! Eight more times. Thwack! Thwack! And I again understood intellectually, but for those of you counting at home, that's 16 Thwacks! At the Denny's afterward across the street, what I also understood was that my back hurt like hell. Again. But Zen is not about intellectualization, and indeed, who is it that hurts like hell if there is no me? The job of zazen is not to recognize hurting like hell, but to strive, always strive, for *kensho*, enlightenment, nirvana. Without striving. But the Buddha found enlightenment sitting alone under a Bodhi tree. And if he was alone, then there was no jikijitsu, and so the question is begged, "Who hit the Buddha?" And if no one hit him ... Well, you get the picture.

Buddhadāsa said two things that resonated with me. First, he said that *if* we had been reincarnated, *if* we were still in this game of samsara, this game of repeating lives and repeating re-births, we couldn't know who we had been in that past, and *if* we were to be reincarnated in the future, we couldn't know who we would become. There was only here and only now, and *if* we wanted to attain enlightenment, this was the time. And he said that we were constantly achieving nirvana in our lives every time we reached a state of not-Self, every time we forgot to remember that we were. I was confused. But then he gave us an example: He said when we watched a movie, and the movie was so good that we just watched the movie and forgot to be aware that we were watching the movie, that in that moment it was no longer "I am watching a movie" but simply "watching a movie," and then, then, we have attained not-Self, and not-Self was enlightenment. The trick was not in the getting there. The trick was staying there.

In a directed meditation at Suan Mokkh, an American monk, Bhikkhu Santikaro, reminded us: *You have nowhere to go, nothing to do, no one to be.* Only here, only this, only me.

In the lobby, June's and my conversation between two becomes a circle of one, our legs moving together, our knees touching, our faces prodding the moment. Do I want to go to dinner? she asks. She has already promised herself to two others at the Sailom. The restaurant is Indian. Good and cheap. She's promised. Will I come?

At 5:30 P.M., a large white taxi pulls up, and three travellers burst in out of the rain carrying huge duffel bags and armfuls of unpacked Vietnamese military souvenirs. Then four more arrive. ROOMS! They want ROOMS! YES! Australian voices. Or New Zealand. Yes, they will share, that is not a problem. Away from the registration, their discussion is oddly familiar. At the airport they were given only three-day transit visas and not the expected fourteen-day tourist visas. It was not a worry. They would just overstay and pay a fine. Matter-of-fact. No problem. No ethical dilemma or question of repercussion. Done. An obvious decision. Maybe the Can-Aussie was right.

The man with the visa solution hears June say Vangviang. Three long strides and he is towering over our circle.

"You get the Vangviang bus from behind the morning market. Every day. Seven A.M. 500 kip. There's a guesthouse in Vangviang.

Quite good," and he turns his back and is gone. He looks familiar. Still, faces repeat in Asia, and the traveller's route in that repetition becomes less an adventure and more a carnival. You see people over and over. Like Paul. He looked familiar. Maybe all white folks look the same.

43
To Thailand

J une is gone. Two hours ago to Vangviang. A legal fugitive.
After dinner last night we walked together to our floor and I
looked into her eyes and said good-bye and good night and wished
her a good trip and luck at the airport and I meant none of it. What
I meant was to reach out, to embrace the moment, to embrace her.
Out of our closeness of that single day, of that single evening. Out
of our humanity.

Wednesday, March 7

Now I know. I would cheat on Cassie. I decided
that if the opportunity presented itself, I'd
sleep with June . . . but over dinner with her
two friends, we lost momentum and I never felt
enough desire to try to re-find it. And now she
has gone.

Last night at the top of the stairs, I wanted to
reach out, to hold her, to . . . not for sex, but to
acknowledge the closeness we had discovered in
that day, to acknowledge our humanity. I wanted
to reach out, to deny the lost momentum, to touch
what was almost there.

I have cheated on Cassie. That June and
I didn't sleep together isn't the point. I never
asked. She never refused. It was simple. Letting

fear dictate decisions always is. At least in the short-run. And then she turned and walked alone to her room, me towards mine.

And so I wonder. Who have I cheated on more? Me or Cassie? In fear I denied the moment. What am I remaining faithful to? There must be a Mark whose behaviour simply *is*, a behaviour that doesn't require an overt act of faithfulness.

Cassie would never have known. I would have known, but what would I have known? There is no integrity in fear. The betrayal is not to Cassie. It is to me.

Who am I fooling? The betrayal is to both of us.

I meant to reach out. Instead I stood and fumbled as she looked back at me and filled the awkwardness saying I was a good listener, that I had been a help, that there was nothing she could do, and now, that was okay. And if I had reached out? If I had taken her in my arms, if I had acknowledged my desire, my loneliness? If I had acknowledged the moment? Would she have seen that moment and our humanity the same way? Are my rose coloured glasses framed in fear?

Fear is a choice. It is an illusion that I choose to choose. And so what if we had one more day? One more night? What if there were no more "what ifs".

What if I could live without fear?

The questions are moot. Her door at the end of the hall is open, the room empty and lifeless. Nothing remains to suggest she was there: no warmth, no imprint in crumpled white sheets, no indentation in the pillow. A camel hair coloured wool blanket is folded neatly at the foot of the bed. Gone. Was she ever there? Is my memory just playing tricks with me again? And now I am gone too. Two paths diverged in Vientiane. Where is the Mark whose behaviour simply is, a behaviour which requires no act of will to achieve? Where is he? *What if we had one more night?*

What does embracing today have to do with "what if" except to deny it?

What if I'd known that thirteen months later, Cassie and I would fail. What if I hadn't fought the intuitions that told me Cassie was a time and a place, and that times and places change. That in four days' time, I would collect eight letters from Cassie addressed to me Poste Restante, the GPO, Bangkok. For many, many minutes, many, many times, I would read and re-read her words. And it would be so clear, so clear. So obvious. Cassie and her life were a world away from me and Laos.

The city is cold and damp and grey, a monotone of lifelessness, a monotony of emptiness. The bakery feels harsh and impersonal, the coffee more obligatory than joyful. New precipitation weights the atmosphere and, for the first time, it feels like a March day and not the deception of summer. It is a good day to leave.

On the road running east from the Talàat Sao, across from yesterday's sãam láw tricycle drivers, is a line of serious car taxis and a congestion of velvet-painting-on-fire-engine-red sãwng tháew (pronounced *song tao*) pick-up-truck share taxis. A group of sãwng tháew drivers stand talking, their rolling poster-art vehicles clustered behind them, parked in random disarray around some invisible spot, their attention to the arriving and not the leaving.

My call for a taxi to Thaduea returns shuffling, murmured discussion, a solitary "No" and a collective shaking of heads and turned backs and hidden-faced laughter.

"Yes," I nod. "Thaduea. How much? How many kip?"

My repeated question simply begets their repeated response with more murmured gazes and more laughter. There is no interest in either Thaduea or me. The mirror replaced by the cage, I am denied even the basic courtesy and respect that exists between seller and buyer.

An uncomfortable wait produces a shout of "2500 kip" and more laughter. *Take it or leave it. Sabadee. Fuck you.* Part game, part insult, the weighting is decidedly towards the taunt and today,

I am willing to indulge neither. Bargaining is not a synonym for insolence and indifference. Taxiing passengers is their job.

"No. Too much." *Fuck you,* and I walk away. There is no resistance.

A single sãwng tháew driver breaks away from the clique, following after me. "Hello! Hello! O.K. Thaduea. 2000 kip," he says. I keep on walking.

"Hello! Hello! 2000 kip."

At least he is willing to bargain, to recognize me as a person. And he wants the fare, unlike the others who seem content to stand around and talk and wait for the locals that won't take as long and they think will earn them as much money.

"Yes. Thaduea". *Fuck you. 500 kip.* "1500 kip." It is not a question. We settle on 1800, and just like that we are off.

There is a solitude to the road that was not there eighteen days earlier, a forlornness that cuts through my veneer and leaves me vulnerable. Perhaps it is the smothering overcast. Perhaps it is riding alone in an open pick-up that seats eight, exposed to a chilling wind on a morning without sun. Perhaps it is as simple as *being* alone, once again sharing an experience with myself instead of someone else. Alone the ride feels stripped of accomplishment. The death of a cycle. It is over already.

There is almost no traffic. An old couple flags us over for a short, three kilometer ride. They pay 200 kip. At least the driver is making the trip worthwhile.

As we stop to let them off, a red Toyota sãwng tháew passes us carrying five brown monks in uttarāsanga robes the rich colour of pumpkin under this piled charcoal sky. Each holds a wood skeleton money tree, the kip notes held on with clothes pegs and paper clips, the branches flapping wildly in the breeze. As their sãwng tháew slows for their wat, a single branch flies off, scattering kip notes across the road, the bills spinning and whirling away in the truck's sucking ducktail draft. For an instant the monks turn toward the notes. I wait for the slap on the cab roof to stop and retrieve the lost alms, but it never comes and the truck continues on into the wat, the monks' attention already turned away from the money and into the bumps of the driveway. Beggars can be choosers.

Like Kasi and Vangviang before it, Thaduea from this side is much less imposing than I remember. There is no guard tower, no police sentry, and the perimeter fence is a powder blue trellis archway overgrown with ivy and roses in a deep green hedge. In front on both sides of the dirt road are long lines of taxis. I separate three 100 baht bills from my cash reserve and slide them into my front pocket.

The immigration counter is a confusion of people. From their passports, most are Thai, but there are two other Western men as well, neither of whom I had seen before. Dressed in cream cotton slacks and shirts, they resemble me only through genetic makeup. I assume either wealth or delegation members. Like the Vientiane sǎwng tháew drivers, they don't look like they particularly want to acknowledge me, but then, what is *their* assumption? Behind the counter sit three passport control officers in starched and pressed olive uniforms and caps: two women and one man.

As each passport is stamped and returned, other arms thrust towards the counter, a rage of voices rising with the attempts to satisfy the urgency. There is no civility. Each arm tries to outdo the other, to prove its position as its owner acquired it. Even here there are winners and losers. In spite of the confusion, we are not that many: perhaps only ten. The urgency is unwarranted. There is no plane to catch, no connection to be made, no pregnant surge of people waiting behind soon-to-be-opened-doors to dislodge us.

At the counter a passport is returned, and a woman's arm shoots over my shoulder, her body shoving into mine, her body too far away to find the counter, her arm too short to make up the difference. I'm two deep behind a pack of eight. I don't stand a chance, it's not my turn, and she's behind me. The arm belongs to a middle-aged Thai woman, well-dressed and wearing make-up in the style of self-deception as opposed to enhancement. It's not that she's so important as much as she's better than the rest of us.

The woman official returns another passport. Over the short black heads in front I extend mine and win, the official glancing up towards me as I do, then as quickly away, fumbling to find my picture and name. She has turned my passport upside down, and there are too many stamps in languages she can't read for her to find the Laotian visa quickly. At least that's what I think I see. She sets my passport down and writes something in a large blue accounting ledger.

"You are late," she says. "You are three days late." In her first utterance, Bill's guarantee of disinterest has crumbled and I feel my mouth dry in its erosion. "Where were you?" she asks, and I am lost in the question, confronted and unprepared in the anticipation of "Why?"

So I lie. About the time, not about Louangphrabang, not about the trucks. I tell her I just arrived back in Vientiane today, trying to convince her I am only two days late, that Sunday didn't count, that there was nothing I cold do.

Unblinking and unresponsive, she sets my passport aside and takes the well-dressed woman's document from the swarm offered in my rejection. Open. Stamp. Sign. Return, and the Thai woman is through. More passports are thrust begging towards the official. She reaches for the ledger and picks up my passport again. She stares at the picture, then at the visa, flipping back and forth between the two.

"You are three days late. Where were you?" she repeats. "Why do you come here three days late? You should go on Sunday."

There is a moment when the parameters of experience evaporate and the unknown and its realm of possibilities present the only alternative. At once all that is known is lost and all that is possible probable. It is that moment of lost control which flushes blood through the face until in its heat the eyes burn and water, a heat that dries the mouth so that it contracts the lips in a contortion that immobilizes speech. Words fight to escape as the brain sputters, its "thought-sound" synchronization lost to this simultaneous occurrence.

This is that moment.

"I was in Louangphrabang," I repeat. "I wanted to get a ride Sunday, but there were no trucks, so I got the first ride I could and I just got here now. There was nothing I could do.

"Is there a problem?"

"Wait here," she says, and standing, she turns and walks down a narrow outer balcony into an office at the rear of the building. It is neither a command nor a request. "Wait here." I finger the three 100 baht notes folded in my pocket, separating them because, like Bill, I want her to tell me the fine and pay it, rather than produce a wad of cash and volunteer a plea for pity.

The door opens and emotionless she returns, her eyes refusing to meet mine that follow her questioningly.

"Ten baht please." She hands me an exit card. "Sign here. And next time, don't be late, please."

There is a surge of passports to the counter. *Next time don't be late, please.* No fine, no reprimand. Ten baht is the exit fee. *Next time, don't be late. Please.* Bodies swarm forward squeezing me out like an air bubble in a turned-upside-down bottle of shampoo, like a shy fart.

At the river, two ferries are loading. The made-up entrepreneur sits in one, two monks in a second. I am directed to the monks. For all her hurry, she hasn't left yet. Buddhist monks can't touch women. I assume they put me in this boat because I'm male. We're filling up faster. Across the river, Nong Khai sits in a haze, a shimmer of sun burning through the mist and humidity.

The town is a long, narrow mass of store fronts and guesthouses—THE MEKONG RIVER VIEW GUESTHOUSE in huge capital letters, undeniable through the haze—the skyline a confusion of shapes and stories, a mismatch of squared roofs, air conditioning units, fire escapes, hydro pylons and Buddhist wats, the muddied, disunified backdrop for hundreds of television antennae, an inspired confusion of outstretched arms demanding owner recognition. TV envy.

Behind the coveted façade is the blare of restaurant radios and the urgency of greasy, restaurant-scrap-stained streets and the sputtering of motorcycles and the sweet sickliness of uncontrolled exhaust fumes that stick to the lining of the nostrils like bloated road-kill.

It is the West again, replete with ice cream cones and newspapers and two English dailies and Pepsi advertisements that both titillate and persuade. The West, filled with Westerners arriving, each day more, to sit and stare across the river and in that stare find romance and thrills and wanderlust in and over bottles of cold Singha beer and warm Mekong Whisky, to exult how exotic it was to be here, so far away from home. So close to the river. A border. A delineation. Natural. Absolute. Except since when has Thailand become the West? Perspective, perspective, perspective.

An armed patrol boat speeds by, a wash of foam spreading out behind its squared stern, its flag flapping soundlessly from behind the gun emplacement. Asia juxtaposed before my eyes.

Now full, the ferry draws low into the river, the wooden railings inches above the surface. We push off from the shore, leaving the other boat to wait. I dangle my fingers over the edge into the water. It is cool. Refreshing. Alive.

In ten minutes, the Thai side, cement stairs and familiarity. Here, now, silt and the prints of bare feet. The smell of life. Natural. Behind us Laos Customs, looking like so many huts in so many villages in the north: dull, dark, dirty, wooden and ancient. Unpretentious. Welcoming. Organic. Further south along the riverbank, the new Laos immigration checkpoint, the white façade draped over in huge official bars of Laotian blue and red looking like a Barnet Neuman painting. Clean. Neat. Yuppie Communism. I am glad for the old one, the wooden cottage with the rose covered trellis and trimmed hedges and the wooden staircase of broken steps that ascended the bank from the edge of the river.

Where is old Asia? Is it in the darkness of the Tibetan monastery at Namche Bazaar on the footsteps of Everest, watching with dilated pupils the flicker of ghee lamps at the altar of a soot covered Vajrayana Buddha, listening to the guttural intonation of nones, the room filled by the scent of yak hides and burning ghee and incense, the dampness and cold creeping into my stockinged feet, the dry rasping coughs of chants echoing off the walls? Is it in the young Tibetan monk in the layers of blackened, soiled robes who asked me for batteries for his flashlight? Or is it over there in Nong Khai, a forgotten, unremarkable frontier town where in the innocence of a sultry Friday night I waited in the back row of a concrete movie theatre forty minutes past the advertised curtain time as the stairways and fire exits were crammed with folding chairs to accommodate the overflow demand for a badly dubbed *Honey, I Shrunk the Kids*? Or is it in Japan, where lost behind the dot-matrix screen of technological wizardry and vacationless work years, Western haberdashered Japanese salarymen sit on *tatami* mat floors and drink *sake* brewed by 25th generation hands and eat *sashimi* on palmfulls of hand-harvested rice soaked in 20th generation crafted vinegar, watching sumo warrior *rikishi*, naked but for a perfect silk *mawashi* loin cloth and mink-oiled *chunmagei* hair, throw handfuls of salt high into the air, purifying the *dohyo* and appeasing gods rooted in *Shinto* animism and not twentieth century philosophy? Or does it exist only in my mind, in the romance I give Asia here and now? My new Asia will one day be another's old, my present Asia someone else's romance. My romance was once another's new. And so the circle goes. It is all illusion.

The driver cuts the motor and we coast the final few boat lengths into the broad cement steps of the immigration centre that mingle with the lapping river like the steps of a Varanasi ghat. The skiff barely anchored, passengers flurry to unload, rocking the boat violently in the slapping, shallow water. Slowly I think. Slowly. The concrete steps congest in movement and bags. Porters wearing numbered orange plastic vests fawn and fight to collect baggage, dodging each other and the disembarking legs in their obsession.

At the landing's foot the river flows, the same simplicity of current that mesmerized me almost three weeks earlier. Dirty brown, the water laps and peaks and breaks transparent and silver in the midday sunshine. All the same. All different. Does anything change but perspective?

At the end of the stairs, another boat, a new boat, drawing low in the water, prepares to leave, its passengers rocking the hull as they settle for the ten minute cruise to where we have just left. I strain to see if there are any foreigners on board, but the new boat is crowded and the faces turned away and lost under the wooden canopy. I place one foot out of the ferry, straddling the steps and river, the reaction against the water sudden and absolute, the boat slipping away from under me, pulling me backwards towards the water and Laos. A numbered man in an orange vest bends to pick up my pack. I shake my head.

About the Author

Mark Boyter is a traveler, educator, marathon runner, and recovering academic. As a traveler, he spent years in Asia and the Middle East, combined with shorter stints in Europe, South America and Africa. In Asia, he discovered Buddhism and Zen, both of which have informed everyday of his life since. As a teacher, he taught in Japan, the UAE, and Canada. He holds a MA in Teaching degree. As a runner, his races have been more local in nature, but in that locality have given him an ever deepening marveling for the capabilities of the human body and spirit. It also gave him fabulous legs. Throughout, Mark has carried a deeply felt sense of spirituality and place. He lives happily in Vancouver, sharing his life with his long time partner and her three cats.